Merry christmas
love Emlyn nadine Dale 2009 !!

COLOUR COMMENTARY

MY GREAT HOCKEY JOURNEY

BRIAN McFARLANE

This one,
more important than all the rest,
is for you, Joan,
the love of my life for fifty years and
counting

Library and Archives Canada Cataloguing in Publication

McFarlane, Brian, 1931-
         Colour commentary : my great hockey journey / Brian McFarlane.

ISBN 978-1-55267-600-4

         1. McFarlane, Brian, 1931-. 2. Sportscasters--Canada--Biography.
3. National Hockey League--History. 4. Hockey--Canada--History.
5. Authors, Canadian (English)--20th century--Biography. I. Title.

GV742.42.M34A3 2009a   070.4'49796962092   C2009-903289-9

This collection produced for Prospero Books.
Originally published as *Brian MacFarlane's World of Hockey*.

Key Porter Books Limited
Six Adelaide Street East, Tenth Floor
Toronto, Ontario
Canada M5C 1H6

www.keyporter.com

Printed and bound in Canada

09 10 11 12 5 4 3 2 1

Every reasonable effort has been made to trace ownership of copyrighted materials.

Photo credits
4. Mecca/Hockey Hall of Fame; 7. Portnoy/Hockey Hall of Fame; 25. Imperial Oil–Turofsky/ Hockey Hall of Fame; 26. Imperial Oil–Turofsky/Hockey Hall of Fame; 36. Priere de Mentionner, National Photography Collection; 42. Graphic Artists/Hockey Hall of Fame; 48. National Collegiate Athletic Bureau, New York; 51. Eastwest photo; 54. C.T.M. Pictures; 57. TV Guide; 62. Imperial Oil–Turofsky/Hockey Hall of Fame; 76. Get Stock; 81. Robert Shaver/ Hockey Hall of Fame; 95. Robert Shaver/Hockey Hall of Fame; 99. Robert Shaver/Hockey Hall of Fame; 100. Robert Shaver/Hockey Hall of Fame; 101. Robert Shaver/Hockey Hall of Fame; 105. Harold Whyte for Grant-Whyte Photography; 109. Imperial Oil–Turofsky/Hockey Hall of Fame; 110. Ann Hamilton; 114. Imperial Oil–Turofsky/Hockey Hall of Fame; 117. CBC Still Photo Collection; 118. Hockey Night in Canada (Canadian Sports Network); 125. Toronto Star; 127. Robert Shaver/Hockey Hall of Fame; 133. Imperial Oil–Turofsky/Hockey Hall of Fame; 137. Imperial Oil–Turofsky/Hockey Hall of Fame; 141. Dave Sandford/Hockey Hall of Fame; 143. Imperial Oil–Turofsky/Hockey Hall of Fame; 144. Imperial Oil–Turofsky/Hockey Hall of Fame; 147. Portnoy/Hockey Hall of Fame; 151. Graphic Artists/Hockey Hall of Fame; 155. Dave Cooper; 157. Imperial Oil–Turofsky/Hockey Hall of Fame; 158. Paul Bereswill/Hockey Hall of Fame; 172. Paul Bereswill/Hockey Hall of Fame; 174. O-Pee-Chee/Hockey Hall of Fame; 177. Graphic Artists/Hockey Hall of Fame; 178. Imperial Oil–Turofsky/Hockey Hall of Fame; 180. Paul Bereswill/Hockey Hall of Fame; 183. Portnoy/Hockey Hall of Fame; 184. Portnoy/Hockey Hall of Fame; 187. Paul Bereswill/Hockey Hall of Fame; 190. Frank Prazak/Hockey Hall of Fame; 195. Imperial Oil–Turofsky/Hockey Hall of Fame; 196. Imperial Oil–Turofsky/Hockey Hall of Fame; 198. Imperial Oil–Turofsky/Hockey Hall of Fame; 201. Imperial Oil–Turofsky/ Hockey Hall of Fame; 202. Portnoy/Hockey Hall of Fame; 205. Mecca/Hockey Hall of Fame; 206. Portnoy/Hockey Hall of Fame; 209. Hockey Hall of Fame; 214. Mecca/Hockey Hall of Fame; 217. Portnoy/Hockey Hall of Fame; 240. Doug MacLellan/Hockey Hall of Fame

Also by Brian McFarlane

It Happened in Hockey

More It Happened in Hockey

Still More It Happened in Hockey

The Best of It Happened in Hockey

Stanley Cup Fever

Proud Past, Bright Future

Hockey's Glory Days

The Leafs

The Habs

The Rangers

The Red Wings

The Bruins

The Blackhawks

COLOUR COMMENTARY

MY GREAT HOCKEY JOURNEY

BRIAN McFARLANE

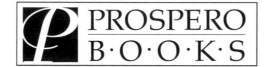

PROSPERO
B·O·O·K·S

Brian McFarlane, Bobby Clarke, and Maurice Richard

Contents

Introduction

Hockey, when played by the elites of the game, can be a beautiful tapestry of skating, shooting, passing, and playmaking. That's why fans like me love the game. We particularly enjoy the Stanley Cup playoffs, the Olympics, the World and Junior championships. An added bonus is being able to watch our sons and daughters, our grandsons and granddaughters play the game.

It's a game that triggers emotions. As a spectator and player, broadcaster and journalist, I can't count the number of times I experienced the joy of victory and the agony of defeat. And the exhilaration that comes from broadcasting some of hockey's most thrilling moments.

The game has changed dramatically since it first gripped me seven decades ago. Today's players are bigger, stronger, and better conditioned. Unlike the Original Sixers, they wear helmets, visors, and the best of protective equipment. Gone are the days when players, including goalies, went bare-headed, when pros were paid a pittance, when at least one NHL team (Boston) had no skate sharpening machine, when the seventh best goalie in the world might find himself playing in the American League. I remember NHL games on *Hockey Night in Canada* when an injured goalie left the game and was replaced by a team trainer or a junior goalie plucked from the press box.

Still, those were memorable days. Six teams playing each other fourteen times a season. Great line combinations: the Production Line, the Punch Line, and the Million-Dollar Line. Great individual performers: the Golden Jet, the Big M, the Rocket, Terrible Ted, and the China Wall.

The game has always been rough. And always appealed to Canadians like no other sport for that very reason. Today's game can be violent and dangerous even though bench-clearing brawls, prevalent in the past, have been eliminated. Stiffer rules and hefty fines have been adopted to keep hot-tempered brawlers in line. But brutish behaviour sometimes prevails. It can turn a stunning spectacle into an ugly, bloody, unfortunate scene.

Todd Bertuzzi's premeditated assault on an unsuspecting Steve Moore ended the latter's career. In the seventies, I recall interviewing colourful Henry Boucha of the Minnesota North Stars just before Boston's Dave Forbes of the Bruins butt-ended him in the eye. Forbes was charged with aggravated assault, but was acquitted. Boucha, an Ojibwa who wore a red headband, never fully recovered and soon retired from the game.

My broadcasting colleague Dan Kelly was in the booth on September 31, 1969, when St. Louis Blues rookie Wayne Maki was struck by a high stick wielded by Bruins' tough guy Ted Green. Maki retaliated and crushed Green's skull with a stick swing of his own. Kelly said, "It was dreadful. Green almost died. It took five hours of surgery to save his life."

Years ago, I predicted that it would be only a matter of time before an NHL player dies from a blow suffered in a hockey fight. Most of the current players are heavyweights—some super heavyweights. Many can punch like the late John Ferguson. I cringe when I see helmets come off and exposed heads strike the ice or the Plexiglas panels.

Henry Boucha's NHL career was terminated after Boston's Dave Forbes butt-ended him in the eye.

Backyard Rinks and Rubber Ice

As a kid, I loved hockey more than anything. By the time I was four years old, in Whitby, Ontario, I was on skates at every opportunity. I didn't knock shingles off the house practicing my shot, à la Gordie Howe—we never owned a house. And I didn't use my grandmother as a goalie, the way Wayne Gretzky did. Nor did I ever flood the kitchen floor hoping to create a real indoor ice surface—as Wayne Cashman once did while his mom was taking a nap.

A big ditch across the street was my first rink. It was about as big as a birdbath—well, marginally bigger, but it seemed like an ice palace to me. On bitterly cold days, my mother allowed me out on the ice on one condition: that I wear a thick scarf over my face if the temperature fell below zero.

"But why?" I whined. "Hockey players don't wear scarves."

"Because your father let you out one day when we lived up north in Haileybury. You were just a toddler, too small to open the kitchen door. It was about 20 below and you froze your face and ears. Your father had the radio on and didn't hear you crying to get in. Now when it gets really cold, you get white spots on your cheeks."

I stood still while she inspected me.

"Skates tight enough?"

"Sure."

"Got your long underwear on?"

"Of course."

"Gone to the bathroom? Last time you stayed out so long you almost wet your pants."

"Mo-om! I went a minute ago."

"Okay," she laughed. She pulled my leather hat with the earflaps over my head and tied it under my chin. Then she wound the long ratty scarf around my face and neck, knotting it securely in back. She zipped up my jacket and helped me on with my mitts.

"Go play hockey," she said, patting me on the back and propelling me out the door into the blast of cold air. And like every mother of every player ever born, she couldn't resist some final advice. "Don't get hurt!" she shouted as I took a shortcut across the drifts covering our front lawn, crossed the rutted street, and glided onto the solid ice covering the ditch—my very own make-believe arena. Oblivious to the gusts of wind and swirling snow, I would stay there till dark—skating, shooting, practicing. My breath would condense on my scarf, soaking it and causing ice particles to form. Snow would fall and I'd sweep it aside with the blade of my stick. Two chunks of snow served as my goal posts and I would shoot my little puck between them—time and time again. A hard, rising shot would disappear in a bank of snow and I'd have to reach deep into the hole it made to recover the puck. I was always willing to pay the price—lots of snow up my sleeve and inside my mitt.

In the gloom of the late afternoon, I'd hear one of my sisters shout, "Brian, supper!" I'd pick up my puck and retrace my steps, arriving at the back door calling for help: "Someone open the door. Hurry before I wet my pants!"

In my day, a beginner needed only hand-me-down skates, a stick, a puck and a patch of ice to get started.

I never minded skating alone. But it was much more fun if I could persuade my sisters, Pat and Norah, to join in. Or whenever some boys who lived down the street came along to share my patch of ice.

It took a lot to keep me off that ice. The longer the winter, the better I liked it. I used to feel sorry for kids living in far-off places like Africa and South America. There was no ice, no hockey there. I was so happy to be born a Canadian, living in a place where snow and ice prevailed for several months of the year.

One day I complained of feeling sick and my mother wouldn't let me go out to play.

"Your face is flushed," she said, feeling my forehead with the palm of her hand. "You can't play hockey if you've got a temperature. Why not take a nap instead?"

Reluctantly, I lay on my bed and plotted a means of escape.

When she went into her bedroom I crept into the kitchen and placed my head in the refrigerator. I stood there for several minutes, then ran to my mother.

"Mom, I'm all better. Feeling great."

Once again she ran her hand across my forehead.

"Why, you do feel much cooler. All right. You can go out for a while."

As I recall, I skated around for a while, barfed into a snowbank, came home, and went straight to bed.

In time, I discovered that other kids were playing hockey—a dozen or more to a side—a few blocks away at the local park. Where the ground sloped, water gathered, was trapped, and froze into a long corridor of ice—perhaps 200 feet long by 30 feet wide. Most of us kids would put on our skates at home in the kitchen while our mothers tsk-tsked at the sound of metal blades clumping over linoleum floors. Then we'd fly down the snow- and ice-covered streets, stumbling over bumps and potholes and into the park. We'd join a game in progress—there was always one going on—and have the best fun of our young lives.

"You go that way, kid," an older boy would say, pointing north. The next player to arrive would be told to go the other way. There were no positions, no referee, no age or size restrictions, no timeouts, no substitutions, no rules, and, perhaps best of all, no parents to tell you what you were doing wrong. What a joyous time in my life! I had discovered the fascination of hockey. By then we were all using magazines for shin pads, our mittens instead of hockey gloves, and sticks with blades that were often bare of tape and perilously thin—sticks called toothpicks, eroded by a hundred games of road hockey, which we normally played in our street shoes.

At the park, we quickly learned the hazards of engaging in unsupervised group activity. A body check delivered with glee by an older, heavier boy would leave you sitting stunned on the ice, gasping for breath and fighting back tears. One of your teammates—also older, showing no sympathy—would shout, "Get up off your arse, you damn sissy. Get back in the game!"

"But he hit me in the stomach. It hurts."

"Don't be such a crybaby, kid. Hit the bugger back. Hit him in the jewels."

Jewels? What are jewels? I asked myself.

You'd jump up, wipe your tears and your snotty nose on your sleeve, and get back in the play. The next time the player who dumped you came close, you'd elbow him into a snowbank and laugh as he landed face-first. He'd emerge, red-faced and defiant, shaking the snow from his hair and the nape of his neck. He'd give you a dirty look, then skate away. You'd have learned a valuable lesson: hockey is not for the timid, not for the squeamish. If someone knocks you on your butt, it's kinda fun to wait your turn to get him back, to get even.

In time, you even learn what jewels are.

We didn't always play on the ice in the park. The Hatch kid lived in a big house down the street, and his backyard rink was something to see: boards all around, a bench for changing skates, and a well-maintained ice surface—slick, fast, and flooded with the garden hose every night. The Hatch kid had the best equipment we ever saw: new skates, a new stick, shiny new shin pads—he even owned a pair of hockey pants! Occasionally we'd be invited to play hockey on that rink of his and those times were special, really special.

One day, with winter waning and the March ice soft under our blades, two of us stayed too long at the rink, trying to stretch out a season that was rapidly coming to a close. It was well past suppertime and we knew our parents were going to be mad. Homeward bound, we passed a deep ditch covered by tissue-thin ice. My friend said, "Hey, it's 'rubber ice.' If you slide across it real fast it'll bend and crack but it won't break. Watch!"

I thought he was kidding at first, but he took a short run and slid safely across the ice. I could see the ice bend and shift under his weight, but it held him. He laughed and said, "Your turn."

I hesitated. It seemed like a long way across. But he'd more or less dared me. I took a few steps back, ran toward the ditch, and launched myself onto the ice.

Crack!

Suddenly I was up to my ears in water. The shock was so sudden, the water so cold, the result so breathtaking that I screamed for help. My friend thought my plight was hilarious. Laughing, he held out his hockey stick and I was able to scramble out of the pool.

"Now I'm in for it," I said.

I ran home and confessed to my parents that I'd been a fool and a numbskull and promised never to do it again. After an admonition, a hot bath, and a mug of hot chocolate, I was sent right to bed—without any supper. A cruel punishment, I thought, for a boy who would need all the nourishment he could muster if he planned to become a big-league hockey star.

Dad Was a Stone-Age Broadcaster

I often say I was born in Haileybury, Ontario, but that's not quite accurate. We lived in that pleasant town, where my grandfather was principal of the local school, but I was actually born five miles away, in the hospital in New Liskeard.

My father was a freelance writer who churned out exciting hockey fiction as well as mystery and adventure stories. He also kept detailed diaries of life in the 1930s and '40s. I feel extremely fortunate to have a written record of so many events from my childhood. For instance, on August 10, 1931, my father wrote:

> Amy [my mother] woke up with pains at 6 a.m. I got [brother] Dick to drive us up to the hospital in New Liskeard at 9 a.m. We stayed with Glad [Amy's sister] until noon, then to the hospital. I came home to Haileybury and Dr. Arnold called at 6 p.m. to tell me the news—the birth of a boy. Nine pounds, 3 ounces. Up to see Amy tonight. The baby is a young husky.

I read on. Dad describes how sister Pat was not impressed over having a "baby brudder." How Pat saw me being breastfed and was quite mystified. How Dr. Arnold circumcised me on August 19. How my mother stayed in hospital for eleven days—an eternity by today's standards. I'm referred to as "the baby" or "the wee lad" for several entries. Wait a minute. Where the hell is my name? I read through entries for the rest of August and move into September. By this point my dad is writing about going fishing and having no luck. Going deer hunting and seeing no deer. Winning 80¢ in an all-night poker game. Hey, Dad, remember me—"Baby"? When do I get some identity here? By mid-September Dad is out in the woods, partridge hunting. He sees a bird, only to find his gun isn't loaded. On the 21st, Mom is out playing bridge and "Baby slept until she came home." "He is the best wee soul imaginable," my father writes. That's great, Dad, but who the hell *am* I? What's my name? Finally I find what I'm looking for—on October 1, 1931. Following an entry about a visit to the house from Gilbert LaBine, who went on to riches in the mining industry, my dad writes, "Decided to call the baby Bryan. He weighs 14 pounds, six ounces."

Bryan? I'm almost seven weeks old before they give me a name, and even then they haven't decided on the spelling! When did they change it? Or was it supposed to be Bryan—with a *y*—all along? All I know is if they'd waited much longer I'd have been able to pick my own name and select my own spelling. And write it out.

I came by my love of hockey honestly. Haileybury, and the nearby mining town of Cobalt, were steeped in hockey history. Both had been charter members, along with Renfrew and the Montreal Wanderers, of the National Hockey Association, formed on December 2, 1909. A couple of days later *les Canadiens* joined the circuit, and the most successful hockey franchise in history was born. Eventually, in 1917, the league would be reorganized as the NHL we know today.

At the turn of the century, the Haileybury and Cobalt teams were owned by mining moguls who'd struck it rich in the area and were offering fabulous salaries to the top hockey stars of the day. Names like Cyclone Taylor, Art Ross, and Newsy Lalonde were scrawled on the walls of the visitors' dressing room in the old Haileybury arena. The Haileybury team lasted only a year in the top pro league, but the region had given in to the hockey craze.

Later, my dad would work for the *Sudbury Star*, and he witnessed some of the best amateur hockey of the era. In those days, the word "amateurism" was used rather loosely. It was a poorly kept secret that players worked at good jobs in the community—arranged for them by the teams—and that they were being paid under the table to play hockey. When the local Senior team, the Sudbury Wolves, was scheduled to play a rival like Sault Ste. Marie in a rink that seated about 2,000, hundreds of fans would line up all night in frigid weather to wait for the box office to open the morning of the game. Many would build bonfires to avoid dying of exposure.

Newspaper accounts of the games ran to a full page, but even that wasn't enough to satisfy the fans' appetite for instant information. Those who couldn't make the 200-mile journeys to out-of-town games—not to mention those who couldn't get a ticket when the game was played on home ice—would pack movie theatres and clubs and wait for play-by-play reports provided by the Canadian Pacific Railway's telegraph operators.

Because my dad followed the Wolves to their road games, he was conscripted to dictate the action to a nimble-fingered man on the telegraph key. All my dad had to do was talk—and refrain from swallowing his gum in moments of sheer excitement. He was, in effect, a stone-age hockey broadcaster in an era when radio was little more than a wailing fiddle coming through space every night from, of all places, station WGY in Schenectady, New York.

After a few games, he started to spice his coverage with colourful witticisms during delays in the action, and he used prizefight terminology to describe the frequent bench-clearing brawls. Back in Sudbury they would interrupt curling bonspiels and Hollywood movies at the local theatre so that my dad's accounts could be read aloud to a hushed, hockey-mad audience.

Trouble was, the information he was giving to the CPR and its clients wouldn't be seen in the paper he worked for until the next day. His boss, Bill Mason, seethed over this perceived conflict.

Mason found a clever way of resolving the matter. One day he asked my dad how much the CPR people were paying him for his game reports.

"Five bucks a game," my dad replied.

"Disgraceful," Mason told him. "They're robbing you blind. I've heard your work and you've got a gift for that sort of thing. Go and ask for twenty bucks."

My dad approached the CPR's Dan Bowen (whose grandson is the current Leaf broadcaster, Joe Bowen) and asked for a $15 raise.

"We can't pay that," Bowen told him.

"Well then, how about a $10 raise?"

"Impossible."

"Five?"

"No, no, no. And if you're not happy with the current sum, we don't want you working for us. We'll simply have the telegrapher double up and do both jobs from now on."

"So that's what happened and apparently nobody noticed any difference," my dad said. "And that's how I learned an important fact of life: nobody is indispensable."

We always lived in rented houses, in Haileybury, and later in Whitby, where we moved when I was four, and in Ottawa, where I spent my teenage years. My dad could never raise enough money to buy a house—nor even a car. Neither of my parents could even drive. To get around we walked, rode our bicycles, or hitched rides with friends. When we moved to Ottawa, we took buses and streetcars. But mostly we walked—to school, to downtown, everywhere.

If we were destitute, or close to it, at times, the McFarlane kids never knew it. We always had wonderful Christmases. Every day was a happy one. We were rich in friends, blessed with the natural wonders around us, and given the freedom to enjoy whatever small-town life thrust in our paths. I did well at school and liked all my teachers. I attended Sunday school and sang in the church choir. I went fishing in the creek. There was the excitement of Halloween and the annual Whitby Street Fair.

The town of Whitby was a year-round haven for energetic kids. By the time we were nine or ten years old, we were taking off in all directions. In summer we'd head to Lake Ontario, where we'd cross a pebble-strewn beach and leap into the frigid waters. Local streams also provided a chance to splash around in deep pools of clear water. Then we'd play softball in the park and my dad—always a good sport—would be dragged from his typewriter to serve as umpire.

"Get your dad to ump," they'd tell me. "He doesn't have a real job like the other dads."

There's only one moment from my childhood that I could complain about. On Valentine's Day, the girls at school would prepare special box lunches filled with sandwiches and cake. The boxes were wrapped in white tissue, to which red hearts punctured with arrows were pasted. The boys would bid a small amount of money—up to 25¢—on each box, not knowing who it belonged to. The highest bidder on a box would then enjoy the privilege of sitting next to the girl who'd prepared it—and would blush and endure much giggling and teasing from his classmates as he devoured the contents.

I made it my goal to bid on the box lunch prepared by Lorna Sullivan, and I relied on my sister to help me.

"Okay," she said, "I've asked around and the box Lorna has prepared is a shoe box, about this size, and it's wrapped in red tissue—not white—with a big red bow on top."

"Got it. Thanks, Sis."

The following day—Valentine's Day—the teacher started the bidding. Suddenly she held up a box—a shoebox wrapped in red tissue, with a bow on top.

I threw up my hand and began bidding. I was sure that in a few seconds I'd be sitting next to Lorna Sullivan. Ten cents, 15¢, 25¢.

"And the highest bidder is—Brian. Now let's find out who Brian will be sitting next to." She consulted a list while I held my breath.

"It's Debbie Morgan."

Debbie Morgan! I almost fainted. Debbie Morgan (not her real name) was immense—the fattest girl in the entire school. She could barely squeeze into her seat. There was no escape. I'd have to sit with her. Debbie Morgan grinned at me as I perched on the side of her seat. I pictured all my classmates—Lorna Sullivan among them—snickering behind my back as I began to choke down a sandwich. After school, when I told my sister about this embarrassing disaster, she said, "I told you to look for a box with a red ribbon on top. You bid on one with a *white* ribbon. So it's your own fault you missed out with Lorna. Besides, Debbie's a nice girl."

I agreed she was. It was just that there was so much of her. There was no room to sit next to her.

"Why didn't you sit in her lap?" my sister suggested.

One day I went missing, and that set off a few alarm bells. I'd become absorbed in reading comic books in some school chum's basement and lost all track of time. When I hurried home, long after dark, all the lights were ablaze in my house, and a dozen cars were parked around it.

"What's going on?" I wondered as a dozen people raced toward me. A large man grabbed me by the arm and propelled me up the hill and into our house.

"Here he is!" people shouted. "He's home—alive and well. Tell the police to call off the search."

Search? My mother, who'd been frantic with worry, clutched me to her.

"We thought you'd drowned—or were kidnapped," she cried. "Where in the world have you been?"

"Reading comics—in my friend's basement."

Neighbours dispersed. Cars pulled away. A couple of large policemen gave me frosty looks. The panic subsided. I was safe at home.

It wasn't the first time I'd pulled a vanishing act. In Haileybury, where I was born, I wandered off toward Lake Temiskaming one day. Another, smaller, search party found me beside the lake, tossing pebbles into the water. A 1933 entry in my dad's diary reads, "Brian is two years old and runs away so often that I am fixing up the backyard so that we can keep him penned up in a makeshift corral."

At least I was easy to recognize whenever I'd wander off. I had long golden curls that would often prompt a concerned citizen to call my parents and say, "We've found your little girl."

My mother, weary of correcting the gender confusion, marched me into the local barbershop and my curls soon piled up on the floor. My dad wrote: "He seemed almost a stranger when he came home. A boy now, a baby no longer and I feel sad. Nearly everyone approves, but I can't be enthusiastic."

My father, Leslie McFarlane, a writer and filmmaker, was the first author of the wildly popular Hardy Boys books under pen name Franklin W. Dixon.

3

The Ghost of the Hardy Boys

Freelance writing was a precarious way to make a living in the twenties and thirties, when my father decided to make a career out of it. In his cramped little study, with no door to shut out the hubbub that a noisy, growing family created, he would chain-smoke his Buckinghams, or puff on his pipe, and pound away at his reliable Underwood. Editors in far-off places would scrutinize his work, and accept it or send it back. In a few days, a cheque for $20 to $50 would arrive in the mail, his reward for his efforts to be published in *Argosy*, *Maclean's*, or one of the many pulp magazines of the day.

Pulp magazines—dedicated mainly to sports and adventure stories—were printed on rough paper that yellowed over time. Often he got paid by the word—at a rate of 1¢ or 2¢ per word—and I would wonder why he didn't write a whole lot of small words so that they would pile up quickly and the returns would be greater. I also wondered who sat and counted his words at the publishing house. What kind of job was that?

Dad's diaries reveal that he polished off eight young adult novels in 1926. Each of them was between thirty and forty thousand words in length, and he earned a flat rate of $100 for each of them. He also scored with a twenty-five thousand-word novelette that netted $525. Total earnings for the year—$1,350. The following year he cut back to five books, did more magazine work, and pocketed $1,815.

Most of my readers will be thoroughly familiar with the books he wrote at that time. Remember the Hardy Boys? Millions of avid readers throughout North America devoured the thrilling adventure stories starring brothers Frank and Joe Hardy, with titles such as *The Tower Treasure* and *Hunting for Hidden Gold*. My dad wrote those books, accumulating little treasure, and certainly no gold, for his efforts.

Leslie McFarlane had worked on several newspapers when he was young, beginning as a teenager in Cobalt, Ontario. When he was twenty-four, he was with a paper in Springfield, Massachusetts, and it was there that he saw an ad one day: "Writer wanted for series of juvenile books. We'll supply the plot outline and you fill in the book." He answered the ad, included an adventure story he'd written and sold to a men's magazine, and got the following response from a giant in the world of young adult fiction, Edward Stratemeyer.

April 29, 1926
Dear Mr. McFarlane:

Your letter of the 20th. inst. to hand asking about writing for the Stratemeyer Syndicate, of which I am proprietor.

I have looked over your story in "Adventure" and frankly, I do not know whether you could do any of the boys' stories or detective stories we need or not. Your tale is very good of its kind but not at all the sort we are handling.

All of the manuscripts we handle are written to order for us, on our own outlines and casts of characters, the author simply "filling in" as it were. We buy all rights for cash and we pass on a manuscript inside a week. All Syndicate stories are published under our own trade-mark pen names, Franklin W. Dixon, Roy Rockwood, etc.

All told we have about thirty series of books running, for boys, for girls, and for little children. Also a line of detective stories, for older boys and men. A few lines are issued in paper and the others in cloth at a popular price.

By this same mail I am sending to you, with your copy of "Adventure," two paper-bound books, a "Dave Fearless" and a "Nat Ridley"—the first a boys' sea and wild adventure yarn and the other a detective tale. We are having additional titles written in each line. Each book is to fill 216 text pages. For these stories, written on our own complete working outlines, we pay one hundred dollars each. On our cloth-bound books we of course pay more.

The next Dave Fearless we shall want (inside of a month or five weeks), will be a story of a young diver's adventures off the coast of Brazil trying to get at a treasure in a sunken submarine. We also want another Nat Ridley—a robbery in Wall St. with action in it and near New York City, to come a little later. Complete plots for each are now ready.

If after looking over the books sent, you care to tackle one of these, let me know. As this stuff is all printed under our trade-mark pen names it need not interfere with your magazine stories. Many of the well-known authors do this work "on the side." But I should want to see four or five sample chapters before giving an order to complete a manuscript.

Yours truly,
Edward Stratemeyer

My dad dashed off three or four chapters, sent them to Stratemeyer, and was hired.

Although he would never meet Stratemeyer in person, it was the beginning of a relationship that would last for the next twenty years.

After he wrote two Dave Fearless books, Stratemeyer notified my dad that he was about to introduce a series called "The Hardy Boys." He'd invented a character, a detective named Fenton Hardy, who had two sons named Frank and Joe.

Under the name Franklin W. Dixon, my dad wrote more than twenty of the Hardy Boys books, starting with *The Tower Treasure* in 1926. He got $100 a book. The fee wasn't negotiable, and there were no royalties. And all of his work came out under aliases: He wrote some of the Dana Girls books under the name Carolyn Keene, and he was Roy Rockwood for a series of Dave Fearless books.

Dad quit his job at the newspaper in Springfield, figuring he could write a book a month. Twelve books a year would bring in $1,200—not bad money for that era. So he moved up to Sudbury, rented a small cabin on Ramsey Lake, and started writing his books. He soon found that he needed a supplemental income, so he started writing short stories for magazines—sports and adventure stories, the kind of writing he enjoyed far more than the Hardy Boys.

The publisher—Stratemeyer—was a kind of Henry Ford of juvenile fiction. He had a book factory in New Jersey where he produced the Hardy Boys, the Dana Girls, and the Nancy Drew series, as well as the Bobbsey Twins, the Motor Boys, and Dave Fearless. He hired freelance writers to channel all these adventure stories through the pipeline. Then he published and sold millions of books and made millions of dollars.

When Mr. Stratemeyer died he left his authors a small percentage of the money they had earned him for writing these books. My dad picked up another couple of hundred dollars at that time.

When I was growing up, I didn't really have any idea that my father was the famous Franklin W. Dixon. One day, years later, he recalled an incident from the early 1940s. "Brian, you came into my study one day and noticed a row of Hardy Boys books on my shelf. You asked me if I read them when I was a kid. I said, 'Son, I *wrote* those books.'"

I remember I was incredulous. "Dad," I asked him, "why didn't you tell me? Every kid I know reads the Hardy Boys. We trade them back and forth. Why didn't you tell me?"

My wife Joan and I were in Haileybury, Ontario, when the town honoured my father, author of the Hardy Boys series of books.

The Ghost of the Hardy Boys

Home of LESLIE McFARLANE

HAILEYBURY

"I guess it didn't occur to me," was his reply.

Dad admonished me not to tell my friends he was writing such "nonsense." He often referred to the books as "those cursed juveniles." He never thought they amounted to very much, and because he was never shown any sales figures, what he didn't know was that every kid in Canada and the United States was reading them.

He might not have cared much for the Hardy Boys books, but from then on I took a lot of pride in what he was doing. Sometimes I'd tell my friends that my dad was writing the Hardy Boys books, but I'm not sure they believed me. How could they when his name never appeared on the covers? Only in midlife did he begin to let it be known that he had also been Franklin W. Dixon. People started coming to his door, asking him to autograph their books.

I remember a journalist, a writer named Robert Stahl, came to see him many years ago. Somehow Stahl was aware that my father was the author of the Hardy Boys. He interviewed him and the story appeared in *Weekend* magazine. Stahl did quite a good job of it, too.

Mr. Stratemeyer did not want the world to know that there was no such person as Franklin W. Dixon or Carolyn Keene or any of the other authors he'd invented. And I know he asked my dad never to reveal he'd written any of the books. But in the 1970s my dad decided to write his memoirs, and he called his book *The Ghost of the Hardy Boys*. "I don't care about the secrecy thing anymore," he told me. "For the little money they paid me, I'm not going to keep that secret any longer. The hell with it." I know the Stratemeyer people were upset with him when he revealed all in his memoirs.

Dad really didn't like writing those juvenile books. They were a lot of work, and the price went down to $85 a book after the stock market crashed in 1929. He told me once they kept him from doing all the other stuff—books and magazine articles—that he knew he could do better. So I think he was quite an angry and frustrated writer when he wrote the Hardy Boys.

In 1934, Dad wrote: "Stratemeyer wants me to do another Hardy Boys book. I always said I wouldn't do another of the cursed things, but the offer always comes when we need cash. I agreed to do it, but asked for more than $85, a disgraceful price for forty-five thousand words." Another time he wrote, "The plot is so ridiculous. I'm constantly held up trying to put some logic into it. Even fairy tales should be logical." But even though he called it "loathsome work," he did feel bound to put as much effort and quality into them as he could. There was a lot of good writing and fun in those books, his characters were well developed, and I know he used challenging words occasionally, words that young readers would have to ask their teachers or their parents about. I notice that Lucy Maud Montgomery did the same thing with *Anne of Green Gables*, something I appreciated when my kids were reading those books.

He was never proud of Frank and Joe Hardy, but I know Dad was pleased that others seemed to think so highly of them. Hundreds of people have told me personally that the books meant an awful lot to them when they were growing up. Even today, when I make my banquet speeches and it's mentioned that my dad was the author of the Hardy Boys, people come to me afterward and tell me how influential the Hardy Boys series has been on their young lives, how the series triggered their interest in reading.

Once a book was finished, Dad would never take it off the shelf, never read it again. As far as he was concerned, it was part of his past and he had his $100. And he really needed that money. Growing up, I never felt that I came from an impoverished family, but when I read his diaries today, I realize that things were very grim financially. He writes about taking me for a walk one day, and my shoes fell apart on the main street of New Liskeard. He was so upset because he couldn't afford to buy me new ones. There were even times he couldn't afford to send his scripts out because he didn't have the postage. "I had to borrow ten cents from Brian's piggy bank for stamps," he writes. Another entry reads, "Almost finished the damn juvenile today when my typewriter ribbon disintegrated. Will have to stop. I have no money to buy a new one." His writing was interrupted because he couldn't buy a simple thing like a new typewriter ribbon!

All the while, the Hardy Boys books were becoming the bestselling boys' book series in history. In his *Weekend* article, Robert Stahl called my father a giant of modern literature, pointing out that the series had sold around seventy-five million copies. I'm sure that sales are well over one-hundred million by now.

Years ago, I suggested to my father that he surely had grounds for a lawsuit against the publishers, that it was dreadfully unfair that he had received no royalties. Even the smallest royalty would have been enough to buy a house and a car.

He shrugged. "How can I sue them when I knew perfectly well what the deal was? If I didn't write the books there were a hundred out-of-work writers anxious to take them on."

My dad could write a book in about three weeks. He wrote *The Secret of the Caves* in five days in 1928 because he was almost dead broke and needed money fast.

His last Hardy Boys book was *The Phantom Freighter*, which he wrote in 1946 when we were living in Ottawa. By that time he was employed by the National Film Board, writing and producing documentaries. He'd had enough. That was it. There were no hard feelings, no pleas from the Stratemeyer people for him to continue, and certainly no retirement gift or party. Dad simply quit after twenty years and more than two million words.

It's unfortunate that his other significant achievements were overshadowed by the Hardy Boys. He was with the CBC for many years and wrote dozens of highly acclaimed radio plays. He won several awards for his work. One year he was named Canada's top playwright. When he was with the film board, he was nominated for an Academy Award®. Later on, he went to Hollywood and wrote for *Bonanza*, the *U.S. Steel Hour*, and other series, and yet everybody says, "So, your dad was Franklin W. Dixon."

"Imagine," he used to say, "being singled out for that."

Years later the Stratemeyer syndicate came along and stripped the books down, to streamline them and modernize them, probably for economic reasons. Robert Stahl showed my dad an old Hardy Boys book, then he showed him the same title in a modern, re-edited form. There was really no comparison. He said parents who read the books years ago and enjoyed them were telling their sons, "I'm going to get you a Hardy Boys book because they are delightful adventure stories," but what they bought wasn't the same book at all. Not the one they remembered from their youth. My dad said they had gutted the books. He called it a literary fraud. And then they made a couple of TV series of the Hardy Boys, one of them with cartoon characters. I recall my dad saying that they polluted the airwaves with that for a year or two. He was quite strong in his opinions.

I have a complete set of the Hardy Boys books. I collect them at flea markets and garage sales. I even found a set with the dust jackets on, which I've had framed and passed on to my children. Now, with six grandchildren, my search continues.

I try to buy the books for a dollar or two. Sometimes I mention that my dad wrote the books, but only after the sale is made. They fetch big money in secondhand book stores—as much as $40 for a copy with a dust jacket intact.

My father owned lots of books, and was always at the library borrowing others. And, perhaps unknowingly, he gave his three children a valuable gift: regular trips to the town library. My sister Norah was the chief beneficiary. On the CBC radio network a couple of years ago, during a tribute to our father, she reminisced about her visits to the library.

"My father took me to the Whitby Public Library at a very early age and introduced me to a wonderful librarian named Miss Best—I thought she had a great name for a librarian. And it became almost a daily event for me. You could only take out three books at a time. So I would race home and read the books and be back the next day asking Miss Best to recommend more. This would happen day after day, and I've followed that pattern for most of my life."

"What about this legacy of writing that exists in your family?" the interviewer asked. "What did you learn from your father?"

"My dad did a wonderful thing for me," Norah replied. "I started writing at a pretty early age. I would write these things in pencil and he would immediately take them to his typewriter—his old Underwood— and he would type these things up and I would see them transformed into print. Remember, I was very young. Then he would say, 'All right, where are you going to send this?' I hadn't thought of sending it anywhere. So he would encourage me to mail them off to all sorts of publications, including newspapers. Sometimes they would be published and often they wouldn't be. But I remember how exciting it was when I received a dollar—or a couple of dollars—for what I had put to paper."

My dad's encouragement paid off. When she was just sixteen, Norah won an international short-story writing contest sponsored by *Seventeen* magazine. Got a $500 prize and her picture in the Ottawa papers. She went on to write several delightful novels, has won several awards for her work, and I'm very, very proud of her.

4

"Best Wishes, Syl Apps"

My dad was never an athlete but he knew sports. He followed all of the major sports and was a real fan of hockey and baseball. When I was five years old, my sisters and I were allowed to stay up late one night to listen to Foster Hewitt describe a game from Maple Leaf Gardens. Why? Because my dad was a guest on the broadcast that night. Even at that age, I realized that rubbing elbows with Foster Hewitt was a very big deal. I wonder how I'd have reacted if someone had said to me, "Someday, Brian, you too will be on the broadcasts at Maple Leaf Gardens."

I imagine I would have uttered the five-year-old's equivalent of "Get outta here."

On March 6, 1937, my dad wrote in his diary that "Mr. Passmore of the MacLaren Advertising Agency called up this morning to invite me to be guest announcer on the Imperial Oil hockey broadcast next Saturday night at $50 for the date. I went to Toronto this afternoon to arrange details."

On Friday, March 12, he went to the Royal York Hotel, where MacLaren had arranged a suite for him. He describes his first adventure into broadcasting the following day:

> Up early this morning to meet Percy LeSueur [a CBC commentator and former Ottawa goaltending great] and we talked and went over material for the broadcast. Passmore and Prendergast came up in the afternoon. Eight o'clock was on me before I knew it. Up to the Gardens and met King Clancy, Charlie Querrie and others, then up to the gondola. First period was over quickly which cut down on our time on the air so we had to discard our material and ad lib—a fearful experience for an initiation. Not until I told a story in the second intermission did I manage to loosen up. After the game it was down to a microphone in the dressing room corridor. Introduced [Chicago goaltender Mike] Karakas, [Leafs centreman Syl] Apps, and [Jimmy] Fowler and finished my chatter with LeSueur. After it was over my knees melted. Sheer nerves. Back home, Amy and others thought the broadcast was quite good.
>
> Everybody in Whitby seems to have listened with great interest.

What amazes me about my dad's report on his CBC debut is the fact he makes no mention of the fact the game he covered was historic. It was the game in which the Chicago Blackhawks introduced an all-American lineup. He mentioned Mike Karakas (from Aurora, MN) in goal, one of four bona fide U.S.-born big leaguers on the Hawks. The others were Alex Levinsky (Syracuse, NY), Doc Romnes (White Bear, MN), and Louis Trudel (Salem, MA). But Hawks' owner Major McLaughlin added five more Yankees to his roster that week—all rookies. They were Ernie Klingbeil (Hancock, MI), Butch Schaefer, Al Suomi, and Milt Brink (all of Eveleth, MN). McLaughlin boasted his team would become the "New York Yankees of hockey." Some called his experiment the most farcical thing ever attempted in hockey. But the Leafs were lucky to win that night by a 3–2 score. And my dad was there to see it. Too bad he was never invited back.

Dad hadn't been paid his $50 by the end of the month, so he was forced to write to MacLaren Advertising, asking for his cheque. It arrived, in due time. Some things never change: they were just as casual with payments and contracts three decades later, when I worked for them.

Leaf captain Syl Apps, my boyhood hero. He gave me my first autograph.

Legendary hockey commentator Foster Hewitt. My father worked with him long before I did.

Colour Commentary: My Great Hockey Journey

I chuckled over another of his diary items that winter: "Brian has inherited Pat's old skates. His pride in them is almost pathetic."

My dad took me to my first game at the Gardens the following year. It was a Memorial Cup final game between the Oshawa Generals and the St. Boniface Seals. Dad had written an article about the Generals' great star, Billy Taylor, so naturally I rooted for Oshawa. But St. Boniface had an equally stellar player in defenceman Wally Stanowski. Years later, Wally—a delightful man, full of laughter and humour—would be a teammate of mine on the NHL Oldtimers. Taylor's NHL career, unfortunately, would be cut short a decade later when he and Don Gallinger drew lifetime suspensions from the league for gambling on games.

The game that day was overshadowed in my mind by the majesty of the Gardens, the home of the Maple Leafs. So vast, so sparkling, so noisy, so exciting—filled to capacity for a Junior playoff game.

"Up there," my dad said, pointing skyward, "is Foster Hewitt's gondola."

I stared long and hard at Foster's cubicle so high over the ice. Did I think that day that I might one day be a resident of that famous site, that I might even share space—and a microphone—with Foster in that hallowed spot? Honestly, it never occurred to me.

During the intermission a swarm of men in blue sweaters attacked the ice. Near the boards, they swept it with brooms. Down the middle, they scraped it. Blue barrels on wide wheels were rolled onto the ice and the men pulled them around the ice in neat ovals. As the barrels dripped water onto the ice, the skate-marked white surface turned to a glassy, dark slate blue. Music blared and crowds filled the hallways. There was cigarette smoke everywhere. Men in topcoats and fedoras gathered in groups and I saw large sums of money being passed around.

"What are those men doing?" I asked my dad, afraid to let go of his hand for fear I'd be swallowed up by the crowd.

"They're making bets on the game," my dad replied.

"People bet on hockey?" This game I loved was full of surprises.

No trip to any museum, to a Santa Claus parade, to an amusement park, impressed me as much as that first visit to Maple Leaf Gardens. Years later, talking to his friends, my dad would recall that game, that matchup between Wally Stanowski and Billy Taylor.

"I remember taking Brian to that game," he would say. "But he seemed more interested in the hot dogs and the ice cream bars I kept feeding him than the game itself."

I denied his observation heatedly. I had no memory of any hot dogs. But come to think of it, the ice cream bars were irresistible.

Not long after that, my dad took me by the hand one evening and marched me down to some smoke-filled hall in Whitby. I think it was the first time I realized that most grown-up men smoked stinky cigars, and often used language as foul as the stogies they smoked. The air was putrid, but in the centre of a large, noisy group was my hero—a tall man wearing a handsome topcoat and a neat fedora. It was Syl Apps, the captain of the Toronto Maple Leafs. My dad elbowed his way into the group and tugged on Apps's sleeve.

"Syl!" he shouted over the din, "My son would like your autograph."

Apps turned and looked down at me. He flashed me a big smile and took the piece of scrap paper I held up to him. I watched as he wrote, "Best wishes, Syl Apps." No boy ever treasured an autograph more. The encounter might have lasted fifteen seconds. Certainly not more. But it was a momentous occasion, better than meeting the King of England. Apps had made a friend for life.

On the way home, I held out my scrap of paper. "Look! Mr. Apps gave me two extra words—Best Wishes." His generosity overwhelmed me.

After that meeting I asked for and received a blue sweater for Christmas. It had a small maple leaf on the front. My mother, knowing of my affection for the Leaf captain, carefully cut out the numbers 1 and

0 from a piece of white felt. She arranged them carefully on the back of the sweater and stitched them neatly in place. From then on, I proudly wore that sweater to the park when I played, in honour of my only hockey hero.

Decades later, when I was a young broadcaster at CFRB, I'd occasionally sit next to Apps in the press box at Maple Leaf Gardens. One night I made him chuckle when I told him the story of that first encounter with him in Whitby—and the sweater I treasured.

I loved Whitby. We had a collie dog named Tony and a nice house and lots to do. And I've already mentioned the crush I had on Lorna Sullivan, a cousin of my hockey-playing pal Doug Williams. One night we went skating together at the local rink. I called for her at her parents' apartment and I recall, much to my embarrassment, the noisy flushing of a toilet while I waited for Lorna to collect her white skates. It was, I suppose, my first-ever "date" and I had 50¢ to spend—enough to cover two admissions. We skated round and round to recorded music played at full volume—the "Skater's Waltz" and other appropriate tunes. Then, a few weeks later in Sunday school, there was a devastating announcement: "Boys and girls, I'm sorry to tell you we'll be losing one of our most popular class members next week. The Sullivan family is moving to Toronto and we're really going to miss our friend Lorna."

Oh, how my heart ached at the news. I went home that night and thought about Lorna. I leaned out my bedroom window, looking up at the stars. On the radio someone was playing "Moonlight Becomes You" and I experienced, for the first time, the pending loss of someone dear to me. I never saw Lorna Sullivan again.

Moonlight becomes you,
It goes with your hair
You certainly know the right thing to wear . . .

There are certain songs, and certain people, one never forgets.

5

The Star of McNabb Park

When the Second World War came along, my dad tried to enlist, but he failed the physical. There was always the suggestion that his heart was not strong and I often feared his sudden death. But his writing skills did not go unnoticed: the minister in charge of the Department of Munitions and Supply in Ottawa needed a speechwriter and so my dad was recruited.

The idea of moving to the big city of Ottawa left me with mixed emotions. I would miss all my friends in Whitby and was not at all certain I would be as enthralled with my new home.

During the war, housing in Ottawa was at a premium. My family moved into a small house at 8 Christie Street, which we shared with one of my dad's relatives—a widowed aunt—and her son. It was extremely crowded—seven people in a three-bedroom house with just one small bathroom. I would be bunking in with my distant cousin Barnett Ogden. Not a good start.

My reservations about the move were assuaged when Barnett told me there was a park down the street—McNabb Park—that had an outdoor hockey rink, encircled by a skating rink. In the summer there was room enough to play three or four ball games at the same time. Perfect.

I spent most of my spare time in that park. Skates on in the kitchen, a few strides down Bronson Avenue, and onto the slick ice where dozens of hockey players were always zipping around. You could usually find two or three games in progress. Bigger guys played against bigger guys, while the smaller fry formed their own games. Put the puck anywhere against one of the boards at the end of the rink and it's a goal.

"Who's that kid over there?" I asked. "The kid who stickhandles so well, but never passes the puck?"

"Oh, that's Larry Regan. He's a puck hog. Says he's going to play in the NHL someday."

"Fat chance," someone sneered. "You've got to pass the puck in the NHL."

A dozen years later Regan was named the NHL's rookie of the year after a banner season with the Boston Bruins. I wonder when, in his career, he decided to become a passer.

Lesson one at McNabb Park: keep your head up. The biggest guys will barrel right over you if you get in their way. I forgot that in one of my early forays onto the park ice, and I woke up on my back, staring up into a mass of unfamiliar faces. Each face had a double. I was staring at a bunch of Siamese twins.

"Is he dead?" I heard some kid say.

"No, just knocked out. Help me get him up."

I was pulled to my feet. My tongue and lips were cut and my head was sore.

"You better go home, kid," someone said.

"No, I can play," I answered, leaning on my stick.

Play commenced and I thought it odd that I saw two of everything. Two players carrying two pucks. Two kids standing in the goal area. I appeared to have two sticks in my hands. I decided to go home.

"A concussion," the doctor determined after he was called and examined me in my bed. "Complete rest for a few days. And I'll have to put a couple of stitches in his tongue."

I'm sure that critics of my broadcasting skills would suggest that it's too bad they didn't amputate the damn thing.

One of the toughies in McNabb Park was a kid named Mickey McFarlane. I never asked if we were related because I didn't want to know. He had learned to smoke, how to blow perfect rings in the air, and how to siphon gas out of a stranger's car—things the rest of us who played in the park hadn't really considered up until then. Mickey mocked me one day when he saw me jogging around the park, getting ready for the hockey season. And Mickey could run like hell.

"You're slow as molasses!" he yelled at me. "I dare you to race me—twice around the park."

The other kids waited for my answer.

Nervously, I said, "Okay, twice around."

He tossed his cigarette butt aside and we started out. Mickey dashed ahead, opening up a big lead—twenty, then thirty yards before we'd completed our first circle. Then I closed the gap and soon passed him. With a couple of hundred yards to go I looked over—he was gasping. I sprinted the rest of the way and when I crossed the finish line I looked back. He was sitting on the grass, completely winded.

"Son of a bitch," he said later. "I know I'm faster than you are."

"Yeah, but I'm in better shape," I said.

I learned a valuable lesson that day. An athlete in top condition will always have the advantage over one who isn't.

I had my first fist fight at McNabb Park. Don Kerwin, who lived up the street, accused me of something and I denied it—whatever it was. We began to punch at each other and the battle lasted about fifteen minutes. I remember how frightened I was at first because he had a reputation as a tough kid (his kid brother Gayle would later fight in main events at Madison Square Garden) and I'd never been punched in the mouth before. I began by trying to avoid his shots, then I got in a few of my own. I heard a grunt of pain and discovered the exhilaration of landing a couple of solid blows. We kept punching each other until our arms grew weary and the other kids broke it up. We both emerged bloody and bruised and when I arrived home my parents wanted to hear all about it. My sister Pat shot out the door and was back again in minutes.

"I marched right up to the Kerwins' front door and demanded that Don come down here and apologize," she reported.

"You what?" I demanded, horrified. "I can't believe you did that. It's none of your business."

"Is he coming?" Norah asked.

"No, his dad said his head was hurting and he had to go right to bed." Now *that* made me feel better. Only then did I figure I'd won that fight.

At school one year there was a city-wide contest. The student who wrote the best essay about growing up in Ottawa would have his composition broadcast over the CBC radio network. Then it would be sent to England and Australia for rebroadcast in those countries.

I entered the contest and, to my complete surprise, was declared the winner.

Two men from the CBC came to my school and whisked me down to the studios in town for a recording session. I stood in front of a huge microphone and read my piece. For some reason, the CBC kept the recording, and it was played back for me fifty years later when I was being interviewed about either hockey or the Hardy Boys—I've forgotten which. Here, then, is the radio debut of Brian McFarlane.

MY DAILY LIFE IN OTTAWA

My name is Brian McFarlane, I'm twelve years old and I live at number 8 Christie Street, Ottawa—which is the capital city of Canada. I live here with my mother and father and my two sisters. I am going to try to tell you something about Ottawa and what it's like here.

To start with, I'll tell you about our house and its surroundings. Across the road is a store, where we buy most of our food and groceries. Just down the street is a playground, and around the corner is a school where my sister Norah goes.

Our home is made of brick and has seven rooms. It is two stories high and has a flat roof, just like many other houses in Ottawa.

Sometimes on cold winter mornings my mother wakes me up and I have to go out and shovel away the snow that has fallen overnight on the front walk. But snow and cold weather mean plenty of sports, such as hockey, skiing, and sleigh riding. We have snow and cold weather all winter long in Ottawa and that's how I like it.

We have good hot meals in winter. I have just finished my breakfast of grapefruit, porridge, bacon and egg, toast, and hot cocoa. In winter our clothing has to be warm and I wear a lot of it. I wear a parka, which is a short, windproof coat with a hood. There is fur around the hood and when you get in the snow you look something like an Eskimo.

Our school is called Glashan School and is eight blocks away. My best subject is literature. That may be because my father is a writer. On the grounds there is an outdoor skating rink where we also play hockey. The team on which I play won the school championship this winter.

Two of the places we like to visit on Saturday and Sunday are the National Museum, where we can see the bones of prehistoric animals; and the Military Museum, where we can see weapons of war. Other times we visit the Parliament Buildings and go up into the Peace Tower, where we get a wonderful view of the whole city, part of the Ottawa River, the City of Hull, across the river in Quebec Province, and the Laurentian Highlands in the distance.

In spring it's fun to go out in the country and watch the farmers make maple sugar. The first thing they do is to cut a small hole in the trunk of a sugar maple tree. Then they insert a metal funnel from which the sap drips into a bucket. Afterwards, the buckets of sap are poured into large kettles and boiled over a blazing fire. While it is still hot, a bit of it is poured into the snow where it hardens into a very delicious taffy. This is an extra treat because most of the boiled sap is either put into containers as syrup or allowed to harden into blocks of maple sugar.

In the summer we often take our lunch and have a picnic at Britannia, just outside the city on the Ottawa River. We can swim and dive there and have plenty of fun. We have a canal in Ottawa called the Rideau. It is not used by any big boats now although many people enjoy canoeing there in the summer. It is lined with trees, grass, hedges, and rock gardens, and it is very pleasant down by the canal on a hot summer afternoon.

On my way home from a ball game or hockey game I may stop in at my favourite store, which is owned by a man named Bob Wells. Then I will have a soft drink, or perhaps a hot dog, which is a wiener sausage in a bun. Not far away there is an ice cream parlour where I sometimes have a banana split, which is a banana served in a dish with ice cream and fruit.

When I am at home in the evening, after my schoolwork is done, I listen to the radio until bedtime at 8:30, or I will read a book or look at the comics in the evening newspaper. As a hobby, I collect matchbooks. I have hundreds of matchbooks from many distant cities such as New York and Chicago and Vancouver. I also build model airplanes. The last model airplane I built was a Russian fighter, and the one before was a Spitfire. Now I am building a Fairey Battle and a Hurricane. Soon I hope to be able to go out to Rockcliffe airport and see many types and sizes of bombers, fighters, reconnaissance, and commercial planes they have there.

I am in grade eight now and when I pass I hope to go to Glebe Collegiate, where my sister Patricia is in grade ten. Just yet I am not sure what I want to be when I grow up. If the war is not over I would like to be a pilot in the Fleet Air Arm. Like many other boys I would like to be a professional hockey player but I have also been thinking I would like to be a schoolteacher or a foreign correspondent or a sports announcer.

In Ottawa I was always employed part-time, always making a few extra bucks doing odd jobs. I cut grass and shovelled snow with my friend Norm Cottee, I delivered papers, and by the time I was in my teens I was able to work during the summer in service stations. Or I'd slug it out working in a lumberyard or delivering ice.

One day I saw an ad in the paper: Salesperson wanted for book promotion. I answered immediately and was called in for an interview. I was seventeen years old.

"We're looking for college men," the interviewer told me. "Are you in college?"

"I'm enrolled at Carleton," I lied, looking him straight in the eye. I was in grade twelve at the time.

"Do you think you'd be a good salesman?" I was asked.

"Sure I would."

A few more questions and I was hired. I was to be part of a five-man sales team that would cover the downtown business core of Ottawa. I was instructed to approach young women only—at their desks, in the company cafeteria, on a smoke break—quietly and discreetly. If they were in groups of two or three, so much the better. And I would deliver a memorized spiel which started something like this.

"Hi, I'm here from the B&M Reader's Service, and we're conducting a survey to see how many young women are receiving some of the popular magazines we distribute. Mind you, I'm not here to sell magazines but to give them away—free. We'd like to add your name to our circulation list so we can charge more for the ads for our magazines. So we'll send you five magazines of your choice—free—all you pay for is the postage."

Once I'd persuaded them to select five magazines, I'd tell them the postage was a mere 72¢ a week. But that added up to $15 a month. Then I'd try to squeeze another $2.50 cash from them as my "commission"—to get the order started, I'd tell them.

Sometimes, three or four working girls would order simultaneously. If one said yes, often they all did.

I would depart with my commission and I'd get another dollar from the B&M Reader's Service for every commitment.

It was an interesting summer job. Some days I'd make as much as fifty bucks, other days nothing. But for a bashful teenage kid with acne it was a marvellous way to develop self-confidence as well as a gift for the gab. I'll wager there are young people out there today, knocking on doors, using similar spiels.

6

The Inkerman Rockets

Hockey took a firm grip on me while I was at high school. It wasn't enough to play on the school team and practice once a week: I would slip away early in the morning and hustle down to the Auditorium, sneak inside, see which team was at practice, and ask if I could join in. Often they were school teams with small rosters and I was allowed to fill in on a line. After their workout they would hurry off to class, and I would either wait for another team to appear, or skate by myself until an arena worker would bellow, "Get off the fucking ice!" Then I'd head off to school, always ready with a note, signed by my mother, to excuse my absence or my lateness. I could forge her signature perfectly.

On January 9, 1945, my dad wrote: "Brian brought home his C.A.H.A. card today for me to sign. He is very proud that he has made the grade as right wing on the Hornets." A few weeks later he added: "Brian's team lost in the semi-finals this morning 7–6 but he got five goals and an assist. In the two-game playoff, in which his team scored 11 goals, he collected 8 goals and 3 assists."

I remember very little of those matches, except that they were always played outdoors, often on snow-covered ice in sub-zero temperatures.

In his diary the following winter my dad wrote:

Over to the Auditorium today to watch Brian play with the Glebe juniors. He has improved a good deal over last year and is developing nicely. He scored four goals out of the team's five. But it was a costly game. A high stick caught him in the face and broke off three of his front teeth. Dr. Nixon put stitches in his tongue.

A few days later he writes:

To the hockey match with Brian tonight. A junior game between Inkerman and Ottawa and it was one of the best junior games I have ever seen. Brian's report card was pretty bad—he was 20th in a class of 32. The only subject in which he got a high mark was art! He won first prize in the art competition for his painting "Northern River."

I played Midget hockey at rinks all over the city, then was invited to play for an excellent juvenile team called the Marshalls. We lost the city championship by a goal, playing outdoors on soft ice covered by about an inch of water. A year later, at seventeen, I found myself in the Ottawa Junior league, playing for the Montagnards.

I was awestruck when the Monties recruited me, because I didn't think I was ready for Junior hockey. Before the season had started, I'd wangled a tryout with the Inkerman Rockets, and the coach, Lloyd Laporte, had shown no interest in me. I wasn't big, wasn't fast, wasn't tough. Couldn't shoot hard or stickhandle very well. But I could make plays and score, and I had a tremendous desire to improve and to play at the highest level possible.

The Inkerman Rockets played in and won three junior playoff series in 1951. Then we ran into Jean Beliveau.

Rocket reunion: Inkerman Rockets Lou Pelino, Ed Nicholson (holding the photo), me, Orval Porteous, and Roger Hunter surround esteemed coach Lloyd Laporte.

I was even more thrilled when I led the Monties in scoring, and I was elated when I was selected to the second all-star team at centre ice—right behind Bill Dineen of the St. Pats, a player so talented that he went on to play with Gordie Howe, Ted Lindsay, and the Detroit Red Wings.

Only then did I begin to think I was ready to move up a notch. I figured I was ready to play for the Inkerman Rockets. So did Lloyd Laporte. He drove into Ottawa one night, talked to my parents, and offered me a spot on the Rockets. I would have to live, attend school, and play home games in Winchester, a town about five miles down the road from Inkerman, which had no rink. If I signed, Laporte said, he would pay me $25 per week. I signed without giving it another thought, even though a great old pro, Bucko McDonald, had invited me to play for the Beavers, an Intermediate team he coached and managed in Sundridge, Ontario.

No village as small as Inkerman, Ontario (population 108), had ever produced a Junior team as good as the Rockets. And a small village it was: a couple of stores, a post office, a few houses. I imagine it's not much different there today.

In one of those houses lived Lloyd Laporte, a schoolteacher who had moved to Inkerman from Collingwood, Ontario. Laporte loved hockey and he enjoyed helping boys get started in the game. So he built a small rink in the schoolyard. Young lads played shinny on the rink and, eventually, Inkerman entered a team in the nearby Winchester Town League. Laporte was the coach.

At season's end, with $48 in the kitty, Laporte drove to Ottawa to buy sweaters for the next season. In a sporting goods store, he found a bargain: On sale were a couple of dozen red and white sweaters with a big *R* on the front. All he had to do now was come up with a nickname that started with *R*, and that's how the Rockets were born.

I was fifteen or sixteen years old when I first saw the Rockets play. It was a playoff game on the egg-shaped ice surface at the old Ottawa Auditorium. Most of the Rockets were little fellows, but my, how they could skate. Still, I was certain they would be no match for St. Pats, the powerful Ottawa city league champions. But the farm boys whipped the city players that day, led by twins named Erwin and Edwin Duncan, as well as a little spark plug on defence by the name of Leo Boivin. Leo was just embarking on a career that would take him all the way to the Hockey Hall of Fame. He could skate backwards as fast as anybody I'd ever seen.

I was so impressed with the visitors in the tattered sweaters that I told my dad, "That's the team I want to play with someday."

I had no idea where Inkerman was. The next day I looked it up on the map. Finally, after a fair bit of hunting, I found a little pinpoint halfway between Ottawa and Cornwall, just a few miles from Winchester.

Laporte came calling the following year. He chose two of us from the city league—John McDonald, and me. McDonald was a big defenceman who was the talk of the neighbourhood because he'd signed a C-form with the Toronto Maple Leafs. At sixteen he looked like a future All-Star, while I was just another skinny forward. Years later, Laporte told me I was the player he coveted more.

In Winchester I roomed over the barbershop with Lev McDonald (no relation to John), a good centreman who went on to become an All-American at Hamilton College in Clinton, New York. It wasn't long after that that the booze caught up to Lev. He never finished college, his marriage turned sour, and he lost a good job in Toronto. Years later, he would turn up periodically on my doorstep at one or two in the morning, pleading for a place to sleep and a little companionship.

The Rockets played against tough Intermediate and Senior teams all season and we were heroes to the rural fans when we played our home games—on natural ice!—in the old Winchester Arena. Whenever trouble broke out and our opponents started beating on us, a dozen of our mackinaw-clad fans would leap over the boards, tackle the visitors, and pummel them into submission.

Our road games could be just as frightening. The other teams in our league didn't like being embarrassed by us fast-moving youngsters, so they'd belt us at every opportunity. Only our young legs saved us from many a thumping.

It was never any fun playing in Cornwall, where Ray Miron—who would go on to manage pro teams, eventually becoming Don Cherry's boss in Colorado—had assembled a fast, tough squad. The fans there despised us.

One of Cornwall's toughest players was a big, mean defenceman named Bruno Bourgon. One night Bruno tangled with Orval Porteous, one of our third-liners. They each drew five-minute fighting penalties and were sent to cool off in the penalty box, where they were separated by a burly timekeeper. Suddenly, Orval hoisted his stick over his head, leaned over the timekeeper, and smacked Bourgon across the skull. You could hear the crack of stick meeting scalp throughout the arena. Down went Bourgon, out cold, and bleeding profusely.

Porteous was a hero to the Rockets and their fans that night. He got a one-game suspension for almost decapitating poor Bourgon—not much of a penalty for wielding his stick like an ax. And I'll credit Bourgon for showing admirable courage: Late in the game, he returned to the ice, looking like some character out of a horror movie with his head completely bandaged. Thank God he was still in a daze. If he'd been his ugly old self, he would have killed a few of us.

It was in Cornwall that I suffered an embarrassing on-ice moment. I was circling behind our net when I heard a "clang." I looked down to see my metal cup, which had somehow slipped free of my jock, bouncing crazily in front of me. I ignored the damn thing and dipsy-doodled down the ice until the whistle stopped play in the far corner. Just as the referee was about to drop the puck on the ensuing face-off, he said, "Hold it, boys." I looked around to see one of our defenceman stickhandling up the ice—with my cup on the blade of his stick. He swirled into the face-off circle, scooped up the cup in his glove, and handed it to me. "Mac, you dropped this thing back there," he said with a grin. The crowd howled as I skated to our bench and tossed the metal protector to the trainer.

In between games in that brutal Intermediate league, Laporte frequently arranged for us to play exhibition matches in towns throughout the Ottawa Valley and in the States. We played a memorable two-game series in upstate New York one weekend against the Clinton Comets. It was a long bus ride to Clinton, and some of the boys were feeling no pain by the time we arrived. At the border, they'd bought those little bottles of booze, the kind they used to serve on airplanes—Southern Comfort, rye, and gin.

Imbibing didn't seem to hamper our play at first; we won the first game easily. Afterward it was party time. The Rockets were in no shape to battle the Comets in the Sunday afternoon rematch. We played so badly that we should have been ashamed of ourselves. Our goalie, Ron Diguer, was so hungover that we had to push him into the shower to sober up—half an hour before the game.

The Comets beat him for 8 or 9 goals and we never stood a chance.

Winters were colder fifty years ago than they are today. There were some nights long ago in the Ottawa Valley that we'd play in temperatures of 30 or 40 below. One night we huddled around the woodstove in our dressing room (imagine having a stove in a dressing room!) until it was time to play. Only two forward lines went out—one to start the game, the other to sit on the bench. The third line stayed in the room trying to keep warm. We all wore extra sweaters, and most of us donned toques and earmuffs.

One night in Maxville we made the mistake of tying a rough game as time ran out. Our opponents were so incensed that they lashed out at us with sticks and fists. One bruiser hit me so hard with his fist that my jaw ached for a month. When overtime was proposed, Lloyd Laporte just laughed and said, "You can have the game and the 2 points, gentlemen. I'm not going to have my kids beaten to death in the overtime." We went home, counting ourselves lucky to get out of there with our lives and thankful that the fans hadn't thought to slash the tires on our team bus. The ashen-faced referee beetled off ahead of us. He'd been roughed up by one or two disgruntled Maxville players and paused at the arena office just long enough to snatch up his $10 pay for the game.

Some on-ice officials in that era learned to deal with the irate fans who'd wait for them outside the rink by wearing their skates on their hands. The sight of the flashing blades usually scattered the mob, and an angry fan bent on punching the referee in the nose often had to settle for hurling snowballs at the back of his head instead. Most referee-haters felt their aim was improved when they accompanied their icy missiles with a stream of colourful curses. "Words sting, but they don't cause stitches," a referee told me once.

We won most of our games and when spring rolled around we were in splendid condition, full of confidence and primed to beat the Ottawa Junior champs. One year it was St. Pats, another time it was Eastview St. Charles. What a thrill it was to come into the city for these series. The old Ottawa Auditorium filled to capacity. The aroma of hot dogs and popcorn. Perhaps—or did we imagine it?— even the whiff of manure in the air, deposited in the aisles by the stomping of a thousand farmers' feet. All of them belonging to Rocket fans, of course.

"That Goalie Hall's Not So Hot"

I almost missed the excitement of the best season the Rockets ever had. In 1950, I'd been invited to play for the Stratford Kroehlers in the Ontario Hockey Association, considered by many to be the finest Junior league in the world. The Kroehlers paid the Rockets an $800 transfer fee to get me. It would turn out to be a poor investment.

Before making the jump, I wanted some assurance that I would be a regular on the team, and I was promised that, barring injury, I would be. I found a boarding house and registered in high school. The trainer handed me a new pair of Tacks and I began looking forward to a November date in Toronto against the Marlboros. It would be the fulfillment of a lifelong dream—a chance to play at Maple Leaf Gardens.

Training camp in Stratford was delayed several days because they couldn't put ice in the arena for one reason or another. In the meantime we played softball and took part in a fitness program designed by rookie coach Pinky Lewis, who was a former trainer with the Hamilton Tiger-Cats. Pinky was the first black man I'd ever met who was involved in hockey.

In the early going I was on the first line, playing wing on a line with Bob Bailey, one of the OHA's best centres. Not only did I have to adjust to a new position, I also had to learn to deal with Bailey's eccentricities. In practice one day, after I messed up a couple of passes he felt I should have controlled, Bailey lost his temper and hurled his stick at me. Not directly at me, but close enough. The stick sailed over my head and landed in the stands. Bailey glared at me, didn't say a word. But I got the message.

I felt Bailey was a cinch to make the NHL—and he did, playing 150 games with Toronto, Chicago, and Detroit. Scored 15 goals and is mainly remembered for a prolonged, nasty, stick-swinging fight with Rocket Richard.

One of our early-season games was in Windsor, against the Spitfires. Ted Lindsay visited our dressing room before the game to give us a little pep talk. If someone had told me then that Ted and I would hook up more than two decades later on the NBC telecasts—and become fast friends—I would have thought they were mentally unbalanced.

During the game, Bailey sent me in on a breakaway—and I scored. I skated to our bench and told my mates, "Hey, guys, their goalie's not so hot." Later, I found out the Windsor goalie's name was Glenn Hall. Glenn went on to become one of the best goalies in NHL history.

The new skates the club had given me fit poorly and I soon developed sore and raw tendons that hampered my play. I didn't complain because I understood a couple of the unstated rules of the game: no bitching and no bragging. Guys who bitch or brag are not appreciated.

One Friday night in Stratford we stunned the powerful Barrie Flyers, the best team in the league. Their talented lineup included such stars—and future NHLers—as Jerry Toppazzini, Leo Labine, Real Chevrefils, Doug Mohns, and Jim Morrison. We edged them 3–2 and were flushed with success. But in the rematch at Barrie we ran into real trouble and were trailing 8–0 after two periods. We slumped in our dressing room after the second period. Pinky slammed the door in disgust when he left the room.

For some reason, Pinky had benched me and another player, Ron Murphy (not the same fellow who played eighteen years in the NHL), for most of the game. I chose this moment to open my big mouth. "Hey, Murph," I called over in a stage whisper, "if this game goes into overtime, we'll be ready."

The trainer darted out of the room and told Pinky I'd been cracking wise in the dressing room. As the third period began, Pinky waved me over. "We've got a penalty. Let's see if you and Murphy can kill it off." It was pretty obvious he was out to embarrass us.

The puck was dropped and I shovelled it over to Murphy. He threw it back. We banged away at it, and suddenly it wound up in the Barrie goal. I don't recall which one of us scored, but I remember Pinky's reaction as if it were yesterday.

"Get off the ice," he ordered as we came to the bench with big grins on our faces. "Both of you. You're through for the night."

I think it was about then that I realized I would have to leave Stratford. I wasn't having much fun playing hockey there, and that had always been the reason I put on skates and carried a stick. I had already set my mind on getting out when Pinky approached me a few minutes before that game with the Marlies at Maple Leaf Gardens.

"I'm going to try someone else on right wing today. A kid I'm bringing up from Junior B. He's a troubled kid—just out of jail—and this kind of a shot will be good for him."

"What about your promise that I'd play in all the games?" I reminded him.

He shrugged.

My dad had come some distance to see the game that day and he too was disappointed that he wasn't able to see me play.

While the team changed after the game, he and I sat in the stands. When I told him I was going to quit Stratford and go back to Inkerman, he said, "You realize some people are going to call you a quitter. They'll say you couldn't hack it."

"I've thought of that," I said. "What do I care what they say? This team is badly coached and not going anywhere. And the coach reneged on a promise to me. It's not much fun being here."

My dad said, "You have to do what you think is right. But think about it for a day or two. Never make a decision when you're really angry."

I took his advice, but a couple of days later I still hadn't changed my mind. I told the manager I was through in Stratford and returned to my home in Ottawa.

I rejoined Inkerman at half the salary, but I had twice the fun. Lloyd put me back at centre, where I felt I belonged, and gave me two fine wingers, Ed Bjorness and Moe Savard. Even though it was early December before I played my first game with Inkerman, I was voted team captain and managed to score 50 goals.

One thing about Stratford I'll always be grateful for is the opportunity I received to try my hand at newspaper work. I approached Chick Appel, the sports editor of the *Stratford Beacon Herald*, and asked him if he had any writing assignments he could give me. To my surprise he said, "Sure. Cover the big high school football game on Friday."

I did—in the pouring rain—and he said he was pleased with the results. It was my first published effort.

In my final season with the Rockets we knocked off the Ottawa champs, Eastview St. Charles, then stunned a strong South Porcupine Combine team. Orval Tessier was one of the South Porcupine stars, and some of the Combines had tears in their eyes when we eliminated them in a thrilling series.

After the win over South Porcupine, we journeyed by train to Halifax for a showdown with St. Mary's, the Maritime champions. Tom Foley (who later became a host on *Hockey Night in Canada* in Montreal) and Terry Kielty of CFRA joined us on that trip and broadcast the games back to Ottawa. They were two of my media heroes.

In the fifties, few players wore helmets and goalies like Johnny Bower and Glenn Hall played without masks.

The series was the strangest see-saw battle I was ever involved in. We took a commanding lead in the opening game and looked so good that Lloyd told us to ease up. "Play a defensive game," he ordered. We stopped motoring and Halifax popped in half a dozen goals. We hung on for a 9–7 win. We partied for two days after that. The boys got into some Navy rum and some late-night card games and chased a few girls around the hotel. Not surprisingly, we lost the second game, 5–3.

Back in Ottawa Lloyd admonished us to shape up and we responded by pounding St. Mary's. By this point my dad suspected that the Rockets might be playing to stretch out the series and maximize the gate receipts, which were considerable. "There's something fishy about this series," he wrote in his diary. He was even more suspicious when Halifax whipped us soundly in game four. But we got our act together to take games five and six and sent Halifax packing.

I was feeling poorly before the last game of the St. Mary's series, and I complained to the team doctor, pointing out that I had bumps on the back of my neck. He took a look and said, "Looks like a couple of ingrown hairs to me. Don't worry about it." Seems to me I scored a pair of goals in that game, but I was too dazed to be sure. Afterward I went right home to bed. My family doctor was called and his diagnosis was the measles.

"No hockey for at least a week," he ordered.

Oh, I was miserable. Stuck in bed with some kid's disease during the most important part of my life. Unable to travel to Quebec City for our biggest challenge ever—against Jean Beliveau and the Quebec Citadels, the Memorial Cup favourites.

Quebec shut out the Rockets in the first game of the best-of-five series. I was up and out of my sick bed just in time for game two at the Ottawa Auditorium. Laporte took me aside. "I know you're not in game shape, but I want you to stop Beliveau," he said.

The challenge excited me. How proud I'd be if I could keep the greatest Junior player in the world off the scoresheet. After the teams warmed up, I skated out for the opening faceoff. I was head-to-head with Beliveau—well, not exactly: I had to keep looking up, up, up to see his head. He was a giant—the biggest player I'd ever faced. Was I intimidated? Well, I guess. And the referee hadn't even dropped the puck. When he did, Beliveau won the draw cleanly and skated away with it. After that, he might have let me have the puck once or twice, when he got tired of stickhandling through our whole team.

He took one shot from the blue line that rocketed toward Diguer, our goalie, who was normally a pretty cool customer. Beliveau's drive had him diving to save his life, and luckily it sailed over the net.

I chased Beliveau around the rink on wobbly legs. Once he was leading a rush along the far boards and I saw an opportunity. I rushed over and delivered a body check that was probably illegal. I threw everything I had at him—shoulders, elbows, and gloves.

He tossed me aside, sent me flying on my ass, and kept right on going.

I couldn't have stopped Beliveau that day with a bulldozer, and neither could any of the other Rockets. He was sensational. We lost the series in three straight games.

But we'd done well: We'd played twenty playoff games and were among the last six teams left in the hunt for the Memorial Cup, coming as close as could be expected. Laporte's Rockets made more money in playoff gate receipts than the Barrie Flyers, who won the Cup that season. And we put Inkerman on the hockey map in such a way that oldtimers still talk about the "Valley boys."

I'll never forget the Rockets' final game with Quebec, my last with the team. In a pre-game ceremony the Quebec fans presented Beliveau with a new Nash car. We watched enviously from the sidelines. In the third period, with the game out of reach, Lloyd gave our backup goalie, Ed Nicholson, a chance to play. We were always a little nervous when Nicholson played (which wasn't often) so we watched in wide-eyed amazement when he stopped Beliveau on a breakaway—threw out his glove and caught a hot drive that Beliveau intended for the upper corner. When Nicholson made his astonishing save, we all jumped off the bench, hauled him to his feet, pumped his hand, and pounded his back. The entire team.

The Quebec fans, I'm certain, had never seen a team celebrate such a save. In the nearby faceoff circle, Beliveau watched our act, a half smile on his face.

My left winger in that final season was an American—Ed Bjorness from Brooklyn. Ed was one of the first U.S.-born players to come to Canada to improve his skills. We took the train to Maniwaki, Quebec, one weekend for a game. Bjorness had never been on a train and noticed that we were travelling on a stretch of line that had only a single track.

"There's only one track," he observed. "Shouldn't there be two?"

"Yeah, it's a problem, Ed," one of the guys said. "In Canada we can't afford two tracks. Coming back, the train has to back up all the way. It takes twice as long as it does to get there."

In Winchester one night, some of us arrived at the rink early. In the dressing room we found the skates of a player I'll call Ace. We were upset with Ace that week—he hadn't been hustling, hadn't been skating the way we felt a Rocket should. Some of us decided to teach Ace a lesson. We elected to "fix" his skates—to make him go faster, you see. We banged his skates on the steam pipes until the blades were nicked and burred. It would be impossible for anyone to use those skates without stumbling and tumbling.

We dressed hurriedly and got on the ice before Ace. During the warm-up we all waited for Ace to make his appearance. When he did, we were amazed. He skated around with the rest of us as if nothing was wrong.

At this point one of our best players, Cliff Baldwin, made his way through the gate and hit the ice. Boom! Down he went. He got back up and boom! He was down again. Last we saw of Cliff, he was crawling off the ice on his hands and knees. Had to have his blades sharpened. He told us later the blades were all nicked and burred, a real mess. We never did tell him we'd doctored his skates by mistake. Cliff suffered the fate meant for lucky old Ace.

They organized an Inkerman Rockets reunion in Winchester one weekend a few years ago, and aging Rockets returned from far and near. What a treat it was to see them all again. Well-deserved tributes flowed to our remarkable mentor Lloyd Laporte, the man who outfitted his first team in $48 worth of sweaters, who'd made the Rockets hum. And how those of us from the 1950–51 team beamed when Lloyd told us he figured our team was the best one he ever coached. Hall of Famer Leo Boivin was obviously the best player Inkerman had produced, and Ron Diguer was the top goaltender. "Diguer was a wonderful goaltender," Lloyd often said. "I'm surprised he didn't have a major-league career."

Decades have passed, gone like a puck in the crowd. It's been nearly fifty years since we danced on our blades, delighting the fans with our youthful exuberance, skill, and energy. The playoff excitement we brewed each spring, with Laporte frantically stirring the pot, was truly incredible. We were the small-town underdogs playing David to the city slickers' Goliath.

"We came into Junior hockey with nothing and we left with nothing," Lloyd Laporte once told an Ottawa reporter. But the Rockets did make their mark. They even rated an entry in *Total Hockey*, the voluminous official encyclopedia of the NHL. You can look it up.

8

The College Man

I have often said that playing against Beliveau changed my life—and for the better, I hope. If he's that good, I remember thinking, and there are a couple of hundred Juniors in Canada who are almost as good, what chance do I have of making the NHL?

During my last year with Inkerman, the Rockets were invited to play an exhibition game against the tough Lake Placid Roamers, a Senior team, on the campus of St. Lawrence University in Canton, New York. The game was held at Appleton Arena, the new home of the university's hockey team, and as I recall, it was a brutal affair that featured about a dozen fights.

After the game I chatted with Olav Kollevol, the St. Lawrence hockey coach. He was determined to ice a high-calibre team, one in keeping with the beautiful new arena. Olav suggested I'd be welcome at St. Lawrence University, and he piqued my interest even more when he told me the school had a radio station. I was very interested in attending a U.S. college. It was a chance to get an education and to go on playing hockey. He suggested that I come back one day soon and take a tour of the campus. I drove down after the hockey season to look around, and I fell in love with the place. Hell, if it was good enough for Kirk Douglas, it was good enough for me.

But would *I* be good enough for St. Lawrence? The next step was an interview with the director of admissions, a man with a distinguished-sounding name—J. Moreau Brown.

I was ashamed of my high school grades, and with good reason: they wouldn't gain me admission to most respectable colleges and universities. But somehow Mr. Brown and I hit it off and I squeezed in. Years later, he would tell me, "I took a big chance on you, McFarlane. But you left a good impression with me and I went with my hunch."

I didn't let him down.

Back in Ottawa, I got on a bus one day and there, across the aisle, was Mr. Bruce, my high school vice-principal. He looked over at me and said, in a loud voice, "Well, McFarlane, we haven't seen much of you in class lately. What in the world are you going to do with your life?"

"Sir," I replied, "I'm going to St. Lawrence University next year—on a scholarship."

Well, that broke him up. He laughed aloud and, pointing a finger at me, he said, "You? Going to university? That's a good one." I could feel the stares of everyone on the bus as my face kept getting redder. All the while, I was thinking, "Why, you old fart! I'll go down to that university and I'll come back some day and wave my college degree right under your nose."

So between Mr. Brown and Mr. Bruce I felt I had a lot to prove. I buckled down, and my grades improved. I was elected president of my class every year at St. Lawrence—and my sister Norah was vice-president. I was captain of the hockey team, and was listed in *Who's Who in American Colleges*. My photo appeared in *Sports Illustrated* and on the cover of the annual *NCAA Guide*. I made Kixioc, the highest honours society, and the dean's list as well as the All-America team in hockey. Almost fifty years later, I remain the only player in the school's history to score more than 100 goals. The feat didn't mean much back then because we were pioneers in college hockey. There were no records or standards to aim for, no context for that achievement. Only now am I able to take some pride in it.

My only regret is that I never met Mr. Bruce again. He passed away when I was a sophomore, so I never got the chance to prove to him that I was college material after all.

Two memorable things happened to me during my first week at St. Lawrence. After registering for classes, I was given a red beanie to wear on my head and a sign with my name printed on it, which I was to wear on my chest. Believe me, I was not impressed with this orientation week tradition.

That afternoon there was a football game at Weeks Field, and I gathered with some other Canadian students in a row of seats behind some attractive freshman girls. We began horsing around, cracking wise, having a good time. Some of the boys were away from home for the first time, and so they were especially exuberant. The girls in front were not impressed with our antics.

After the game there was a freshman dance at the student union. There was a lot of commotion and laughter as the girls and boys, all meeting for the first time, all wearing their oversized name cards, mixed and mingled. I'd never been much of a dancer in high school. At the so-called prep dances, I'd always wait until the last waltz to ask someone to dance, and by then it was often too late, as the girl I approached would invariably be chosen by someone else a second or two before I arrived on the scene.

On this night at St. Lawrence there was an intermission, and an entertainer of some sort—a magic act, perhaps—took the stage. All the freshmen gathered round in front. Some guy nudged me. "There's a real pretty girl," he said, pointing to a brown-haired young woman with large hazel eyes who was standing just in front of me.

Whoever that fellow was, he turned my whole life around with those few words.

"You're right," I answered, and I made up my mind to ask her to dance. Her name tag read "Joan Pellet, Hillsdale, NJ."

For once I didn't hesitate when the music began. And no one else got there first. We introduced ourselves then danced. Something very special happened in those few minutes—in a word, I was smitten.

The same couldn't be said for her.

"You're one of those fellows I saw at the football game," she said, a hint of disapproval in her voice.

"Hmm, yeah," I said. "I guess."

Desperate to change the subject, I said, "You're going to think this is a line, but it's not. I'm really serious. How often in your life do you meet someone you're instantly attracted to? That's what's happening to me right now. Why not let me walk you back to your dorm after the dance?"

"I don't think so," she said.

I was a little taken aback by her rejection. I know I hadn't left a very good first impression, but couldn't she feel the current of electricity between us?

Later I learned she already had someone to walk her home—the guy she'd come with, her date!

Geez, we'd only been on campus a few hours and she'd already found a date!

It wasn't a good start. I saw Joan around campus from time to time that fall, but she'd started dating someone else. Meanwhile I was getting out of a relationship with a girl back in Ottawa. We didn't go out on a date until midway through our freshman year, and by then she was also dating a teammate of mine, Neale Langill, a top hockey player from Montreal. Langill would have become one of the greatest players in St. Lawrence history, but prior to his sophomore season at St. Lawrence he was suspended for having played professionally for a season in England.

Langill didn't like the fact that Joan was seeing both of us, so he came to my room late one night and proposed that the two of us resolve the problem. He said, "It's a little embarrassing that we're both centres on the hockey team, that we're both getting our photos in the paper all the time, and we're dating the same girl. I know you've got a girl back in Ottawa and I don't think this is a very good situation."

I told him that I was breaking things off with the girl in Ottawa, but that if he felt so strongly about it, perhaps he should be the one to go on dating Joan. He seemed satisfied with that answer and went to talk to Joan. He told her about our conversation, and how we'd settled it so that he was going to date her from now on and I was stepping out of the picture. She made it perfectly clear that no one was going to make those kinds of decisions for her—and certainly not a pair of Canadian hockey players. After that, Joan and I began seeing a lot more of each other, and we dated steadily throughout the rest of our college days.

Joan wasn't my only steady companion at St. Lawrence. Somehow I befriended a local dog named Spot (a Dalmatian—what else?) who followed me everywhere. He came to work with me every day in the cafeteria and attended most of my classes. Occasionally he would cause a stir during class by quietly breaking wind—with dramatic results. Students sitting nearby would gag and cough and fan their faces while Spot, asleep on the floor beneath my chair—dreaming perhaps of pretty spotted bitches—would twitch and groan, completely oblivious to the dirty looks thrown his way. Despite his penchant for flatulence, and for chasing cars, he was very popular on campus, beloved by all.

During my junior year he was struck and killed by a hit-and-run driver. Local police tracked the driver to Syracuse, where he was apprehended and charged. A judge fined him $15 for taking Spot's life. Sadness overtook the entire campus. I wrote a story about Spot's life and death and it appeared, along with his photo, as a two-column obituary in the local newspaper, the *Plaindealer*.

I borrowed a small truck and placed Spot's body in the back. I drove down the street next to the arena. The tears I shed blurred my vision, and I wiped out two small posts when the truck skidded on a patch of ice. I kept right on going, now a hit-and-run driver myself. I buried Spot in a grave by the river, where he loved to swim and chase squirrels, where Joan and I often took long walks. We would visit the site often—even after we graduated, when we'd return for various reunions. Anyone who has ever loved a dog—and Don Cherry and Roger Neilson come to mind—will understand how we felt.

I tried to get involved in everything at university. I always had a strong interest in radio and television and was thrilled to be able to call play-by-play of college football and baseball games. I took a tape recorder down to the local jail one afternoon and sat in a cell with a convict who was facing extradition to Texas. I taped a half-hour documentary on his life story and I played it in front of my sociology class. It was a hit with my classmates, and the professor, Dr. Bloch, gave me an A in the course. University gave me a lot of freedom I hadn't felt in high school.

I even sat on a judiciary board, which included half a dozen select students. We would adjudicate the misdemeanours of other students and recommend an appropriate punishment. One prankster who'd spray-painted a sorority house while he was drunk was tossed out of the university on our recommendation.

In our senior year, Joan and I starred in a play together—*Of Mice and Men*. I'd never tried acting before and I thought it would be fun to give it shot. Memorizing my lines was hard work. Joan and I would go for long walks and run through our lines over and over again. I really enjoyed the experience of being up on stage in front of a full house of students and parents. There was one foul note during one of the play's most dramatic moments: the sound of loud footsteps on the stairs at the back of the hall, followed by a door banging open and a drunken student shouting, "Everybody go and get laid!" The door slammed shut and the prankster ran off, laughing like a hyena. On stage, we paused momentarily, then picked up our lines and carried on.

I never had much money in my college days, so a date with Joan might consist of a walk downtown or along the river and an ice cream cone—a big double-dip, which cost 5¢ a scoop. We shared a love of trout fishing, and somehow we scraped together seventy-five bucks and bought a 1939 Mercury coupe. In that car, we'd seek out some of the fine little streams in the area. I'd bring a metal tray from the cafeteria, where I was head waiter, along with some butter, flour, potato chips, and soft drinks. We'd come to a bridge and park the car, bait our hooks, and agree to meet in an hour or two. Joan would fish upstream,

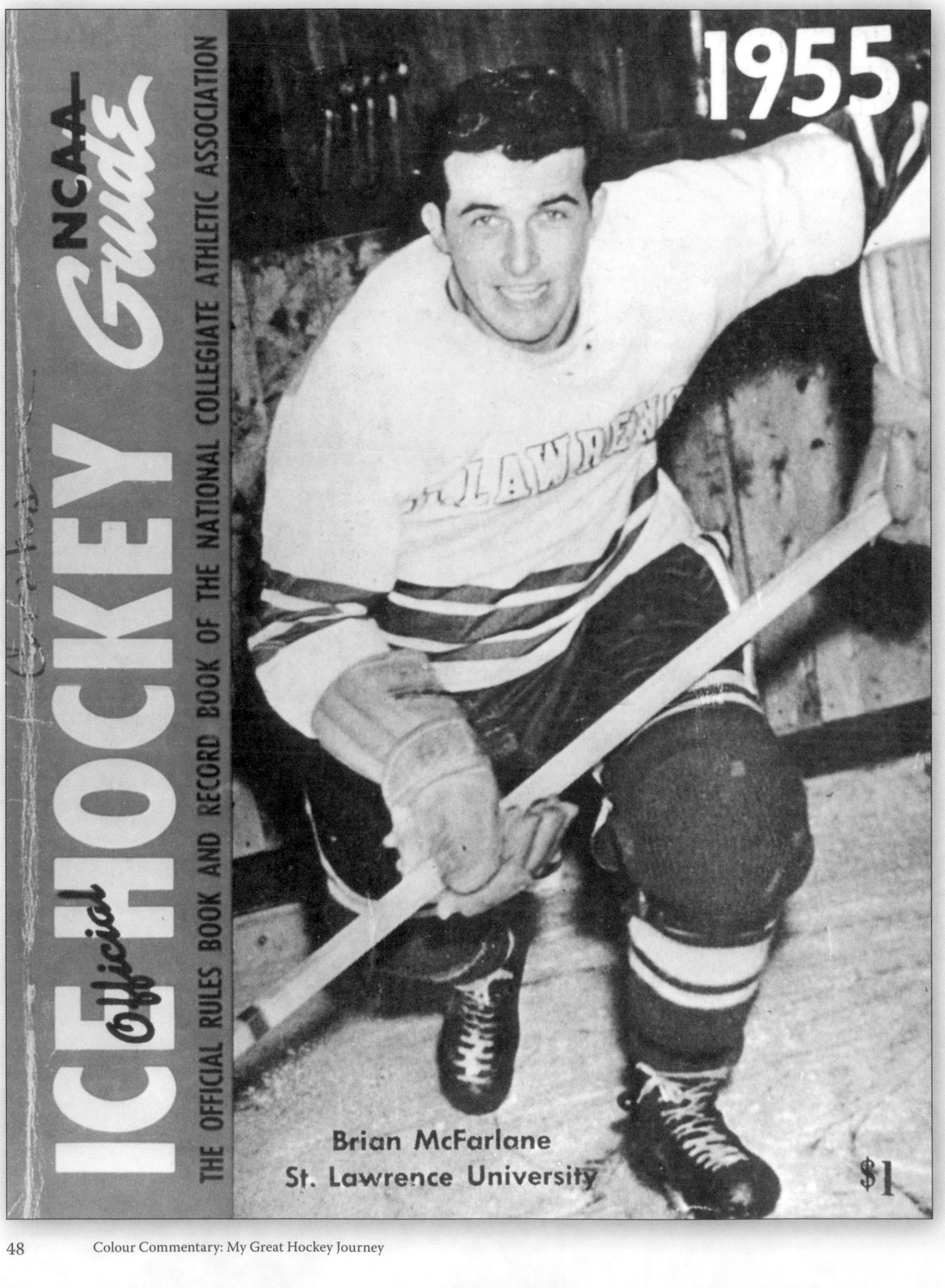

NCAA Guide
Official
ICE HOCKEY
THE OFFICIAL RULES BOOK AND RECORD BOOK OF THE NATIONAL COLLEGIATE ATHLETIC ASSOCIATION

1955

Brian McFarlane
St. Lawrence University

$1

I'd go downstream. We'd clean and cook our catch over a small fire, using the tray as our grill. Spot was always by our side, waiting for leftovers. And we were falling in love. My, those were happy times.

The hockey team did very well while I was there. During my four years, the Saints' record was 64 wins and 19 losses. In my freshman year St. Lawrence and Yale represented the East at the NCAA championships in Colorado Springs. I had torn some cartilage in my knee during the season and wasn't of much use to my team. Then a flying puck cracked my upper jaw in the final game against Yale to wind up my season. We placed fourth in the tournament—Michigan beat us 9–3 and we lost the third-place game against Yale, 4–1—but it was the first time a St. Lawrence team had ever gone that far. We made it to the tournament again in my senior year, 1955, and again, torn cartilage—in my other knee—hampered my play. A strong Michigan team beat us 2–1 in the semifinals. We placed fourth again after losing 6–3 to Harvard.

I enjoyed my years at St. Lawrence and often say that going there was the single best decision I ever made. I encouraged my children to go there, and both my daughters, Lauren and Brenda, excelled on campus. Brenda recently moved to Hollywood and is embarking on a career as a screenwriter, while Lauren is a publisher with *Today's Parent* and other prenatal magazines. My son Michael chose Ryerson, in Toronto, and is now one of those clever computer specialists.

Our St. Lawrence University hockey team
went to the NCAA finals in Colorado
Springs twice, in 1952 and 1955.

9

The Budding Broadcaster

During the summer after my sophomore year, I was fortunate enough to get a job as an all-night disc jockey, spinning records at radio station CFRA in Ottawa. They paid me $125 a month and I acquired some good basic broadcasting experience there. I worked with such local legends as Fred Davis, Terry Kielty, and Les Lye, the morning man, who was very good to me. Sports director Tom Foley was my idol. He was killed in an automobile accident in 1960 at the peak of his career, when he was a rising star on *Hockey Night in Canada*.

During my last two summers at college, I also worked as a TV cameraman at WRGB in Schenectady. In those days, everything was live, and local stations produced all kinds of shows. There was a cooking show and an interview show and a kids' show and a nightly variety show with a singing host and an orchestra. Then there were the early and late newscasts. Every day I'd wheel my camera around the studio, and get more and more caught up in the atmosphere around the television station. I'd spend all my spare time hanging around the studio—watching, listening, learning. All I had to do was push a camera around for two or three shows, then someone else would take over.

The folks at WRGB were real television pioneers. By the time I got there, the station had already been on the air for seventeen years! They treated me grandly and when I left for my senior year at St. Lawrence, I told them that if they ever needed a sportscaster, I'd like to be considered.

When we graduated, Joan and I both pursued careers, and they took us in different directions. She accepted a job as a flight attendant with United Airlines. Her training course took her to Wyoming, and when that was done she was flying all over the country in twin-engine Convairs. Meanwhile, thanks to my second knee operation, I was hobbling around on crutches for the first few weeks of the summer of 1955, anxious to get on with my life—and to land a job in broadcasting.

In the middle of my recovery, I was offered a temporary job acting in a movie for Ottawa-based Crawley Films. It wasn't a demanding role; I played a writer exploring the scenic wonders of New Brunswick in a film called *Picture Province*. For six weeks I travelled with a producer and a cameraman, visiting the Reversing Falls, Magnetic Hill, and other New Brunswick tourist attractions. The film is probably still around somewhere today.

One day in the Maritimes, I got a telegram from WRGB in Schenectady. They were introducing a new nightly sportscast starting in October 1955. Would I like to host it? "I'm your guy," I wrote back. "I'll be there."

My mother died that September in Ottawa after a long battle with cancer, and I took her passing very hard. There was a funeral to attend to and a lot of grieving. Everyone who met my mother loved her. She would have been amazed at the number of people who travelled long distances to be at her funeral, among them my hockey-playing pals from Inkerman and elsewhere. She'd always made them welcome in her kitchen—even the rowdiest ones.

Joan and I celebrated our fiftieth anniversary
in July 2006.

She'd had two great goals in life—to see her children graduate from college and to own her own home. She lived just long enough to witness the former, but not long enough to enjoy the latter.

When I got to Schenectady, they wanted me to walk through the new show. People were concerned because the show had a sponsor—Montgomery Ward—and the host would be required to do stand-up commercials. Could I do that? Well, why not?

Someone handed me a twelve-gauge shotgun and a couple of rifles and told me to ad lib a one-minute commercial about the guns. Ad lib? Guns? I'm no hunter—I knew nothing about guns. My heart skipped a beat. Not knowing what to say, I said with a laugh that "the bullets go in here and they come out there. Give me a hockey stick, a baseball bat, or a fishing rod and I'll do a much better job ad libbing your commercials. And we all know if any of those items are from Montgomery Ward they're going to be first-class products."

"Sorry, guys," I added, "but guns just aren't my thing."

Fortunately, sports *were* my thing and they hired me on the strength of that. My first sportscast on WRGB aired on October 10, 1955. Twice during each broadcast I'd get up from behind my desk, move to a nearby set, and sell something. One night it would be a refrigerator or a TV set, another night it might be men's suits, an electric drill, or snow tires. I had no experience as a commercial announcer, so I learned on the job.

My first guest on my first show was Johnny Podres, a pitcher who'd just won the final game of the World Series for the Brooklyn Dodgers. He lived about 100 miles away and I interviewed him on the telephone. I received permission to send Podres a proper gift to mark the occasion and the sponsor came through with a plaid shirt.

I enjoyed working in Schenectady. Even today, I can remember some of the guests I interviewed on my show—boxer Joe Louis, football great Jim Brown, golfer Mickey Wright.

Some interviews were easier than others. One day I went to Cooperstown, New York, where some of baseball's Hall of Famers were appearing. As soon as I arrived, I spotted the great Stan Musial warming up along the sidelines. I hurried over and persuaded him to let me interview him on camera. I was a huge fan of his, and I was beside myself to be getting the interview for the show. When Stan left, the cameraman came over to me. He was fiddling with his camera and said, "You know, I didn't have the film threaded properly. You'll have to get that fellow over here again."

I almost died. "Do you know who that is?" I asked in disbelief. "That's Stan Musial. You want me to go back and ask him to do this a second time?"

His blank look infuriated me. I had no choice. Approaching Musial, I apologized, told him that there'd been a problem with the camera, and asked if he'd mind reshooting the interview. He grinned and said, "No, not at all, kid." He gave a second short interview and then hustled off toward the outfield. I asked my cameraman how it had looked. He shook his head sadly. "Sorry, I still didn't get it. You better call him back."

I fumed, ready to throttle the son of a bitch.

Now Stan was 200 feet away, warming up and shagging fly balls. I knew how unprofessional I must have looked as I hurried out there, my head hung in shame. "Mr. Musial, I don't know how to tell you this, sir, but I'm afraid that cameraman didn't get our interview again." He laughed and put his arm around my shoulder. "Okay, kid," he said, "let's go over there and try to get it right this time."

I'll never forget Stan Musial agreeing to do that third interview. It was incredibly gracious of him to do what he did for me that day. I've told that story a thousand times and I always end it by saying, "That Musial. He's one of the greatest athletes, one of the nicest people I've ever met." Someday I hope to meet him again. I'd love to tell him how he rates with me half a century later. Better still, I'll send him a copy of this book.

Auditioning for my first full-time job in sportscasting at WRGB-TV in Schenectady, New York. I was asked to ad lib a commercial for guns. I knew nothing about guns.

One of my first TV guests in Schenectady was former heavyweight champ Joe Louis. My very first was with Johnny Podres, who had just pitched the Brooklyn Dodgers to a World Series win.

I helped organize an amateur hockey team in Schenectady—the Generals—and agreed to take on the role of player-coach. Our team of mostly former college players played outdoors on a patch of ice in Central Park. A lumber company donated boards and we assembled a rink with right-angled corners. Before our first game against Syracuse, the park superintendent volunteered to paint lines on the ice, so I gave him a rulebook as a guide. Somehow he became confused and, starting at centre ice, paced off 60 feet and painted a blueline about 10 feet out from the goal. Then he repeated the process in the other direction, leaving us with the largest neutral zone in the history of hockey. For that game, as I recall, we scrapped offsides and played an hour of old-fashioned shinny.

Joan quit her job with United Airlines in the summer of 1956, and we were married a few weeks later, on July 7, in her hometown of Hillsdale, New Jersey. We honeymooned for two weeks in Lake Placid, Muskoka, and Montreal. Believe it or not, by sleeping in a tent we stayed within our $100 budget.

Back home, we moved into a small furnished apartment in Scotia, New York, across the river from the TV station. A year later, our son Michael was born. I filmed him and included the piece in my show that night. I signed off my show with what seems today like a hokey closing line: "Remember, there's always room in the world for one more good sport. Tonight, here's a little film of a brand new sport who was born today in Schenectady." That was Michael's first appearance on television—a not-so-tiny Winston Churchill lookalike, howling at the camera.

In 1957, WRGB decided to drop all sports programming. I was disappointed because I'd enjoyed working there, but I knew that the changes were coming. The way I saw it, I had to decide whether I wanted to go to New York City and try to hit the big leagues in broadcasting there, or return to Canada, my first love, and find a place for myself. I spent a day or two in New York and met with a friend, Bill Creasy, who was a sports broadcaster and a fellow St. Lawrence alum. He encouraged me to be patient. He told me that a new sports network, a fifties version of ESPN, was in development. Because things were still in the planning stages, he advised me to go to Toronto and try to latch onto something there for a year or two to gain more experience. He said I could always move to New York when the new network was about to be launched.

I took a preliminary trip to Toronto, knocked on some doors, and found there weren't many opportunities. I remember hearing that there were sixty thousand unemployed in the city that winter. Christmas was approaching; it was a terrible time to be moving and seeking new opportunities. In spite of all that, I felt good about myself and my ability and I was confident that I would find a job somehow.

I went back to Schenectady, rented a U-Haul, and put all of our belongings in it. We headed back to Toronto, by way of Niagara Falls. I stopped twice along the way, in Rochester and Buffalo, to see if the radio or TV stations there had any job openings. They didn't.

We spent our first few days in Toronto in a cheap motel. Michael was about four months old, and Joan heated his bottle under the hot-water tap in the bathroom. Shortly thereafter we rented a small apartment in Scarborough and used a cardboard box as a table. We had a bed, a crib, and a chest of drawers, but no other real furniture.

I'd prepared a nice brochure outlining my experience. Full of optimism, I took it around to all the radio stations, the advertising agencies, and the CBC. To my dismay, I couldn't get a job anywhere. Christmas came and I had no money for presents. On Christmas Eve I went out and bought Joan a pair of panties and a broom. Something sexy, something functional. Then I stole a Christmas tree off a lot. Well, I didn't really steal it, I just waited until the lot closed and I grabbed a leftover tree. I was beginning to feel a little desperate.

My dad called one day from the film board office in Montreal to say that my cousin, Don Wilder (he would later film the hockey movie *Face-Off*) was producing a movie. Don needed someone to do a voice-over, and the job paid $600. Dad was pretty certain I would get the job, so he encouraged me to drive up to Montreal to audition.

With nothing to lose, I jumped in the car with the family, stayed at my dad's home in Mount Royal, and spent most of the night going over the script. I went to a studio the following day and read for the part, then waited for my cousin's decision, desperately hoping I would get the job. The $600 seemed like an enormous amount of money.

I was bitterly disappointed when Don called to say he'd hired someone else to do the voice-over, even though I knew that the actor he'd hired had far more experience. My dad was furious. He'd given Don his start at the NFB years before and couldn't believe my cousin had repaid him by turning me down.

My confidence was sagging as I drove back to Toronto. I started to wish I'd stayed in the States, where there seemed to be more broadcasting opportunities for young people. A few days later, I saw an ad in the paper, for a job selling pots and pans door to door. I decided to apply. I'd made up my mind that I wasn't going to make it in broadcasting—at least not yet—and our bank balance was down to $90. I interviewed for the job and was hired. When I told Joan I was about to make my fortune selling pots and pans, she put her foot down. "You are not going to do that," she insisted. "You are a great sportscaster. You will get a job in broadcasting. That's what you've always wanted. That's where you belong." End of discussion. So I persevered.

But I still had to pay the rent, so I took bit parts in CBC television productions. I'd sit in the jury in courtroom dramas, while actors playing lawyers argued a case. When the commercial break came up, chances are that was me you saw shaving. I also took modelling jobs. I'd appear in ads, out bowling with the boys, canoeing around Centre Island, or lifting my son Michael into a new car. Cameras would click and I'd get a cheque for twenty-five bucks.

I even appeared as an actor in a commercial for Imperial Oil. In the commercial, I stopped at my friendly Esso dealer on my way to Niagara Falls on my "honeymoon." The ad ran several times on *Hockey Night in Canada*.

One day Joan noticed that George Retzlaff, the sports director at the CBC, had moved into our apartment building. Determined to get me a job in broadcasting, my wife kept an eye out for Mrs. Retzlaff, and every time Nina Retzlaff went down to do her laundry Joan would pile up the dirty clothes and do our laundry, too. It was a foolproof plan that paid dividends two ways. On the one hand, Joan and Nina became good friends. And, while folding towels one day, Joan turned to Nina and said, "You know, my husband is a great sportscaster, and he's not working. Would your husband have anything for him?"

Nina went right up to her husband and said, "George, give that poor young guy a job."

George had an opening that Monday night because Steve Douglas, the regular sportscaster, was taking a night off. I wasn't going to let this opportunity slip by; I called all the radio stations and advertising agencies in town and suggested they watch me on the CBC that night. It worked: the very next day I got a call from CFRB, the number-one radio station in Canada, asking to see me.

Wes McKnight, the station manager and sports director, offered me a job doing the late-night sports for $100 a week. Remembering some advice I'd heard—never let them know you're down and out—I replied boldly that I'd have to think about it. The freelance work was coming in steadily, I bluffed; could they maybe sweeten the pot a bit, to help me make up my mind? McKnight replied that Gordon Sinclair didn't work on Saturdays, so I could do the noon-hour news on Saturdays. Moreover, he could also slot me into a Saturday-afternoon shift as a disc jockey. Now they were talking! On top of that, they would hike my pay another $30. Maintaining my cool front, I told them I'd give them my decision by the end of the afternoon. I walked out of the station, which was on Bloor Street in those days, and I almost did cartwheels along the sidewalk. I couldn't wait to call back and accept the job.

CFRB was a wonderful place to work. In the newsroom, I worked alongside crusty Gordon Sinclair and the personable Jack Dennett.

Dennett, who in time became my best friend at the station, was particularly kind to me, taking me under his wing and giving me all kinds of solid advice. We had dinner together almost every night in one

At the WRGB sports desk. I was happy earning $100 a week as a young broadcaster.

Here I discuss hockey with crooner Bing Crosby in
the early sixties.

of the nearby restaurants. He was not only a remarkable broadcaster but a fascinating conversationalist. I loved hearing him talk about all the broadcasting he'd done for *Hockey Night in Canada*.

It wasn't long before I had a dispute with the curmudgeonly Sinclair. He wrote a column for the *Toronto Daily Star* about radio and TV. After my first Saturday-afternoon stint as a DJ—I hosted a country music show—I picked up the paper, and here's what he had to say:

> Brian McFarlane, a young lad from New Liskeard, was introducing a country record on CFRB yesterday and he suggested the song might remind listeners of Johnny Cash or Marty Robbins. Why didn't he mention one of our Canadian country stars? Why all this emphasis on American singers?

I was somewhat upset. It was my first review and Sinclair was giving me the business. The next day I caught up with him outside Wes McKnight's office and I sprang to the attack. "What's the matter with you?" I asked him. "That crack you made about American singers in the *Star* yesterday was uncalled for and foolish."

"Why didn't you mention a Canadian country-and-western star, boy?" he fired back. "This is Canada we're living in."

"Oh, yeah? Why don't you name a Canadian country star. Come on, name one."

Taken aback by the challenge, he tried frantically to think of one. Finally he said, "Well, you could have mentioned Mayor Mackay of Calgary. Remember him? Rode a big horse in the Grey Cup parade here in '48."

"That's ridiculous," I laughed. "Mackay has nothing to do with music. Is that the best you can do?"

By then, McKnight had heard the commotion outside his door and intervened. "What's going on?" he said.

I jumped in because I was hot. "I'm mad at Sinc because he ripped me in the paper. And it was an unfair criticism."

"Well, he rips everybody," Wes laughed. Turning to admonish Sinc, he said, "Why'd you have to tee off on the kid in his first week on the job? You can find better targets."

Sinc laughed and said he was sorry. "If I'd given it another thought, I might not have done it." We shook hands and became good friends after that. In fact, a week later, he slipped another paragraph about me into his *Star* column: "Brian McFarlane is doing a bang-up job as the new sports voice on CFRB."

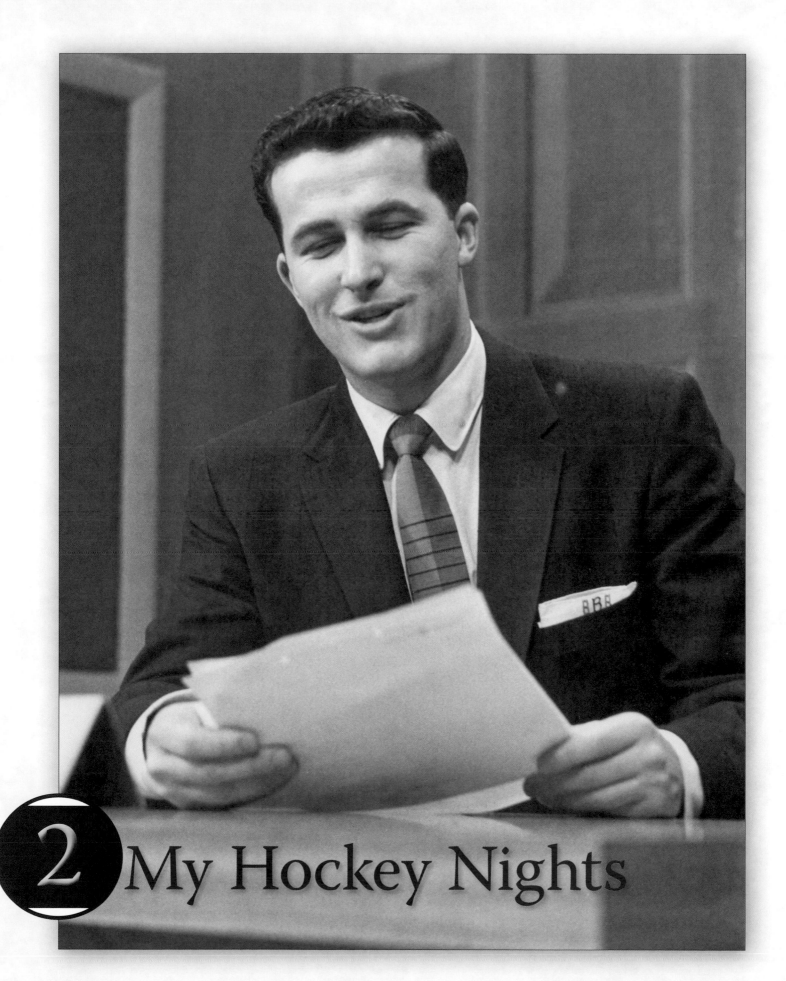

2 My Hockey Nights

"How Are the Tires on Your Car?"

In 1959 *Hockey Night in Canada* was looking for a new host, and I auditioned. I didn't get the job. But later that season I did make my network hockey broadcasting debut—and I got the job as much for my skating ability as for my broadcasting talent. The CBS television network was launching a game-of-the-week broadcast in January 1960. They'd hired Fred Cusick, the longtime play-by-play man for the Boston Bruins, and they were looking for a host and a colour commentator. Someone had come up with the idea that the colour man should do between-periods interviews from centre ice, so the candidate would have to know his way around on a pair of skates.

The network asked Cusick if he knew of anyone who'd fit the bill. "I know someone by reputation," he told them. Fred had been in Toronto and heard my CFRB show *Meet the Hockey Stars*.

"He was a former All-American at St. Lawrence University, so if you're looking for somebody who can skate and demonstrate fundamentals during the intermission, he'd be the ideal guy."

I flew down to New York for an interview, and I was back in Toronto the same night—just in time to do the late sports on 'RB. CBS offered me $200 per game to work eleven weekends that season. I became the first Canadian to be employed by any U.S. network on an NHL hockey broadcast. Needless to say, after losing out to Ward Cornell in my audition for *Hockey Night in Canada* a few days earlier, I was thrilled.

I'd been disappointed when *Hockey Night* hired Cornell. I'd never even heard of him. I found out later that he was from London, Ontario, and that football, not hockey, was his first love. One of the announcers in London told me it was his job to come up with appropriate questions for Ward whenever he had to conduct a hockey-related interview. Was I jealous of Ward? I guess I was. He turned out to be a very friendly, decent man and a solid interviewer. But it always bothered me that he'd watch some U.S. college football game on TV right up until the *Hockey Night in Canada* theme started to play.

Joan and I had planned a small party in our apartment on the Saturday following my interview with CBS. Ray Arsenault, an executive with MacLaren Advertising—the agency owned the rights to *HNIC*—was invited along. When he came to the door, he said, "I'm sorry you didn't get the host's job on *Hockey Night in Canada*. The feeling was you were just a little too young."

"Don't sweat it, Ray," I said with a smile. "I was just hired to do the CBS *Game of the Week*. I'm not too young for them."

His jaw dropped. "Congratulations," he said.

I'd gotten a more humbling response during my visit to New York. After signing with CBS, I met some people at MCA, a major talent agency with whom I eventually signed. When I showed them the CBS contract, they shook their heads. One of them said (rather cruelly, I thought), "CBS must have thought you fell right off the turnip truck if you signed for that piddling amount."

I continued to work for CFRB during the week, but I had to make some arrangements to cover duties on the weekends, when I'd be in New York, Chicago, Detroit, or Boston for a CBS telecast. McKnight had never been a fan of my country music show, but he insisted that I pre-record it so it could run in

Shortly after Ward Cornell (seen here with Leaf captain George Armstrong) beat me out for the host's job on *Hockey Night in Canada*, I became the first Canadian to work network hockey in the U.S.—with CBS.

my absence. "I can't believe I let you put country music on our station," he grumbled. "And now it's fully sponsored. So tape it."

I hired Bob Hesketh, a *Toronto Telegram* sportswriter, to replace me on my weekend sportscasts. I paid him $10 a show. When Hesketh complained to McKnight that the fee was a pittance, Wes called me in. "I hear you're paying Hesketh a mere ten bucks," he said. "How come so little?"

"But, Wes," I protested, "that's all you ever paid me when I filled in for you."

Until his death early in 2000, my friend Hesketh, who attracted a huge following at CFRB with his program *The Way I See It*, always enjoyed telling that story.

My days at CBS got off to a rocky start. I was barred from my first game because AFTRA, the actors' and broadcasters' union in the States, complained that the network should have hired an American announcer to do their games. CBS protested that they hired me because they wanted someone who could skate. "None of the U.S. announcers we considered were skaters," they argued. CBS and AFTRA couldn't come to an agreement in time for the opening game in New York so I was forced to sit by and watch as they did the game without me. All the Toronto papers picked up on the story and it became front-page news. The *Telegram* ran photos of American show-business celebrities next to mine, under the indignant headline, "They Can Work Here. Why Can't He Work There?" It was pointed out that I was a member in good standing of ACTRA, the Canadian counterpart to AFTRA, and that my wife was an American, for heaven's sake. A photographer came to our apartment and snapped photos of Joan and Michael reading the headlines in dismay. By Monday the lawyers and union reps had stopped snarling at each other, the problem had been solved, and my network career was cleared for take-off.

As an afterthought the CBS producers asked me, "You know all the players in the league, don't you?"

"Of course I do," I lied.

During one intermission, I took the camera into the Detroit dressing room and talked to all the Red Wings. Thank God the players' names were written over their stalls or I wouldn't have known Gary Aldcorn from Warren Godfrey. I'd never met any of those fellows.

I was a bundle of nerves before my first on-ice interview on skates. My scheduled guest was the great Gordie Howe. As fate would have it, he was injured late in the first period of the game. When I dashed down from the broadcast booth, threw on my skates, and jumped over the boards, Red Kelly was waiting to meet me. "Gordie won't be here," he said. "You'll have to talk to me." I hadn't prepared any questions for Kelly, but he helped me get through it. From that moment on, I always liked Red Kelly. We are good friends to this day.

The runner or "gofer" on the CBS telecasts was a young man named Chet Forte, a former All-American basketball player who was just a bit too short for pro ball. His job was to make sure the guests showed up where and when they were supposed to. A few years later, Forte gained fame, fortune, and prestige as the director of ABC's *Monday Night Football*.

AFTRA hadn't been able to keep me off CBS airwaves, but my CFRB boss, Wes McKnight, succeeded—thanks to some behind-the-scenes scheming. The Board of Broadcast Governors, forerunner to today's CRTC, was issuing Toronto's first private television license, breaking the CBC's eight-year-old monopoly. McKnight had spent months spearheading a CFRB campaign to land the coveted—and potentially lucrative—new spot on the TV dial. He got it into his head that it was vital that I appear before the board and make an oral appeal on the station's behalf, outlining CFRB's plans for sports programming if we won the license. Without consulting me, Wes called my CBS employers in New York before the last weekend of the NHL season and told them, "We need McFarlane in Toronto on Saturday for the BBG meetings. He's our sports director and he won't be available to work your game in Detroit."

I was really disturbed when McKnight told me what he'd done. I was bitterly disappointed that I didn't get to finish the season with CBS and angry that McKnight had asked the network for my release without consulting me.

At CFCF-TV in Montreal in 1962. The "Chickens," the station's bowling and hockey teams, included TV host Jimmy Tapp, Jerry Rochon (back), me, and Ralph Mellanby, who went on to an Emmy-award-winning career in television.

He tried to brush the matter aside by telling me that, even if I wasn't officially CFRB's sports director, I soon would be. I wasn't sure if I should believe him, because it seemed obvious he was finding it difficult to give up the post. Even as station manager, he had been making all of the sports programming decisions. I had another reason to doubt him: A year earlier, he'd promised me the play-by-play job on the Toronto Argonauts football broadcasts; at the last minute, he changed his mind. "I'll do it for one more year," he said. "Then you can step in."

CFRB's presentation at the BBG hearings was outstanding. But it was Baton Broadcasting—a partnership that included John Bassett, publisher of the *Toronto Telegram*, and Foster Hewitt—that won the license. Later that year, CFTO-TV made its debut.

Montreal had also been granted a new TV license that year, and it wasn't long before I was offered a job as the sports director at CFCF-TV, which the Marconi Company was getting off the ground. I went to Montreal for an interview and they promised me a salary of $15,000 a year, a couple of thousand more than I was making at CFRB. I took the job, hoping that I would have a little more responsibility and decision-making power. By then, McKnight had decided to officially name me CFRB's sports director, but the promotion had come a little too late. I was ready for a change and I looked forward to the new opportunities ahead. Bill Stephenson quickly replaced me at CFRB.

I left CFRB with fond memories and they gave me a nice going-away party. There was even a very practical gift—a set of four snow tires for my car.

Had I known how challenging and frustrating my new role would be, and that it would lead me into deep depression, I might never have left Toronto.

I was met at the Montreal airport by two CFCF-TV executives, Bud Hayward and Vin Dittmer. They took me aside and confessed they'd made a terrible mistake. They were both new to Marconi, and they'd only just been told that they couldn't pay me more than the manager of the tube department at the company's factory. I was stunned. What does a TV station's sports director's salary have to do with some guy making TV and radio tubes? I told them I had to sit down and consider what they were saying. "Look, we're going to dock you a couple of thousand dollars," they said. "But don't worry, we'll get the money back to you under the carpet."

The station eventually did put some carpets down, but when I peeked under them there was nothing there. I should have taken that initial meeting at the airport as an omen of worse things to come. But I'd cut all ties with Toronto, so I had to stick it out.

I hadn't realized until I got to Montreal how lucky I'd been to have learned my trade at such first-class operations as WRGB and CFRB. It became instantly apparent that Marconi wasn't willing to invest heavily in the station, and management had hired an alarming number of people with little or no experience in television, something that made everyone's job that much more difficult. There were a few exceptions. There was Ralph Mellanby, who was just starting out on a career that would earn him several Emmy awards and take him to the top of the world of sports broadcasting. And Gerry Rochon, a talented producer/director. And later, Dick Irvin would join me in the sports department.

Joan and the rest of my growing family—our daughter Lauren was born in Toronto in the summer of 1960—moved to Montreal in the middle of that winter and we rented a house in Lachine. A few months later, we purchased a beautiful home in Gables Court, Beaconsfield. Our daughter Brenda was born in Montreal on July 30, 1962.

While Marconi began construction of our new TV station, we worked out of a temporary studio on the second floor of a building on Laurier Avenue. We were situated over a dance hall, and the boom-boom-boom of the music could be heard in the background during our late-night news-weather-sports package.

Sam Pitt, our executive producer, had planned a lavish hour-long broadcast to mark the launch of CFCF. All the performers—dozens of people, including the news, weather, and sports announcers—were

I dressed as Santa for this interview with Detroit's Gordie Howe.
The Leafs might have signed Santa, but he wore the wrong colours.

to be involved. He even had us lip-synching that familiar number "Another Opening, Another Show." Trouble was, Sam refused—or didn't know how—to edit videotape, a technique that was still relatively new to the industry. It meant that one little mistake by any of us during the taping of the production would bring the session to a halt, and Sam would insist we start all over again—from the top. I think we did that one show a hundred times before Sam was satisfied that we got it right.

We used to chuckle over some of Sam's many memos to the staff. For example, in the studio we employed what is called a giraffe microphone—one with a long neck that extends over the head of the person on camera. One day Sam issued a memo that read, "From now on we will no longer use the kangaroo microphone in the studio." Kangaroo?

I went to Sam once in frustration. "Sam, I'm running a one-man sports department and working seven days a week. I need an assistant. And a secretary would be nice. What's more, when I take a cameraman out to shoot an item for the late sports, he insists on being the director. At the bowling lanes today, he set up halfway down the lane. When I ordered him to shoot from behind the bowlers and zoom in on the pins as they spilled, he was ticked off. And most of the film he shot was soft-focus and unusable."

"Well, Brian," Sam said, "the cameraman always has the last say in such a case."

"No, Sam, I've been taught the director always has the last say."

He leaned across his desk. "Tell me," he said. "How are the tires on your car?"

"What?"

"The tires on your car. I'll bet they're badly worn. I felt just like you do last week—frustrated and upset. Checked the tires on my car and found they were almost bald. Got four new Firestones and I feel like a new man. So go and check your tires. Come back when you've got new ones and we'll finish this conversation."

I walked out in a daze.

I wanted a famous hockey personality to guest on my first show so I called the Montreal Canadiens office. Frank Selke Jr., the team's publicity director and the intermission host on Habs telecasts (and later to become one of my bosses at *Hockey Night in Canada*), took my call.

"Frank, how difficult is it to get a star hockey player for our first telecast?"

He named a fee—$50, I think—and agreed that my choice of Boom Boom Geoffrion was a good one. My first choice—Rocket Richard—wasn't available.

"But this is an exception," he said. "From now on we have a policy of providing guests for you people in order of sweater number. Jacques Plante, number 1, will be your first guest, then Doug Harvey, number 2—"

"Wait a minute, Frank. What if Beliveau scores 5 goals one night and it's Phil Goyette's turn to be on TV?"

"Well, I guess you'll just have to talk to Goyette. He can talk about Beliveau's goals."

I hung up, shaking my head. I think that was the night I started checking the tires on my car.

I finally got permission to hire an assistant. There were applicants from all over the country and I'd pretty much settled on a man from western Canada.

"We can't bring in a westerner!" my boss exclaimed. "It would cost thousands to move him here. Find a local guy, someone who comes cheap."

It just so happened that that week I had done an on-air interview with Dick Irvin, son of the legendary coach of the Toronto Maple Leafs, Montreal Canadiens, and Chicago Blackhawks. I was quite impressed with the way Dick had handled himself on camera.

"You ever think of getting into television, Dick?"

"Yeah, I've thought about it."

I asked my boss if I could hire Irvin.

"Sure. Offer the guy seventy-five bucks a week."

Dick Irvin and I try our hand at film editing in Montreal at CFCF-TV.

"That's pretty insulting. Irvin is making more than that at his regular job. Lots more."

"So? That's all we can pay him."

"Then you offer him the position," I told him.

They called Dick in and he accepted their offer. He was a little shaken when he came to me.

"I thought this glamorous world of television paid more than that," he told me.

"Well, it's a start," I said, happy to have him on board. "And there'll be more money to follow. Trouble is, it's all hidden under the carpet somewhere."

Dick and I got along famously and soon became fast friends. He was a natural for the business. He knew a lot about almost every sport, had many contacts in the city, especially around the Forum, where he was an NHL scorekeeper. He could write copy and had a sense of humour, a definite prerequisite for working at Channel 12.

Dick's presence saved me from going bonkers, at least for a while.

One night we assigned a cameraman to the Forum with instructions to shoot Boom Boom Geoffrion's every shift on the ice. Boom Boom needed just 1 goal for his fiftieth and it was a historic moment, and a costly one in wasted film if he didn't score. In the third period, Geoffrion came close to scoring. A fan leaped up and accidentally struck our cameraman on the hand. He cried out and blew on his fingers, leaving his camera for a moment.

That's when Boom Boom scored and the Forum erupted. I erupted too when the cameraman returned to the station with reels of useless film and no goal. Such things were commonplace at CFCF-TV.

After only a few months on the job, I felt myself beginning to crash. I was on edge and beginning to feel the weight of the workload. I was very unhappy, very uptight, and I needed a change.

One night, just before I was to go on camera, I realized I'd had enough. I found myself perspiring, my mouth was dry, and for the first time I felt a sense of panic at the idea of performing on air. I handed Dick the script. "You do the sports tonight," I said. "I'm out of here." I quit my job the next day and Dick took over.

Stage Fright in Toronto

I went into a real funk after leaving CFCF. I felt that I'd failed as a sports director. I spent many hours walking the beach near our home and pondering my next move. Maybe I should have been selling pots and pans after all.

Finally, I picked up the phone one day and called John Bassett in Toronto.

"Mr. Bassett, you may not remember me but I worked at CFRB in Toronto and now I've quit my job in Montreal and I'm in a bind and I need your help."

He wasted no words. "Yes, of course I remember you. Give me your number. Let me think about it and I'll have someone call you." Our conversation lasted all of fifteen seconds.

The very next day Johnny Esaw, Bassett's sports director at CFTO, called.

"I'm in Montreal on business and I want you to come down to the hotel and see me."

I met Johnny and he offered me a position with him back in Toronto.

"You'll have to agree to do anything and everything," he told me. "News, sports, booth announcing. And I can't pay you more than $8,500."

"Will you pay my moving expenses?"

"Sorry, can't do it."

Johnny's offer was disappointing, but it was clearly a take-it-or-leave-it proposition. In fact, I don't think Johnny would have thought of hiring me if Bassett hadn't pressured him.

I didn't hesitate. I took the job.

My new job at CFTO did not go smoothly. When I wasn't preparing the late sports, I had to sit in a small announcer's booth for hours at a time, giving station breaks—"You're watching CFTO-TV, Channel 9 in Toronto." And I didn't even do that mundane chore well enough to suit one of the bosses. After he lectured me on how to do it better, I said, "Why don't you get one of your top announcers to put the station breaks on tape? That way it'll be the same every time—perfect. And it'll free me up to do more important things in the sports department."

"Oh, we can't do that. The tape might break. Or the operator might forget to play it. Then we'd be stuck."

"Well, the announcer could fall asleep from boredom and miss the station break. Or he could be in the john. Either way there are risks." Within six months all the station breaks were on tape.

I also had to read the occasional newscast. During my first newscast, on a Saturday night, my throat became very dry after a couple of minutes. I reached for a glass of water on the desk and lifted it to my lips. My hand was trembling so badly I almost dropped the glass. Even today, recalling those moments of sheer panic and not knowing what to do about them, I get a sinking feeling in my stomach.

Right after I signed off, Mr. Bassett called and spoke with me. He wasn't angry, just concerned. He offered a bit of advice, told me to hang in there, but I knew I wouldn't be working there long if I didn't conquer my problem.

For a long time after that I was terribly nervous about going on camera. My palms would perspire before every sportscast and I'd have trouble breathing. I tried to hide the problem; I started to use photos and bits of film as little bridges to the end of the telecast, to give myself a chance to catch my breath and struggle through the next few seconds. But I began to worry that I would never conquer my fears, never be comfortable again in front of a camera.

One day I was talking to an actor about my stage fright. He told me he had been asked to perform at Stratford and found he was paralyzed by the fear of performing before live audiences. He went to a hypnotist and she helped him immensely. He was able to perform, and perform well, thanks to her.

"Give me her name," I said.

I underwent several sessions of hypnosis and gradually it began to work. Instead of breathing into paper bags before each show, and agonizing over every minute of my on-camera time, I was able to control my nerves and my breathing.

It was hard to get ahead at CFTO. Tim Ryan and I shared play-by-play duties on Toronto Maple Leaf baseball games on weekends. It was good experience, but the station wasn't paying us anything except mileage expenses—about $3.20 a game, as I recall. Oh, and the ball club let us help ourselves to all the hot dogs we could eat. When I asked Johnny Esaw about getting an actual fee for doing the games, he said, "That'll happen as soon as we get a sponsor." We never got a sponsor.

Tim and I couldn't seem to get any of the little perks that Johnny awarded people like Annis Stukus, Jim Hunt, or Milt Dunnell. They would be invited to sit on a panel on the *Sports Hot Seat* show. Meanwhile Ryan and I would be conscripted to drive the guests in from their hotel or the airport.

I was getting frustrated because I'd been working nights for a lot of years, doing the late sports. It's hard to raise a family properly when you're never home in the evening and gone for much of the day.

Tim Ryan shared my sentiments, and he sent a stack of resumés to various places. Eventually, NHL expansion provided him with an escape: he wound up covering the California Golden Seals. From there he moved to New York and ended up on network TV, where he's been ever since. We would meet, and work together, again in 1973 when we were both hired by NBC to work their hockey telecasts. Each June, for the past twenty-two years, Tim and I have been co-MCs at the famous Canadian Society of New York hockey banquet at the Waldorf-Astoria Hotel.

Each year a former hockey guest is honoured—Howe, Hull, Beliveau, Richard, Dryden, etc. In June 1999 it was Mario Lemieux's turn, and he and his wife Nathalie impressed everyone with their eloquence, dignity, and charm.

Tim and I covered a number of events together at CFTO. One sporting event that stands out in my mind—for the wrong reasons—was the first Toronto Telegram Indoor Games, a track meet at Maple Leaf Gardens. Esaw was away somewhere on business so Tim took charge of the telecast. He and Lloyd Percival worked in the booth while I patrolled the floor area, interviewing the various winners. Because the broadcast was on the full CTV network, I believe we were to make $100 for the night's work.

The highlight of the evening was the half-mile race, in which Toronto's sensational track star Bill Crothers faced some of the world's best. Crothers won the event, triggering an astonishing ovation from the crowd. He collapsed in a heap after crossing the finish line and I dashed over, microphone in hand, ready to thrust it in front of him when he recovered his breath. Suddenly the microphone was pulled away from me. Johnny Esaw, who'd returned from his trip during the meet and was sitting in a rail seat, had sprinted to the scene. "I'll do this interview," he said. "I know this kid like a brother." He dropped to one knee and interviewed Crothers, even though the winner was still gasping and barely able to speak.

I was so pissed off that I left the Gardens. It's the only time I didn't stay around to finish a broadcast I'd started. In the car I told my wife, "I've never seen anything so unprofessional. I can't believe he did that."

On Monday morning Esaw called me in. "I understand you were ticked off on Friday."

"Yeah, I was, Johnny. If you were conducting the orchestra and someone ran on stage and grabbed the baton out of your hand, you'd be ticked off, too."

"Well," he said, "I'm the sports director here and I do what I think is right."

I said, "Johnny, I think you were looking for a way to get yourself on the telecast. It means you earned a hundred bucks like the rest of us."

On another occasion, Tim and I were covering the annual Police Games from Varsity Stadium. There were track-and-field events and a tug of war between the Toronto police and the cops from Detroit. The highlight of our telecast was an appearance of a Canadian high-wire walker—Jay Cochrane. Cochrane attempted to climb a wire from the ground to the top of a TV tower. He would move up the wire at a 45-degree angle to a height of perhaps 80 to 100 feet.

All went well until he got halfway up. Then, without warning, the tower collapsed, sending Cochrane cartwheeling to the ground where he lay in a heap. Tim and I described the dramatic few seconds of his plunge, then looked at each other in shock. We thought he was dead. Cochrane was rushed to hospital where he was treated for various injuries, including two broken legs. The next day our description of his plight was broadcast on one of the U.S. networks. Tim and I earned an extra $100 each for supplying the commentary.

If the name Jay Cochrane sounds familiar, it should. Since his unfortunate debut at the Police Games of 1962, he has gone on to become the greatest high-wire walker in the world. His crowning stunt was walking a high wire between two mountain peaks in China a couple of years ago, higher than any man has walked before.

I didn't dare admit it to Esaw at the time, but he indirectly helped me make a few extra bucks on the side. Whenever a guest for the *Sports Hot Seat* show—a ballplayer, prizefighter, or hockey star—arrived at the CFTO studio, I would tag along behind them with a tape recorder. I'd follow them to the makeup room, perhaps, or even into the men's room, and get a four- or five-minute interview. The next day I would rush down to the CBC and sell the interview to the producer of a radio show there—and collect a much-needed $35.

One day in 1963 I got a call from a young advertising man named Morley Kells, inviting me out for lunch. He was with MacLaren Advertising, and he wanted to know if I had any good hockey ideas, anything that *Hockey Night in Canada* and its main sponsor, Imperial Oil, might be able to use. I told him that Lloyd Percival had once introduced a "Sports College" concept on CBC radio. You'd send in 10¢ and get a little pamphlet—on how to play second base, how to throw a baseball, how to stay in condition—or a crest. I used to write in all the time as a kid. I suggested to Kells that his agency should form a nationwide "Hockey College," with hockey tips and information available to kids and coaches at every Esso station across Canada. We discussed the concept at length and Morley left enthusiastic.

The next day he told his bosses, Bud Turner and David Ray, of our conversation and the day after that I attended a meeting at MacLaren's office at 111 Richmond Street West in Toronto. We talked about parents stopping to buy a few dollars' worth of gas while their sons (we didn't think about daughters back then, but I sure would today) picked up a little booklet—"How to Play Centre Ice," by Dave Keon, or "How to Play Defence," by Tim Horton. The booklets would be in French and English, with Jean Beliveau and other stars of that era involved in the promotion.

When they offered me $20,000 a year to come and work for the agency—as "Dean" of what they would call the Esso National Hockey College—I nearly tumbled out of my chair. It was more than double what CFTO was paying me! I asked them to put the offer in writing and make it a contract. Ray actually scratched his head, looked at Turner, and said, "A contract? Well, I suppose we could do that."

They put some words on paper and I signed it. I was ecstatic and immediately gave notice to a shocked Johnny Esaw at CFTO. "Now look," he said, "if it's a question of money, I can give you an extra thousand dollars."

"Johnny," I replied, "you can't match the offer I've received, so there's not much sense in even discussing it."

Joining a major advertising agency opened a brand new world to me. I had never been a nine-to-five type, never worked in an office, never punched a clock, never had a secretary. It was a difficult adjustment in some ways, but I adapted quickly.

Another novelty for me was an expense account. We'd do a lot of wining and dining of our clients, always on the agency's tab.

When I was still fairly new at MacLaren, Ted Hough, the head of the broadcast division, asked me to organize a going-away party for Ed Fitkin, who was a fixture on the *Hockey Night in Canada* intermissions. He was moving to Los Angeles, where he'd eventually work for Jack Kent Cooke, owner of the L.A. Kings.

I booked the new Riverboat Room at Maple Leaf Gardens for the event and I was given a list of about a dozen people to invite. Hough added more names to the list every day—twelve became twenty, then fifty. On the big night, at least a hundred people showed up.

The bartenders poured stiff shots and soon it seemed everybody was drunk. Somebody's wife took a punch at an overly aggressive radio guy at the bar. A CBC producer, unable or unwilling to find the men's room, used a planter next to the stairwell for a urinal. A young fellow fell down and cracked his head on the floor, knocking himself unconscious. I sent him off to the hospital. It grew late and the maître d' handed me the bill for $915. By then I was feeling no pain, so I said cavalierly, "Just add the appropriate tip and send it to Ted Hough at MacLaren's."

Morley and I threw ourselves into organizing the Hockey College. We held several meetings with the marketing people at Imperial Oil and came away with the feeling they were reluctant to introduce the campaign the next season. A fellow named Burkholder—I remember his spotless desk whenever we'd meet in his office—would say things like, "Fellows, the 'tiger in the tank' campaign is going well. We can't abandon it in favour of a hockey program for kids."

In time we got the green light to spend a lot of money on the promotion. I started to contact people within the Canadian Amateur Hockey Association (CAHA) and within pro hockey, letting them know about our long-range plans. Most thought the idea was very exciting.

Along the way Kells and I also became involved in the production of the hockey telecasts. Morley made plans to have the Esso Hockey College integrated into the first intermission of *Hockey Night in Canada*. We needed a French-speaking representative so I talked with Gilles Tremblay, Jean Beliveau's old linemate, who was with *La Soirée du Hockey* in Montreal. My old friend Dick Irvin, who'd replaced me at CFCF-TV, figured into my plans as an assistant. I approached Father David Bauer about coming on board. We produced a video outlining the objectives of the College. Everybody was enthusiastic.

Our biggest obstacle appeared to be the popularity of Imperial's "tiger in the tank" campaign. It was very strong, a solid campaign, and it threatened to delay our introduction of the Hockey College for another few weeks.

Finally, Imperial Oil decided to postpone the promotion indefinitely. I was taken aback. And now that my project was on hold, the agency had to figure out what to do with Brian McFarlane.

Hockey Night in Canada

I had a suggestion for my bosses at MacLaren Advertising: why not install me in the gondola as Bill Hewitt's permanent colour man?

In those days, *Hockey Night in Canada* employed a different guest colour commentator each week—usually a newspaper reporter like my dad, who had filled the role back in 1937. I always thought the on-air product suffered as a result. How could play-by-play man Bill Hewitt establish any kind of rapport when he was working with a different stranger each week?

Ted Hough and the others shrugged and said, "Why not?" I would like to think I'd earned the job on merit, but in fact it was mainly because the brass didn't know what else to do with me.

Hewitt welcomed me to the gondola in a peculiar way. For the first few games, whenever I spoke, he would reach over and pat me on the back. I'm sure he meant it as a gesture of encouragement, but I found it aggravating. A comment like "The Leafs are playing poorly" would come out this way: "The L-l-leafs are puh-puh-laying poo-poo-poorly."

After a few games, the back-patting stopped and my delivery improved.

As anyone who's ever heard a hockey broadcast knows, the colour man's job is to fill in whenever the play-by-play man stops talking. You rhyme off statistics, analyze how the goals are scored, discuss personalities, and reveal interesting facts about the players and the game. And that's how I approached the job.

But my boss, Ted Hough, had some bizarre ideas about how I should conduct myself on the air. Before my first game, he entered the gondola and said, "Brian, I think you should speak three times a period. That'll be a nice balance between you and Bill." I was stunned. I decided to ignore his edict and broke it within the first few minutes of my career with *Hockey Night in Canada*.

During the first game I worked with Bill, the puck squirted right across the Leaf goal line, from post to post, and it stayed out. On air, Bill turned to me and said, "Brian, as you know, any part of that puck on the line and it's a goal." I was stunned. Surely Bill knew that the puck must cross all the way over the line to count. I certainly wasn't going to correct him while we were live.

During the next commercial break, I said, "Bill, you made a little mistake there. The puck must be over the line to count."

He said, "No, it doesn't."

I grabbed my handy rule book and thumbed through the pages. I showed Bill the rule.

"See here, Bill, it says the puck must be completely over the line or it's no goal."

He studied the page for a few seconds and then said, "Well, they've changed that rule," and went right on with the play-by-play. That rule has been in the books since day one.

Bill and I were in Montreal for a Habs-Leafs game during my first season when I found myself suddenly unemployed—at least temporarily. And it wouldn't be the first time I was fired.

CHUM radio in Toronto had asked me to file a pre-game report from Montreal for their morning sportscast, and I was happy to oblige. Shortly after 8 a.m., the phone rang in my room at the Mount Royal Hotel.

Bill Hewitt, a gentle guy, was my broadcast partner for almost two decades.
Bill was inducted into the media section of the Hockey Hall of Fame in 2008.

Bill and I in the famous gondola at Maple Leaf Gardens. We called the game in 1967 when the Leafs won their last Stanley Cup.

"Brian, this is Ted Hough. I just heard your voice on CHUM and you no longer work for us. You are not allowed to work for anyone but *Hockey Night in Canada*. Unless you call CHUM immediately and tell them you will file no more reports for them, you will not be part of tonight's telecast."

I said, "Ted, I knew of no such exclusivity. Dick Irvin works for a radio station here. And Danny Gallivan files reports for CJAD here in Montreal. Bill and Foster Hewitt have their own radio station. I don't understand—"

"Don't argue with me," he said. "As of now you're fired. Just do as I say. Call CHUM now."

I did, explaining my predicament and telling them I would be unavailable for any more reports. I was reinstated prior to the game that night.

Unlike me, Bill never gave his employers any problems. He knew his job—play-by-play—and he was excellent at it. He didn't contribute much to the other aspects of the broadcast; he was uncomfortable in front of the camera, even more so than his father, Foster.

On road trips, the Hewitts would seldom, if ever, take the same flight as the rest of us. I know they did at least once because I recall Morley Kells quipping, "There's Foster up front. I can relax because God wouldn't dare let a plane crash with Foster Hewitt aboard."

Similarly, Bill seldom stayed in the same hotel as the rest of us. In seventeen years of working with him, I recall dining with him only twice. He never attended a morning skate, never entered a dressing room to talk to the players, never seemed to show much interest in the game before the opening face-off or after the final buzzer. But once the play began, he was right into it—and called the play with accuracy and excitement.

Foster and Bill Hewitt were quite close as father and son, and I came away with the impression that Foster was a controlling influence over Bill's career. But they were good people, and deserving of the accolades they've received. Foster set the standard for all the play-by-play announcers who followed.

Foster made us chuckle one night in the middle of a season. He was on a panel with Jack Dennett, Ward Cornell, and me. The topic was, "Name a highlight of the first half of the season." I've forgotten what the rest of us selected—a winning streak, a big trade, whatever. But I'll never forget Foster's answer: "I think the highlight was my radio station going to fifty thousand watts."

There was a moment of silence. Then producer Bob Gordon interjected. "Uh, Foster, could you make it a hockey highlight?"

Luckily, we were in rehearsal and Foster had a hockey highlight ready when we did the segment live.

Foster used to do the radio play-by-play from the booth next to us. One night, just before we were to go to air, he tapped Bill on the shoulder.

"Bill," I heard him say, "I know we've changed our music policy on our radio station [CKFH] to country, but I heard the most godawful sounds on my car radio driving in tonight. Who the hell is Conway Twitty, anyway?"

Bill replied, "Gee, Dad, he's pretty big in country music. We've got to keep playing his records."

I had to laugh. A few seconds before a Leaf game on national television and Foster and Bill were more concerned about country music than the opening faceoff!

The story of Bill's last night in the booth is a sad one. It was in 1980, and we were covering a meaningless preseason game between Montreal and Toronto. Suddenly he became confused and rattled, delivering a bewildering commentary on the action below. Bob Goldham was the third man in the booth that night and we exchanged startled glances as Bill struggled to remember players' names and positions. During the intermission, executive producer Don Wallace came rushing into the gondola.

"What's the matter with him? Is he drunk?" he asked me. "The Gardens switchboard is lighting up."

"He's not drunk," I said. "But something is wrong with him. I think he's on some sort of medication. Why don't I take over with the play-by-play? Give him the rest of the night off."

"No," Wallace said, "I'll talk to him." He went over to have a word with Bill.

It didn't help. Bill struggled through the rest of the game, after which he took a year's leave of absence. He never came back. The nature of his illness was kept a closely guarded secret.

We visited with him a couple of times at his home near Sunderland, Ontario, and I was shocked when I heard of his sudden death, at age sixty-eight, on Christmas Day 1996. Bill was a nice, gentle man who filled some rather large shoes very well, I thought.

As I've mentioned, one of the things I couldn't get over when I started out at MacLaren Advertising was how freely they spent money. It took some getting used to, especially after the frugal environments at CFTO and CFCF. The agency poured surprising amounts of money into their projects, always accompanied by the standard 15 per cent that was charged back to the client—Imperial Oil, in our case.

Here's an example. One day I suggested we create a feature for a hockey intermission called "Hockey in the Year 2000." We needed some artwork for the feature and I naively assumed one of the agency's staff artists would prepare it. Not so. "We farm all that work out, Brian. Get the best professional artists to do it. Then we add 15 per cent to the invoice and charge it back to the client."

Hmmm, this is quite an arrangement, I thought to myself. Maybe *I* should be providing my services to MacLaren and charging stiff fees for my work. So I had a conversation with Ted Hough. I proposed to leave my staff position so I could form a small company and sell my services to MacLaren on a freelance basis. Hough said, "Well, I was hoping you would join me here in the broadcast department. I need a right-hand man, a full-time assistant. You could learn the business from my side of things and who knows where you might go."

The proposal was very attractive. Ted had a lot of clout. I could envision myself moving up the corporate ladder and eventually becoming an executive producer of *Hockey Night in Canada*. At the same time, I felt a strong desire to remain a broadcaster. I really enjoyed the thrill of covering hockey games. But I took a chance and said, "Okay, Ted. Let me give it a try as your assistant."

I worked with Ted for a week, maybe two. We were never in sync and quite often I couldn't even find him. I would come in in the morning anticipating a good day's work with him, and he would have flown off to New York or Montreal for a meeting. I was like a fish out of water, so I decided to go back to broadcasting. "Ted, this isn't working out," I told him. "I don't think I'm the guy to be your understudy."

"Okay," he said, "can you recommend somebody else?"

"Yes. There's a young fellow named Ralph Mellanby in Montreal. I worked with him at CFCF and he has loads of potential. He's not an on-camera performer; he likes the business side of sports, the production of television. So you might consider him or interview him."

Well, Hough hired Ralph, who's always appreciated the fact that I recommended him for that position. Hough made a good choice: Mellanby has made enormous strides in Canadian and, later, American television. He's very well respected and has won several Emmys for his work. Not only that, among his contributions to hockey was fathering a son, Scott Mellanby, now retired aster twenty-one years in the NHL.

After I left MacLaren, I continued as colour commentator on the Leaf games and I also started my own company, Brian McFarlane Enterprises, through which I produced intermission features for the telecasts and sold my services back to the advertising agency. Jack Vandermay, an excellent cameraman and a friend of mine from my CFTO days, worked with me. I contracted to produce most of the intermission features shown in those days—about thirty-five per season. My contact at MacLaren was Bob Gordon, the producer of the show. Gordon was a good man, saddled with the unenviable task of pleasing both Punch Imlach and Harold Ballard at the Gardens—not to mention his bosses at MacLaren, and especially the sponsors.

I always enjoyed working with Danny Gallivan, seen here with francophone broadcaster René Lecavalier and *Hockey Night in Canada* executive producer Ralph Mellanby.

Sideburns were in when *Hockey Night in Canada* went on the road in the sixties. Here, I'm at the Canadian National Exhibition interviewing Punch Imlach, while Jack Dennett waits his turn to chat with King Clancy.

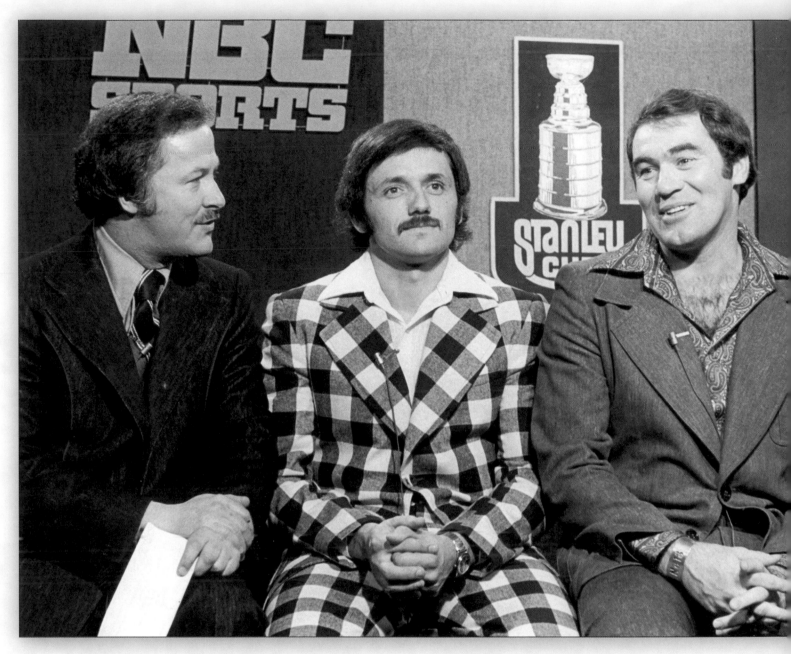

Goalie Chico Resch and Ed Westfall of the Islanders.
Chico's suit dated to B.C.— "before Cherry."

On *Hockey Night in Canada* in the mid-sixties, we were always trying to come up with ways to make the intermissions more entertaining. One idea was for the viewer, the fan, to get to know the broadcasters. That led to the time I went flying with Bill Hewitt. Bill had a terrible fear of flying, so he took flying lessons to try to combat his fear. I volunteered to go up with him to prove that he was a good pilot. Well, between the high winds and the plane carrying the cameraman bobbing along next to us, flying wingtip to wingtip, I was a little nervous and so was Bill. I was happy to return to earth safely and I kissed the ground when we landed.

I even found an ending, a few seconds of vintage film of a pilot crashing through a barn. I said in the voice-over, "There's some film of Bill on his next flight."

But Foster Hewitt saw no humour in the episode and suggested it held Bill up to ridicule. He also persuaded Bill to give up flying.

One day, a week before our Christmas show, I worked out a little skit with Punch Imlach and Leaf captain George Armstrong. They played themselves and I played Santa Claus. The idea was that Santa had come from the North Pole to help the Leafs, who were struggling at the time. The plan was to have Santa zip around the ice (filmed at super-fast speed) and score a few goals on Johnny Bower. Vandermay would film at rinkside, while Armstrong said, "Geez, Punch, we gotta sign Santa. Look at him skate. He can help us."

Imlach would then shake his head and say, "I'd like to sign him, but I can't. He wears Detroit colours." Santa skated over and told Imlach to make up his mind because he was very busy and had to get back to the North Pole soon.

Santa told Punch, "I'm going in to take off my skates while you think about it," and he entered the Leaf dressing room. We stopped filming at that point and, still dressed as Santa, I said to Imlach, "Here's what happens next. You've decided to try and sign Santa. You want to ask him if he'll wear blue and white for a few games. But when you open the dressing room door, Punch, he's not in the room. He's gone. So you turn to Army and say, 'Where did he go?' Then Army will say, 'He's disappeared.' Got it? And really put some emotion in it, look really surprised. Okay?" They nodded. Vandermay set up his camera inside the room, facing the door. I shouted, "Are you guys ready?"

"We're ready." So I shouted "Action!" They pushed the door open. They looked surprised.

Then Punch said, "Where'd the old shit go?"

And Army said, "Why, he's fucked off."

It took a while but we finally stopped laughing long enough to shoot the scene over.

I often wonder how the viewing public would have reacted if the original ending had gone to air.

The viewers seemed to like our new approach and we got a lot of positive feedback. I then suggested we organize a *Hockey Night in Canada* hockey team to play fundraising games. We played everyone from a team of clergymen in Sault Ste. Marie to a women's club in Wallaceburg, Ontario. We even took on the Leafs at the Gardens behind closed doors one morning and beat them, 1–0, thanks to some clever film editing (we cut out all of their goals).

During the 1965–66 season, Eddie Shack was having a great season for the Leafs. After an early-season demotion to the Leafs' Rochester farm team, Eddie was back in Punch Imlach's good graces and on his way to scoring a career-high 26 goals. I was building him up as the Great Entertainer on the telecasts, and I decided I would write a little song about him.

My brother-in-law Bill McCauley was an excellent musician—he'd earned a doctorate from the Eastman School of Music in Rochester, New York—and was serving as music director at the O'Keefe Centre. I told him I'd written some lyrics about Eddie Shack, and he put my words to music in about twenty minutes.

The intermission segment "Showdown" was immensely popular with NHL players and fans until Ballard scuttled it. Here, Howie Meeker and I pose with Darryl Sittler (far left), Rogie Vachon (centre), and Danny Grant.

How many of these past or present *Hockey Night in Canada* regulars do you recognize? Note that Don Cherry, who is always fashionable, was the only one who refused to wear one of those legendary powder blue jackets.

Clear the Track, here comes Shack,
He knocks them down, he gives 'em a whack,
He can score goals, he's found the knack,
Eddie, Eddie Shack.
He started the year in the minors,
And almost gave up the game,
Then boom! He's back with the big club,
And the Leafs haven't quite been the same.

It was a catchy tune and we decided to record it. I'd heard that Eddie was street-smart, a mercenary type always looking to make a buck. So I approached him after a Leaf practice one morning, and told him that I'd written a song about him, and asked if he minded if I recorded it. He told me he didn't care what I did with it. So Bill and I went ahead with the recording.

I'd heard a quartet of Beatle look-alikes one night at the Toronto Press Club. They were called The Secrets. I called them and asked if they wanted to record our song. They were looking for a career boost and agreed to do it immediately. Bill and I financed the recording and booked time at the RCA recording studio in Toronto.

At the recording session, Bill came over to me in shock. "Brian," he said, "these guys are very mediocre musicians." What did I know? They sounded all right to me. Looking back, I should have let Bill choose the band. But we were stuck with them. So they banged away at their instruments and struggled through the song, along with another number I'd written—"Warming the Bench"—for the B-side. The result may not have been the greatest recording ever heard, but RCA Records agreed to distribute it and, incredibly, it shot up to Number 1 on 1050 CHUM, Toronto's top rock station, and stayed there for several weeks. "Clear the Track" fought off all comers—the Beatles, the Rolling Stones, the Beach Boys, and the Supremes.

We planned to feature The Secrets all wearing number 23 Leaf jerseys, and have them play "Clear the Track" during an intermission at a Leaf home game. We were going to put them on the ice to perform. When Ted Hough got wind of that idea, he squashed it in a hurry. "We're not going to let you make money selling records," he ruled. "I'll let you play the record, with shots of Eddie skating around in the background, but that's it. No hype. And nobody's to mention that you wrote it."

"Ted, I'm not trying to sell records," I said. "But if Frank Gifford wrote a football song about a player in the NFL you can bet Howard Cosell and the guys in the booth of *Monday Night Football* would give it a plug, and would have some fun with it." Ted wouldn't listen. He was the boss. We did it his way.

Leaf goalie Johnny Bower had just recently made his mark on the music business with a holiday novelty tune, "Honky the Christmas Goose." He actually sang on the record, which meant he was getting paid a royalty—2¢ or 3¢ a copy. You can bet he was taunting Shack in the Leaf dressing room. "Hey, Eddie, I got a whopping big royalty check today. How much are you getting?"

Shack was peeved and he asked me where his money was. "Eddie," I said, "you gave me permission to write a song about you, remember? Bill and I took all the risks. You're not singing on the record. We're not slandering you in any way—quite the opposite. So you don't get any money. Besides, we'll be lucky to split five hundred bucks from this record."

Eddie wasn't satisfied, and he complained to everyone—including Harold Ballard and a *Toronto Telegram* reporter, that I wasn't paying him anything. I was really upset because I got the feeling he wanted Ballard to turf me off *Hockey Night in Canada* for being such a cheapskate.

I'd written the song as a lark, and it was only helping to increase Shack's popularity, yet here he was telling everybody what a tightwad I was. For years afterward we'd attend banquets together and he would always single me out and tell the audience, "That cheapskate over there never paid me a dime for 'Clear the Track.'" Many people sided with him and thought he should be compensated because

My years with *HNIC* may have been turbulent, but it was a great thrill to be associated with such a unique showcase for the game.

we'd used his name. But Shack had gotten my back up with the hassle he'd created and I refused to give him anything.

For some reason, The Secrets got into the act, griping that Bill and I had "damaged their reputations" with the novelty song, which was a departure from what they really wanted to play. They changed their name to The Quiet Jungle, grew beards, donned black turtlenecks, and faded into musical obscurity.

Just for fun, I looked up my royalty statements from "Clear the Track" and found only two. One was for $230, the other for $2.98. But even today, Shack's convinced that Bill and I made a fortune on "Clear the Track." I often wish "Warming the Bench" had become the hit—it was just as good. "Clear the Track" turned out to be nothing but a headache.

However, it did help me achieve one of the three goals I'd set for myself as a young man: to write one good book, to paint one decent picture, and to write one song. I may write more books, and I've learned to paint in oils, but there'll never be a sequel to "Clear the Track."

Speaking of books, it was about then that I met stockbroker and part-time publisher Chris Ondaatje of Pagurian Press. He said to me, "How would you like to write a hockey book for me, a history of the NHL?" I was flattered.

"I've always wanted to write a book," I answered. "In fact, I was thinking of asking King Clancy if he'd let me write his memoirs."

That conversation marked the beginning of my writing career. I wound up writing both of those books—*Fifty Years of Hockey* and *Clancy: The King's Story*, and about fifty others since then. While I enjoy chronicling hockey's rich history, I find it hard to convince myself I'm a decent writer. It's my dad's influence, of course. And my sister's. And when my daughter Brenda, who's writing screenplays in Hollywood, makes it big, I'll become the fourth-best writer in my own family.

What makes writing worthwhile, despite hearing what my critics say, is hearing from readers who buy my books and tell me they look forward to the next one, and that they collect them. And my publishers, who tell me my sales figures are really impressive. Soon I'll have sold close to a million books in total. So when Mike Rutsey, reviewing books in the *Toronto Sun*, writes, "Thank God I didn't have to read another McFarlane book this Christmas," I can laugh and say, "Up yours, Mike. How many books have you ever sold?"

When people ask me to name my biggest thrill during all my years in the gondola at Maple Leaf Gardens, one stands out above all others.

It was when the Leafs won the Stanley Cup in 1967, the final year of the Original Six, by an ancient Punch Imlach–coached team. They were the oldest collection of vets ever to win the Cup. Toronto met Montreal in the finals that spring and faced the Habs' rookie goalie, Rogie Vachon. Imlach sneered at Vachon, calling him "a Junior B netminder." Vachon and his mates responded by winning the opener 6–2. Imlach's wife, Dodo, watching on TV, said she wanted to kick in her TV set after hearing the commentators praising the Habs and their play.

In game two, Johnny Bower earned a 3–0 shutout over the Habs, despite being belted three times by tough guy John Ferguson, who roared recklessly through his crease.

Bower stopped 60 shots in game three, a match that went into sudden death overtime before Bob Pulford scored the winner in the second overtime period. I can't ever recall seeing and describing thrills to match that overtime.

Terry Sawchuk replaced Bower in game four and looked his age, playing poorly. The Leafs lost, 6–2, and the curtain appeared to be plummeting on Imlach's charges. But Sawchuk, furious with his critics, reached back and played superbly in game five, skating off with a 4–1 victory.

In game six, Bower was too hurt to play but Imlach told him to dress anyway. He wanted Johnny around at the end, if Sawchuk and the Leafs should win, which they did, by a 3–1 score, and with all of

Imlach's old-timers on the ice for the final few seconds. Captain George Armstrong plunked the puck into the empty Hab net and the celebration began.

As broadcasters, we were never invited to Leaf functions in those day, never travelled with the team, nor felt in any way part of the organization. But at home that night, sitting around the kitchen table with Bill McVean, an announcer with CFRB, and Wilf Hayden, a CBC producer, I said, "Guys, let's crash the victory party."

We jumped into a car and drove to Stafford Smythe's house, walked in uninvited, and had a heck of a time. It's the only time I sipped beer from the Stanley Cup.

13

Side Ventures

Early in 1968, Morley Kells introduced me to lacrosse, one of the few games I'd never played. I found the game fast and exciting and I quickly became a fan.

Kells was part of a group planning to form a professional circuit, the National Lacrosse League. He was joined by the late Jim Bishop—then coach of the famous Oshawa Green Gaels—and a group from Peterborough, a lacrosse hotbed. He invited me to a meeting where they were handing out franchises. Kells took Toronto, Bishop grabbed Detroit, and the Peterborough group said they would field a third team.

"We've got to have at least four teams for a league," someone said. "Let's go for Montreal."

"Who wants Montreal?" Kells asked, his eyes sweeping the room.

My right arm rose as if it had a mind of its own.

"McFarlane gets Montreal."

It was done. Approved. I owned a pro lacrosse team. Shit, I thought, what would my wife say about another of my knucklehead decisions?

She took it rather well.

I attended a draft of players and made out all right, snagging the best goaltender available. I'd been told there was plenty of talent in the Quebec Lacrosse League, but I soon learned to my dismay that that circuit was very suspicious of the encroachment of the pros. Any player who even tried out for my club—which I'd named the Canadiens—was threatened with a lifetime suspension from the Quebec league.

I figured at first I'd be able to sell the team within a few weeks—to Montreal interests, maybe Molson's—and keep a small percentage for myself, but no buyers emerged.

Hall of Fame goaltender Jacques Plante was very kind to me, offering Molson's facilities for the press launch of my lacrosse team. When I tried to pay Plante for the buffet and press releases he'd arranged, he refused my cheque and wished me well.

I hired Canadiens enforcer John Ferguson to be my manager and coach and Fergie convinced Michel Blanchard, a star in Quebec, to join my team. Fergie paid him top dollar and handed him a no-cut, no-trade contract. I assigned Blanchard jersey number 9 and we billed him as the Rocket Richard of lacrosse. It was a bit of a stretch—Blanchard sure as hell couldn't fight like Richard.

Sam Pollock drew the line when Fergie said he wanted to play as well. The Habs were on their way to a Stanley Cup victory that spring, and Pollock wanted Fergie to stay focused on the game he was being paid well to play.

Because the Montreal Forum was being renovated, I had to book the Paul Sauvé Arena as my home rink. Because few local players were available, my roster was made up predominantly of English-speaking players. Too bad.

Even so, enough fans turned out to give me hope for the future. The CBC paid us a few dollars to televise a couple of games, we soon had a fan club, and the media gave us plenty of coverage.

We made the playoffs and almost captured the league title, losing to Peterborough in the finals.

Late in the season, my budget was strained to the limit and I had to ask Bruce Norris and the Detroit Red Wings to bail me out. They appointed a new coach and manager, and the league folded after one season. I regret to say that I failed to snare even a single lacrosse ball, stick, or jersey as a souvenir. I lost about $25,000 on the venture and to those who say I was foolish to get involved, I reply, "You may be right. But how often do you get a chance to own a pro franchise for that kind of money—and by simply waving your hand at a meeting?"

By 1969, I was back on shaky ground with my bosses at *Hockey Night in Canada*. They'd decided to hire ex-pros whenever possible to do colour commentary. I was told that Bob Goldham—a good friend of mine who'd been the third man in the booth on many occasions—would replace me on the Leaf telecasts, at least for one season. To Bob's credit he came to me and said, "Brian, if there's any chance they'll have you back, I won't take the job. Our friendship means more to me than that." I was deeply touched but told him there was no chance, and he should take the job. Bob became Bill Hewitt's new partner and I was facing the prospect of sitting out a year, maybe longer. What was I to do?

A few days later, I went to Harold Ballard and handed him a thirteen-page brochure I'd prepared on how the Gardens' image could be improved. "Harold, you should hire me," I told him. "Your public relations department stinks, your press releases are a laughing stock, and you could use a guy like me helping to organize various events and promotions."

For example, I suggested we could move all the old photos out of the front lobby and up to the mezzanine, to be replaced with beautiful colour images of the current stars. Next, I said, we could conduct tours of the building—the Leaf dressing room, the TV studio, and the gondola.

Ballard bought my ideas, but he was reluctant to pay me much to execute them. He offered me $8,500 a year. I told him at that rate I'd have to freelance on the side. "I don't give a shit what you do on the side," he laughed. "You can start tomorrow as our new public relations director."

The next day when I arrived at work, Ballard came to me and said that he'd just spoken to Stan Obodiac, one of his long-time employees. "Stan is so upset I think he's going to have a heart attack," he said. "He thinks he's the public relations director around here and he's pissed off that you're coming on stream. I'll have to pacify the little bugger and let him be public relations director. But don't worry: I'll give you another title as soon as I think of one." After that conversation, I don't think I ever had a title there.

A little later I turned on my television and was shocked to see Stan Obodiac, the Gardens publicity man, in a heated debate with University of Toronto professor John Farina. The prof was castigating Maple Leaf Gardens for its ridiculous policy of not allowing women in the press box. Obodiac defended the policy with excuses like, "The language is often blue in the press box," and "Where would the women sit?"

The next day I approached Ballard and mentioned the broadcast. "We really shouldn't be made to look like fools in regard to this debate over women in the press box. Farina cut Obodiac to ribbons on TV last night. Now, if you really don't want women in the press box, why not say they're welcome if they're qualified members of the Hockey Writers' Association, or that we hope to expand our facilities and make room for them in the future. Say anything, but don't say they're barred. With the women's movement gaining momentum, we're just asking for trouble. We may even be picketed."

"You all through?" he asked.

"Yes."

"Then let's get one thing straight, McFarlane: no fucking women in the press box."

He turned on his heel and walked away. End of discussion.

One night before a Leaf game, four attractive Gardens usherettes slipped out onto the ice, followed by a photographer. They were about to have a group photo taken for the cover of a magazine. Dave Hodge and I moved close to the boards to watch the photo session.

Suddenly, Ballard appeared, bouncing along under his orange coif. He stopped by the Leaf bench, then he turned and roared, "Hodgey! Come on out here with me and we'll fuck these usherettes. You can have the fat one on the end."

Hodge told me a fascinating fact about Harold one day. Hodge was acting as MC at a major hockey event at a downtown hotel and he was sitting next to Ballard at the head table.

"Harold had to take a whiz in the middle of the luncheon, but the men's room was a long way off. So he pulled up the skirt covering the head table, whipped it out, and pissed all over the carpet."

Once I was on board at the Gardens, Ballard put off making any of the changes I had proposed, complaining that they would cost too much money. After a year of getting nowhere with him, I was ready for a vacation. While I was cleaning up my desk, preparing to leave with my family on a trip to western Canada, Gardens' accountant Bob Giroux came to me and said, "I think Harold's going to close down the PR department."

I couldn't believe it. "What are you trying to tell me, Bob? Am I out of work or what?"

"I don't know," he said. "You'd better talk to Harold."

Well, after months working with Harold, I knew how slick he was at dodging people whenever there was any kind of crisis. He wasn't in his office and I wasn't about to chase around the Gardens looking for him. So, I just walked out and went home. To this day I'm not sure whether I quit or he fired me from my ambiguous role at Maple Leaf Gardens.

We left on our trip the next day, hauling a tent trailer. I waited until we were sitting around a campfire near Kenora, Ontario—hundreds of miles from home—before I gave Joan the bad news that I was out of work again. She looked at me and said, "Well, that's great. We can spend another two or three weeks out here!" And that's exactly what we did, travelling all the way to Tofino, on Vancouver Island, and back.

When we got back to Toronto, I decided to explore new broadcast avenues. My wife, an American citizen, urged me to look in the States. "Maybe you should never have come back to Canada," she said. So I contacted the Pittsburgh Penguins, the Chicago Blackhawks, and the Buffalo Sabres. Pittsburgh was looking for a radio play-by-play voice while the other two had openings in both radio and TV. I flew to Chicago for an audition and drove to Buffalo for an interview.

I was soon convinced that Buffalo should be my next destination. I liked the Knox brothers (the Sabres' owners) and the team's PR director, Chuck Burr, clinched the deal when he took me aside and told me, "This is confidential, but I'll be leaving the club for a better job in a few weeks. If you move here, you can do the play-by-play and take over my job in public relations as well."

"Sounds good to me, Chuck. I'll call you tomorrow to confirm all this."

I phoned Pittsburgh and Chicago to tell them of my decision, and I called Burr back the next morning, but I obviously misunderstood just how final the deal was.

"Chuck, I'm delighted to accept your offer. When do I report?"

"Geez, Brian," he said, "I hate to tell you this but the job we discussed just went to Ted Darling. It wasn't my decision. I think [Sabres GM Punch] Imlach got involved and he's never been a big fan of yours. I don't blame you for being upset."

I exploded. "Chuck, I think you're a son of a bitch! You made me an offer. I turned down two other opportunities and now you say the job is Darling's. Screw you." I hung up and called Joan to tell her the bad news. Then we went downtown, met some friends, and drank too much beer.

A few days later, *Hockey Night in Canada* called. "Ted Darling is moving to Buffalo," I was told. As if I didn't know. "Would you like to replace him as our host in Montreal?"

"Why not?" I answered. I didn't have anything else going on.

During that season, I also decided to revive the dormant plan for a hockey college. The first potential client I approached was the ultra-conservative Bank of Nova Scotia. Herb Mortimer of Gruen, the company sponsoring the NHL Oldtimers, suggested I should see the bank's head of marketing, Neil Speicher.

"I mentioned your name to Speicher and he said he knows you," Mortimer told me. As fate would have it, Speicher had been the bank manager in Haileybury when my family lived in the north country. "He said when you were a little kid he drove you from Haileybury to Whitby after your dad moved the family there."

Neil was an interesting fellow who was battling a serious illness and nearing retirement. I told him that most branch managers tolerated youngsters in their bank branches, but few of them showed any personal interest in kids. I suggested that by using hockey as a lure, youngsters could easily be enticed into opening savings accounts at Scotiabank, upon which they would automatically become members of the Scotiabank Hockey College. Each member would be encouraged to stop by the branch once a month to pick up a special bulletin featuring hockey stories and photos, including a centrefold of an NHL star. Stories would stress fair play, fitness, and respect for officials, and provide tips on money management. Every month those who'd made a small deposit in their accounts would be eligible for a draw for prizes like an all-expenses-paid trip to a Stanley Cup game. Kids who remembered the good treatment they got from Scotiabank and the Hockey College would one day become adult wage earners and stick with the bank.

Speicher agreed with the concept, and had me draft another presentation for the bank's top executives. They adopted it on one condition: that we keep the annual budget under $100,000. We estimated the costs of magazines, promotion, and so on, and the figure came out to $104,000. I was disheartened because $15,000 out of that budget was to be my salary. "Look," I said, "take the other $4,000 off my fee."

"No," Speicher said, "we'll find the four thousand somewhere. Let's start the program."

For the next seventeen years I ran the Scotiabank Hockey College program. I wrote and edited the magazine every month and even took many of the photos that appeared in it. As we'd predicted, kids came in by the thousands and opened accounts—about 40 per cent of them girls. Members and non-members alike picked up the monthly magazines at their bank branches.

Steve Payne was our first member to make the NHL, and Toronto Blue Jays' GM Gord Ash was also a member.

Len Woolsey, who succeeded Speicher as head of marketing, decided that Scotiabank should hook up with some high-profile hockey personalities to enhance the program. Gordie Howe and Jean Beliveau came on board and filmed some commercials at the Montreal Forum. Those fellows didn't come cheap.

Jean Beliveau was, and is now, a gentleman. We never asked him to do very much, and he was a little embarrassed. "Brian," he said, "they are paying me all this money and they never really ask me to do anything except maybe go tuna fishing with a couple of bank executives once a year. I don't feel I'm really earning my money." I always appreciated his attitude.

Scotiabank flew Beliveau into Toronto one day to honour him at a dinner party. After the dinner, he took me aside and showed me the special gift they'd presented to him. I thought it might be a small painting or some expensive cuff links. It was a Scotiabank pen, with the logo printed on it, worth all of 98¢.

In the early 1980s the bank asked me to recommend another high-profile player. Darryl Sittler immediately came to mind. He was everybody's hero and he'd just signed a new contract with the Leafs, and I knew it contained a no-trade clause. "If you get Sittler you are getting a good one," I told the bank, "because he is not going to get you in any trouble. And he can't be traded away."

In no time Sittler got into a nasty dispute with his coach, Punch Imlach, and with Leaf owner Harold Ballard. One night before a game, he ripped the captain's *C* off Sittler's jersey. Ballard started calling him a "cancer" on the team. After months of feuding with Imlach, he finally waived the no-trade stipulation in his contract and the Leafs dealt him to the Philadelphia Flyers, getting little in return. So much for my prediction that Sit would never be a problem for the bank and would never leave Toronto.

Over the years the program won many accolades, even though there were those around the bank who just didn't get it, fellows like program manager Harvey Hofbauer, who once asked me, "How do you spell Gretzky in French?" Another banker, who heard I was working on a profile of star defenceman Larry Robinson, asked, "Who's Larry Robinson?"

Still, it came as a shock in 1987 when Scotiabank dumped me unceremoniously. A couple of new marketing people met with me one day and said, "Mr. McFarlane, we're concerned about all this money we are paying you. [I was making about $35,000 a year at the time.] We've decided we can write and publish our monthly bulletin internally, using staff members. But you can stay on with us and we'll pay you $100 per month to write your 'Stickhandling Through Life' column. What do you say?"

I was furious. "What do I say? I say you don't know the history of this program. I came to the bank in 1970 with an idea that now attracts over three-hundred thousand young depositors to the bank every month, with a couple of hundred million dollars on deposit. I say you want to steal my concept and dump me. Then you have the gall to offer me a hundred bucks a month."

They looked at each other with raised eyebrows. "We didn't know the Hockey College was your idea," one of them said.

"You know it now," I told them. "Look, I'm going to make it easy for you. I don't want a few bucks to write a column for you. But you tell your bosses I'm very angry, that I'm going to sue the bank over this. Tell them I'll go quietly for a sum of $150,000 in a settlement."

I thought they were both going to keel over. I hope I scared the hell out of them. I left the bank, never to return. I never sued—I was advised it would be difficult to get a settlement. It wasn't long before the popularity of the program waned. The bulletin became a hodgepodge of articles on every conceivable subject, none of them very interesting. They focused too much on money and savings, boring stuff for most kids.

I saw some of my old Scotiabank bulletins at a major card show in Toronto a few weeks ago. One of them had a youthful-looking Wayne Gretzky on the cover.

"How much?" I asked.

"I'm asking thirty-eight bucks," the owner replied.

In the Swing of the Seventies

The 1970–71 season, which looked bleak for a while, proved to be full of opportunities and excitement. I took over Ted Darling's job in Montreal and I was back into the swing of things at *Hockey Night in Canada*. And the Scotiabank Hockey College was keeping me busy during the week. One night in the Montreal Press Club, I realized what a hot commodity the Hockey College had already become. Frank Selke Jr. asked me how I'd like to come back to Toronto.

"That would be great, Frank."

"Well, we'll bring you back to work Leaf games if you'll give us the Hockey College."

"Take a hike, Frank."

The subject was never raised again.

I never really felt comfortable working in Montreal. Dick Irvin and Danny Gallivan had become part of the fabric of the city, whereas I was the interloper—the guy from Toronto—probably perceived as an incorrigible Leaf fan at heart. I could almost hear people in the Canadiens front office saying, "Why the hell is that Toronto guy hosting our games?"

I once asked Habs GM Sam Pollock if he resented my presence on the telecasts. He pulled out his hanky and launched into a coughing fit. I never did hear his response, though Ralph Mellanby once told me Pollock accepted me because "he's from the Ottawa Valley, isn't he?" When I mentioned my concern to one of the producers, he told me, "All I heard was the Canadiens would rather have *you* host the show than Hodge."

In the summer of 1972, Hockey Canada hired me as a liaison, to act as a buffer between government officials and those associated with Alan Eagleson's Team Canada. I was glad to be involved with the Canada-USSR Summit Series because *Hockey Night in Canada* had been shut out of the broadcasting. Eagleson and Harold Ballard had scoffed at Ted Hough's low bid and awarded the television rights to CTV. It meant that none of us, except Foster Hewitt, would be part of what turned out to be the greatest, most emotional hockey series ever played.

Hockey Canada paid me well to do very little. I acted as MC at a couple of luncheons and followed the series through the first four games. There was obvious friction between the two camps. Eagleson did things his way and he brooked no interference. He hardly acknowledged my existence. I bowed out after the fourth game, turning in my tickets to Moscow, because I felt like a square peg in a round hole, and I felt I was taking money that wasn't well earned. Since then I've often wished I'd been there to see Paul Henderson's series-winning goal in Moscow.

I have often said that three of the best years of my broadcasting career were spent on the NBC hockey telecasts between 1973 and 1975. It was such an honour to be selected to join the broadcast crew and work with people who had covered Super Bowls, World Series, and so many other major events. Unlike *Hockey Night in Canada* and the CBC, where the bosses were quick to point out how fortunate you were to be on board, the NBC people always let us know how pleased they were to have experienced

The NBC broadcast team on the ice in 1974—Brian McFarlane, Tim Ryan, and Ted Lindsay. Years earlier, Lindsay had played with equally good linemates in Gordie Howe and Sid Abel.

Bob Goldham (left) and Dave Hodge interview Peter Puck. Peter was always willing to entertain and educate his fans. (My daughter Brenda is inside the costume.)

broadcasters and knowledgeable hockey men with their crew. They relied on Tim Ryan, Ted Lindsay, and me to suggest the best players to interview, what should be shown during the intermissions, and what rivalries to promote.

At NBC we quickly became a family. We ate together on the eve of a game, we phoned each other during the week, we even had our own NBC hockey team. On the morning of a game, or sometimes the day before, Ted, Tim, and I would suit up alongside other members of the crew (notably our leader, Scotty Connal), and we'd play a team of media guys from the home city involved in the *Game of the Week*. With Lindsay on our side, we seldom lost.

During one of those NBC years, one of my bosses at *Hockey Night in Canada* took me aside and said, "I hear you've been saying nice things about NBC."

"Oh, I have. They're great people."

"Don't forget. We're nice too," he growled.

One of the most interesting characters I teamed up with on NBC was the irrepressible imp of the ice, Peter Puck. The animated hockey puck, created by Hanna-Barbera in Hollywood, with story lines drawn from some books I sent them, became one of the most popular intermission segments in the history of televised hockey. Soon after I began introducing Peter each week, I became known as "Peter Puck's father." It was inevitable that a book would follow, *Peter Puck: Love That Hockey Game*, which sold fifty thousand copies. Later, I purchased the Canadian rights to the marketing of Peter Puck and later still, I negotiated world-wide rights to the character. Someday, in a follow-up book, perhaps, I'll tell the full story of Peter Puck and his hockey travails. Long ago I joined millions of hockey fans who said, "We love Peter Puck!" Don't be surprised if he or one of his rubber offspring makes a comeback soon.

I worked some memorable games for NBC, especially the 1974 Stanley Cup finals between the Philadelphia Flyers and the Boston Bruins. During one of those games I interviewed Kate Smith, whom the Flyers had brought in for a $5,000 fee, to sing "God Bless America" before the opening faceoff. What an ovation the old lady received. She seemed truly overwhelmed by all the attention she got as the Flyers' good luck charm. Uncannily, the Flyers almost always won when they opened a game with her rendition of "God Bless America." It didn't matter whether they played a record or she appeared in person, Kate's record at the time was something like 37–3–1.

One of my most bizarre on-air moments happened during the Flyers' semifinal series with the New York Rangers that year. I was rinkside at Madison Square Garden, holding a wireless microphone. Suddenly a puck shot by New York's Dale Rolfe hit Flyer defenceman Barry Ashbee in the eye. Ashbee fell to the ice, his blood streaming onto the ice. He would lose the eye, and, tragically a few weeks later, die of leukemia. A stretcher was called for, the gates opened next to me, and, without thinking, I followed the stretcher bearers onto the ice. I passed in front of the Ranger bench and Brad Park shouted at me, "Hey, Brian, you're not supposed to be out here!"

I nodded and said, "I know, Brad, but I'm not stopping now." Tim Ryan, high in the broadcast booth, called on me for a report and I chatted with linesman Matt Pavelich. He gave me an eyewitness description of what had happened. Never before had a broadcaster walked on the ice during a game, and it hasn't happened since.

In the *Toronto Star* the next day, I read an interesting article. Under the headline "McFarlane Told to Stay off Ice," it read,

> NBC hockey broadcaster Brian McFarlane has been admonished by NHL president Clarence Campbell for his impulsive act during yesterday's playoff game in New York. Campbell warned McFarlane to stay off the ice after the broadcaster invaded the ice surface to interview linesman Matt Pavelich about an injury—a broadcasting "first."

That's odd, I thought. Nobody had said anything to me about the incident. The following weekend I was back in New York and I passed Mr. Campbell as I headed down a corridor at Madison Square Garden a couple of hours before game time.

I nodded and said, "Hello, Mr. Campbell."

"Hello, Brian."

I was 20 feet past him before he turned and called my name.

"Brian."

"Yes, sir."

"Stay off the ice from now on."

"I will, Mr. Campbell."

The last year that NBC covered hockey was 1974–75, and that year's finals between the Flyers and the Buffalo Sabres took on a surreal quality. Thanks to warm weather and a lack of air conditioning, game three in Buffalo was played in fog so thick that the players seemed to be floating instead of skating. The goalies couldn't see each other—hell, they couldn't see past their own blue line. Things got really weird when a bat flew down from the arena rafters and started circling over the players' heads. Buffalo's Jim Lorentz swatted the poor creature out of the air with his stick, killing it before a full house in Buffalo and drawing the wrath of animal lovers across North America for his murderous act.

Prior to one of our games in Buffalo, our NBC team was given an hour of ice time. I was the first one dressed and there wasn't a soul in sight when I skated onto the ice. I picked up a loose puck and fired a shot at the empty net. I missed and hit the glass. Crash! Shards of Plexiglas flew in all directions. I stood there dumbfounded. I'd broken the glass with my shot.

I raced into the dressing room to tell Lindsay, Ryan, and the others.

Needless to say, they didn't believe me.

"We've seen your shot," Lindsay said, laughing. "No way it would break a pane of glass."

I sought out the arena manager later and offered to pay him for the damage.

"Don't worry about it," he said. "Every hundred thousand shots or so, the glass weakens and breaks."

"Geez, I thought I shot the puck too hard."

"Not likely," he answered, unaware I was kidding.

One of the most memorable interviews I ever conducted took place on the ice of Vancouver's Pacific Coliseum in the spring of 1974. I pleaded with my executive producer, Scotty Connal, to let me chat with the legendary Cyclone Taylor, who lived in Vancouver. I'd met him several times and admired him tremendously.

The only hitch came when I insisted on doing the interview on skates.

"But the man is ninety years old," some of my colleagues protested. "What if he falls and breaks a leg?"

Vancouver Canucks officials had voiced the same fears when it had been suggested that Taylor skate a lap or two during their opening-night ceremonies in 1970, their NHL debut season.

"He won't fall," I assured them. "We'll use a wireless microphone and he can hold onto my arm for support."

Scotty finally gave me the green light. I called Cyclone and he was thrilled with the idea. So there we were, on the full NBC network, circling the arena ice and talking about hockey's "good old days," going back to the turn of the century and even beyond.

Cyclone sparkled during our five-minute skate. His strides were firm, his voice strong, his anecdotes fascinating. It ranks as my all-time favourite interview. The piece drew a tremendous response from the viewers. Letters poured into NBC from all over Canada and the United States. Some viewers called it the most heartwarming thing they had ever seen on TV. Others just called it inspiring. Cyclone Taylor—the old master showman hadn't lost his touch.

Cyclone Taylor in the NBC Vancouver studio after our historic skate around the Pacific Coliseum in 1974–75.

An intermission with Howie Meeker, who was always colourful and
controversial. Here we team up on NBC.

Phil Esposito was a frequent guest on our NBC telecasts. He was hockey's greatest scorer in the early seventies.

Did anyone think to preserve the tape of that magical interview? Foolishly, I assumed that someone at the network would have. But a later enquiry proved me wrong. All tapes of those games—Bobby Orr and Phil Esposito at their peaks; Bobby Clarke, toothless and tenacious, leading the Flyers to consecutive Cup triumphs; Guy Lafleur's electrifying rushes; Ken Dryden's goaltending—all erased, lost forever. Aside from that, everything was first-class with NBC. The three announcers were front and centre at a reserved table at the All-Star dinner and other league affairs. "We're proud of you guys," Scotty Connal would say. "We want you there."

At *Hockey Night in Canada*, we'd take turns being invited to such events. It would be my turn one year, Dave Hodge's the next, and then perhaps Bill Hewitt's.

Before each game, Connal would ask, "You guys need any tickets for the game? How many?" Tickets were rarely available to us at *HNIC*.

Chrysler was a major sponsor of the NBC telecasts and Scotty told us they wanted the announcers driving their cars. "Go to their plant and pick out the model of your choice. Turn it in at the end of the year and select a new one." What a lovely perk for three seasons.

When I was with *Hockey Night in Canada*, I once called Ford, a major sponsor, and asked for a deal on a new car. Shouldn't we be driving the sponsor's product? I suggested. Certainly, was the answer. They referred me to a local dealer, but the price I was quoted was no bargain. Instead, I called a friend in the business and bought a new Chevrolet from him.

One day I was invited to appear on a well-known radio talk show in Boston. The host asked me how I got along with Stan Fischler, the prolific hockey author and TV commentator from New York. I had never met Fischler but I told the radio audience he'd made a significant contribution to hockey, chronicling the game as he did. Only later, when I leafed through the latest edition of *The Sporting News*, did I understand the reasoning behind the radio host's question.

"On NBC television," Fischler wrote, "McFarlane is about as bright as a three-watt bulb."

Now, I've taken some zingers in my time but that one hurt, especially coming as it did from a fellow commentator. I tried not to let it bother me. I considered the source: When *The Hockey News* asked him to pick his all-time All-Star team, Fischler named a forward line of Walt Tkaczuk, Bill Fairbairn, and Steve Vickers—passing over such luminaries as Bobby Hull, Gordie Howe, Phil Esposito, and Frank Mahovlich. He also named Steve Durbano as one of his top defencemen and Aldo Guidolin as his All-Star coach. Guidolin coached one season in the NHL (with Colorado) and compiled a record of 12–39–8 for a .271 winning percentage.

Some time later I was covering a playoff game between Buffalo and Philadelphia. The first period was slow, dull, and disappointing. My guest during the intermission was Phil Esposito, always outspoken and always a welcome visitor to our studio. "Phil," I began, "that first period was so dull it would put you to sleep faster than one of Stan Fischler's hockey books." Phil's face lit up and he pointed his index finger at me. "Now that's a good one!" he laughed. "That's a good one." Months later I was still running into people who reminded me of the night I took a shot at Fischler.

During the 1974–75 season we were all aware that NBC had decided not to renew its contract with the NHL. Scotty Connal arranged a final get-together in Philadelphia for the crew. There was a lot of emotion in the room that night. We had enjoyed three wonderful seasons together. In all my years of broadcasting, I have never experienced a bond quite like it.

Ted, Tim, and I were asked to say a few words. When my turn came, I told the group how much it meant to me to be part of the NBC team and how much I'd enjoyed everyone's company. I surprised myself by talking about the problems I'd had to overcome earlier in my career, how I'd suffered from anxiety and panic attacks before every telecast, and how relaxed, confident, and proud I'd felt as a member of the NBC team. After that night, we dispersed, many of us never to meet again.

Golfing with Bobby Orr. When we finished our round, our foursome agreed it was our greatest day of golf ever.

Scotty Connal died in the summer of 1996. Ted Lindsay and I flew to Connecticut for a memorial service at his home. It was a very sad day. Hockey was a true passion of Scotty's, and millions of viewers have become ardent fans because of his pioneering efforts, including the roaming handheld camera and his coinage of the now-familiar term "instant replay."

We loved Scotty. When I joined NBC, I anticipated that the network might be coldly professional—all business and no fun. It was quite the opposite, thanks mainly to Scotty, and I never hesitate to tell people how much I enjoyed working for him.

15

Hal Wasn't My Pal

Reporters like Al Strachan used to accuse me of being a Leaf "homer" (he dubbed me "Brian McMaple Leaf"), but you'd never convince Harold Ballard of that. I managed to annoy, if not infuriate, him many times with my on-air comments. On one occasion when he threatened to turf me from the Gardens for my "pro-Philadelphia comments," I heard that MacLaren Advertising pacified him with the offer of a new organ for Maple Leaf Gardens. I'd love to have found out if it was an expensive organ or a cheap one. It might have given me an idea of my true worth to *Hockey Night in Canada*.

People who knew him often say nice things about Harold Ballard, pointing out that he was a soft touch to the down-and-out, that he gave freely to charity, that he loved his hockey players, and that he would do anything to bring the Stanley Cup back to Toronto.

I seldom saw that side of Ballard, even when I worked for him. He was crusty, provocative, and sometimes downright obnoxious. He was a racist—he once asked the writer Earl McRae, "If you can call a Chevrolet a Chev, why can't you call a Japanese a Jap?"

He was a chauvinist and a sexist who once called the respected radio broadcaster Barbara Frum a "dumb broad," adding that "Women are good for only one thing—lying on their backs."

He was greedy, cruel, corrupt, conniving, mean-spirited, and a liar. Not to mention a convicted felon.

I often wondered how a warm, friendly, genuine man like King Clancy could revere the man. Why did Tiger Williams extol his virtues? What did my friend Terry Kelly, a member of the MLG board of directors, see in the man? Steve Stavro was a big fan. What was I missing?

As owner of the Hamilton Tiger-Cats football club, Ballard vetoed the sale of the Toronto Argonauts to his former partner John Bassett simply because he hated Bassett's guts.

He drove his son Bill from the Gardens, claiming Bill was plotting a coup to overthrow him.

He forced longtime scout Bob Davidson to quit by cutting his salary by more than half. He fired penalty timekeeper Ace Bailey, who'd been part of the organization since the Leafs were called the St. Patricks and who, in 1933, almost gave his life to the Leaf cause.

When Doug Moore—the chief engineer at the Gardens with more than thirty years of loyal service—dared to ask for a raise, Ballard gave him until the end of the week to empty his desk and get out. In Moore's case, the dismissal turned out to be a godsend. No longer did he have to rush in from Richmond Hill at all hours to fix a leaking ammonia gas line or patch up the ancient equipment that Ballard was too cheap to replace. He went on to perfect a system for making better ice, started a company called Jet Ice, and became hugely successful servicing arenas and curling rinks all over the world. Moore, who died of cancer in 1996, was my best friend.

When *Toronto Star* reporter Frank Orr wrote a few words that raised Ballard's ire, he called the heterosexual Orr a "queer." But not to his face.

When he barred CFRB's Gordon Sinclair from the Gardens for some slight, Sinc promptly bought Gardens stock. "Let's see him try to keep me out of the annual general meeting," he told me. "I'll raise some hell there."

He barred CFTO-TV's Pat Marsden as well as reporters from the *Globe and Mail*.

Imagine sitting next to legendary broadcaster Foster Hewitt.

Doug Moore, who was once the chief engineer at Maple Leaf Gardens, formed
Jet Ice, a successful ice-making company, after Harold Ballard let him go. He
was my best friend. Sadly, he died in 1996.

He ordered the destruction of Foster Hewitt's famous gondola.

He castigated Bobby Hull for removing items from the Hockey Hall of Fame, but when Hull confronted him before a game one night, Ballard backed down and turned on the charm. "Bobby, you're welcome around here any time," he said. Hull, who was working for us on *Hockey Night in Canada* at the time, walked out. "I don't need this bullshit," he said.

When Gordie Howe scored his 1,000th career goal, Ballard refused to allow news of the event to be flashed on the centre-ice scoreboard. "A blind man can score goals in that league [the WHA]," he sneered.

In 1974, Ballard tore a strip off Czech star Vaclav Nedomansky, who had signed with the Toronto Toros of the WHA. He called Big Ned "a coward for running away from his homeland to grab big money in Canada." A decade later, when the Leafs signed two Czech players, Miroslav Frycer and Peter Ihnacak, Ballard had changed his tune. "It takes real guts for these two fine young men to leave their homeland and seek a new life in Canada."

As a hockey executive, Ballard was a disaster, largely because his prejudices and vendettas clouded his judgment. He had a particular problem with "religious" players, a bias that resulted in two of the Leafs' worst trades.

One day in 1975, when general manager Jim Gregory was out of town, Montreal GM Sam Pollock called Ballard to ask about "that religious kid" Doug Jarvis, a Leaf prospect who'd scored 133 points in his last year as a Junior. He offered to take Jarvis off Ballard's hands in exchange for an undistinguished minor pro named Greg Hubick. Jarvis cracked the Habs lineup that fall and played in all 80 games. He would go on to win four Stanley Cups and appear in an NHL-record 964 consecutive games. Hubick would score 6 goals in a 77-game NHL career.

Ballard also forced his GM, Gerry McNamara, to trade third-year pro Laurie Boschman, a born-again Christian. Boschman would play in more than 1,000 NHL games and score 229 goals while racking up more than 2,200 penalty minutes.

Ballard also made little effort to keep several productive Leafs from slipping away to the WHA, including goaltender Bernie Parent, defenceman Rick Ley, and fan favourite Paul Henderson. He alienated Leaf captain Dave Keon, one of the most popular Leafs ever, to the point that Keon vowed never to return to Maple Leaf Gardens.

His biggest gaffe was recruiting the ailing Punch Imlach to come back and manage the Leafs in 1979. He stood by while Imlach stripped the heart out of a promising Leaf squad by trading Lanny McDonald, Pat Boutette, Mike Palmateer, and Tiger Williams. Imlach also got into a bitter feud with Darryl Sittler, which ended with the Leaf captain waiving a no-trade clause in his contract and departing for Philadelphia.

When Imlach underwent bypass surgery in 1980–81, Ballard didn't fire him. But Punch got the message when he returned to the Gardens and discovered his parking space had been taken away.

During the 1980s, Ballard's Leafs, managed by Imlach, McNamara, Gord Stellick, and Floyd Smith, paraded a motley collection of duds onto the ice. No Leaf player finished among the top ten scorers throughout the decade. No Leaf player won a trophy. No Leaf team gave any indication it was ready to challenge for the Stanley Cup and four of them missed the playoffs altogether.

When the NHL realigned its divisions in 1981, Ballard jumped at the chance—some say he was paid handsomely—to place his Leafs in the lackluster Norris Division with Detroit, Chicago, Winnipeg, and St. Louis. Even in that undistinguished company, the Leafs finished last five times, and second-last four times, over the next eleven years.

Despite this dreadful track record, Ballard was inducted into the Hockey Hall of Fame in 1977 as a builder. That's a mystery that can never be explained. What did he ever do to improve or enhance the game in any capacity? Ballard was no builder. He was more like a one-man demolition company.

One of the few highlights of Ballard's regime was that the Leafs paved the way for European players in the NHL when they brought Borje Salming and Inge Hammarstrom to Toronto in 1973. The Leafs also had an opportunity to land two of the greatest Swedes in the WHA, Anders Hedberg and Ulf Nilsson, when they became free agents in 1978. Both men, and their wives, liked the idea of a move to Toronto. But after spending one day in Ballard's boorish company they reconsidered and signed with the New York Rangers.

Ballard was afflicted with diabetes late in his life, but he continued to eat sugary cereals for breakfast, and huge amounts of ice cream and chocolate bars throughout the day.

"Diabetes is all in the mind," he'd snort, failing to convince either King Clancy or myself. We would learn to stick our hides with insulin-bearing needles on a daily basis.

Jim Proudfoot of the *Toronto Star* relates the following: Ballard crashed the funeral of a woman who had toiled faithfully at the Gardens for years. During the ceremony he wept copiously. Yet that employee's son found out while he was settling her estate that she had never received any of the pension she was entitled to. She'd kept the matter secret, being the sort who never complained, while the millionaire Ballard effectively stole her money. Yet he had the gall to send her flowers every Christmas.

Lastly, and regrettably, Ballard was a criminal. He was imprisoned in 1972 after being found guilty of forty-seven counts of fraud and theft totaling $205,000. He was also found guilty of stealing from the Toronto Marlboros and using the Gardens, a public company, to finance personal expenditures.

Did anyone ever come out ahead in a battle with Ballard? Carl Brewer did.

Remember when Punch Imlach brought Brewer out of retirement in the middle of the 1979–80 season? Brewer, then forty-two, played in 20 games after signing a standard player's contract for $125,000. However, Imlach neglected to have Brewer sign a termination contract, which would have expired at the end of the season. Brewer claimed the Leafs had to keep on paying him through 1985–86.

It took eight years and numerous court battles before Brewer settled for back pay of $27,400.

Along the way, Brewer discovered that the name of the hockey club, the Maple Leafs, had never been registered. Brewer impishly registered the name and became its owner, at least temporarily, until Ballard went to court and convinced a judge to rule that the name belonged to his hockey club.

Was all the aggravation Brewer caused the Leafs worth it? "Sure it was," he says. "For the million laughs I received, it was worth it. And it cost Harold a bundle. I know because Ballard's lawyer, by mistake, sent his dockets and his bill to my solicitor halfway through the proceedings. That bill alone was for $150,000."

During the 1981–82 NHL season, I used a few calculated, if ill-chosen, words about Darryl Sittler and his dispute with the Leafs on a midweek telecast from Minnesota. Over the years I had never been close to many of the NHL stars, but Sittler was different. We had worked on a book together—*Sittler at Centre*—and I'd gotten to know him reasonably well and to admire him. His battles with Leaf coach/general manager Punch Imlach were highly publicized and they'd taken their toll. He was under great stress and he was depressed. He also felt that he was underpaid. At the time, Montreal's Guy Lafleur was making double Sittler's salary, and Darryl was not even the highest-paid Leaf: Wilf Paiement and Borje Salming earned more.

Two other NHL clubs, Philadelphia and Minnesota, promised Darryl a raise to $250,000 per year over four years, if he could get the Leafs to trade him. But Toronto was demanding the moon in return for Sittler. Days passed, then weeks, and still no trade.

Sittler was ready to explode. He visited two doctors and both advised him to take a break, to either give hockey a rest or risk a complete breakdown. He told Gerry McNamara, who'd replaced Punch Imlach as general manager, that he would not be travelling with the team to Minnesota for their next game.

It was big news when the club arrived in Minneapolis–St. Paul without Sittler. Some Leaf officials were all but calling him a quitter, and it riled me.

Two of hockey's most colourful personalities—Harold Ballard and Eddie Shack.

Words fail me in describing my emotions at the 1995 Hall of Fame induction ceremonies. I couldn't have been in better company than with longtime friend Bill Torrey, who helped guide the New York Islanders, and later the Florida Panthers, to greatness.

Producer Bob Gordon devoted a full intermission to the story. He asked Dick Beddoes, Danny Gallivan, Dave Hodge, and me to form a panel and discuss the Sittler "defection." The others all seemed to agree that Darryl should have been there. But I said, "Whoa, doesn't a guy have the right to take a day off? Even if he's a hockey star? If I'm on the panel I'm going to take Sittler's side."

"That's fine," said Gordon.

"But it's not fine. If I do that, Ballard will hit the roof."

"So what do you propose?"

"Why don't we tape the segment instead of doing it live? If I say something really inflammatory you can edit it. Or we can do it over again. Or you can throw it out and have the other three guys talk about Sittler without me."

Gordon agreed to tape the segment. All afternoon I deliberated over what to say, and during the taping my words didn't come out the way I thought they would. I recall saying, "I think the Leafs and Imlach have treated Sittler shamefully. Why don't they treat him with respect, like Bobby Clarke in Philadelphia, to get the best out of him?" But Darryl remembers it differently. He recalls me saying, "Why didn't they deliver him from his misery long ago?"

Two days later—a Friday—Frank Selke Jr. told me I would not be working the game at the Gardens the following night. Ballard had banned me from the Gardens.

"We'll go to bat for you," Selke promised. "We'll talk to Harold."

I'm sure they did. So did Hodge and Beddoes. Ralph Mellanby said recently that it was Beddoes who persuaded Ballard to let me come back, that my *HNIC* employers were convinced I was gone. A compromise was reached: Ballard would let me back in to do certain segments of *Hockey Night*, but I was never to enter the broadcast booth again. And I never did, except on two special occasions.

Years later, they were stuck for a colour commentator for some reason and I was invited back. I enjoyed myself and did a good job. I know I did because when I left all the crew gave me the thumbs-up sign. And in 1995, after I was inducted into the media section of the Hockey Hall of Fame, I was invited to open the show on camera, wearing my old powder-blue *Hockey Night in Canada* blazer. Then, at centre ice, I assisted my good friend and fellow inductee Bill Torrey with the opening faceoff, and later I chatted with Bob Cole and Harry Neale in the booth. What an emotional night!

Ralph Mellanby likes to tell the story of a telecast opening I handled after Ballard tossed me out of the gondola. One crisp fall night, I was outside the building, facing a camera and taping an opening: "Tonight from Maple Leaf Gardens, the Toronto Maple Leafs meet the blah, blah, blah . . ." A crowd gathered and Ralph heard one guy ask another, "Who's that guy with the microphone?"

"That's McFarlane."

"Oh, yeah? What's he doing out here?"

"He has to work out here. Ballard won't let him in the building."

"Yeah? Well, he's going to get bloody cold out here when winter comes."

I often ask myself two questions: How solidly did *Hockey Night in Canada* back me when Ballard confronted them? And why did the tape go to air in Minnesota when I'd specifically asked Bob Gordon to scrap it if I said anything inflammatory? It's quite possible Gordon concluded my comments wouldn't bother Ballard. I hadn't mentioned him by name. But I couldn't have angered him more if I'd shoved Sittler's stick up his butt.

In his book *Sittler*, published in 1992, Darryl writes: "Beddoes asserted that I had done the team an injustice. His reward for being Ballard's house broadcaster was to write Ballard's official biography a few years later. To this day, I appreciate Brian's support and courage, which probably cost him his career with *Hockey Night in Canada*."

Well, it cost me a major portion of my career. But not all of it. For the next eight years I hosted games out of Winnipeg and Montreal.

16

Contract Problems

During the summer of 1983, Frank Selke Jr., asked me to come into the office and discuss the coming hockey season. Something in his tone prompted me to ask, "Is there something new?"

"Yes, there is," he said. "It looks like you won't be doing 'This Week in the NHL' this season." "This Week in the NHL" was our first-intermission show, a roundup of the week's events in hockey. For several seasons, Dave Hodge and I had co-hosted it—we used to call it the "TWIT" show.

"The feeling is that Hodge isn't getting enough exposure on the telecasts," Frank added. "There were times last year when you were seen as much or more than he was. Come on in and we'll talk about it."

Frank explained that there had been some discussions about the on-camera time I'd been given the season before. Hodge had not complained, he assured me, but others had and it was decided to limit my role. I'd do "NHL Update," an off-camera segment in which I'd narrate snippets of scores and highlights from other games, and *The NHL Tonight*, the post-game show. The CBC produced the postgame show separately from *Hockey Night in Canada*, which my Canadian Sports Network bosses owned. And, they said, since I'd done such a good job as host on the local midweek games in Winnipeg, I would be given an increase for those games.

When all was said and done, I realized that this amounted to a substantial raise. I was astonished. At first I thought Frank had erred in his calculations. We talked about minor perks like hosting the All-Star game (I hadn't been assigned to one in ten years), and the number of playoff assignments (roughly the same as the preceding year—very few) and I left his office feeling much better than I'd anticipated. I made up my mind to sign the contract he offered without argument. I figured it was the first time in eighteen years that I'd been offered a fair contract for my services, and more surprisingly, a contract that was offered prior to the season. *HNIC* had an annoying habit of not settling its contracts until the last minute—and sometimes well into the season.

One December, when the season was almost eight weeks old, I still hadn't been given a contract. I was so frustrated that I asked the player agent Bill Watters to represent me and negotiate with *HNIC*. Bill made a luncheon date with my boss, Ted Hough, who was president of the Canadian Sports Network (CSN), later to be called Molstar.

Shortly thereafter I was scheduled to work a midweek game in Minnesota. Ted Hough called me at home, just as I was preparing dinner for the kids (my wife Joan was busy at college, taking a two-year course that would give her a fitness instructor's degree).

His voice was cold and hard. "Brian, you are not to get on the plane and go to Minnesota tomorrow morning. You will not be working the game there."

"Whoa, Ted! What's going on?"

"I thought the purpose of my luncheon engagement with Bill Watters tomorrow had something to do with international hockey. But now I hear it has to do with your contract with us."

"That's right, Ted," I confirmed. "I should have had a contract from you before the season started, not eight weeks into it. So Bill Watters agreed to act as my agent. What's the problem?"

Two of the game's most dynamic—and most popular players—Gordie Howe and Johnny Bower—on camera with Frank Selke Jr.

"You know very well we don't deal with third parties. I will not be meeting with Bill Watters for lunch and you will not be working for us on future telecasts."

I couldn't believe it. I'd been fired again. I could feel the bile welling up inside me. Resisting the urge to scream at him, I said, "Ted, I am very upset about this situation and want to mull it over for a minute. What's more, I've got something on the stove. Let me calm down and I'll call you right back."

I hung up and turned off the stove. I paced up and down the living room, grumbling to myself. The kids gave me puzzled looks but said nothing.

Then I called Hough back. "Ted," I said sweetly, "you say you don't deal with third parties or agents. But didn't Howie Meeker use Gerry Patterson to represent him? And didn't Ralph Mellanby, your executive producer, use the same Gerry Patterson to negotiate his contract? I don't understand the inconsistency here. It seems discriminatory to me."

There was a long pause. "All right," he said, "you've made a point. I'll meet your man Watters. Consider yourself reinstated. You may go to Minnesota and we'll talk about this again when you get back."

I hung up and danced a little jig around the kitchen. There were more puzzled looks from the kids. "I've won a small victory," I told them. "I can't believe it." With Hough and CSN, over eighteen years, I couldn't recall ever winning a victory, big or small.

Two days later, when I returned from Minnesota, I heard from Watters. "Brian," he sighed over the phone, "I can't believe this man Hough. I met him for lunch and I've never met such an obstinate son of a bitch in my life. I'm telling you right now, if I don't get out of your life today you'll never work for *Hockey Night in Canada* ever again. They'll gas you for sure. I've dealt with every general manager in hockey, and some of them are real bastards, but this guy Hough is in a class by himself. So you're on your own. Good luck."

A few days later, I went in and signed the long-awaited contract. I didn't like it, but I signed it.

Hough shrugged off the delay by saying, "I've had a tardy pencil." His pencil, or Selke's, was still at turtle speed when the 1984–85 season began. Once again, no contract arrived, although Selke told me it was in the mail. A few days later, when it still hadn't arrived, I called Frank and he told me to come and see him. Meanwhile, Dick Irvin had called me from Montreal.

Irvin said, "Can you believe this? All these years with *Hockey Night in Canada* and it's the same old story. The opening game two days away and not even a phone call about our contracts."

"What else is new?" I said.

Hodge called, too. He was angry and frustrated because his agent, Gerry Patterson, was getting nowhere with Selke. Hodge was worried that *HNIC* wouldn't keep any promises regarding the number of games he was to work. Hodge also said he was insulted by the raise Selke was offering, considering the extra workload he was bearing.

I felt like saying, "Hey, Davey, you talked with Ralph Mellanby and requested extra work last season. You may not have intended to hurt me with that request, but when Mellanby handed you my old job on *The NHL Tonight* it cost me $400 a show. So it's hard for me to sympathize." But of course I didn't utter a peep.

Instead I told Hodge I was meeting Selke and would get back to him.

I went in to see Selke on Thursday. That day I had planned to go to Buffalo with Mellanby, Don Cherry, and Bob Cole to watch the opening game of the season between the Sabres and Canadiens. Selke showed me a copy of the contract he'd prepared and asked me to take it home, look it over, and get back to him with any comments. He apologized for his tardiness in getting my contract settled. He said he'd given me an increase of $100 a game over last season but he was under strict orders to keep raises under control—no more than 5.7 per cent. (I later heard from a reliable source that Cherry had gotten 15 per cent.) Selke mentioned the problems he was having with Hodge, and that he wasn't prepared to meet Dave's demands.

I left Frank's office feeling rather upset. I cancelled my plans to go to Buffalo that afternoon because I was certain I'd say something to Mellanby that I'd end up regretting. I called Joan and asked her to do some quick calculations and meet me for dinner. We met and she gave me the bottom line: If I accepted Frank's offer I'd be doing fewer games and making $10,000 less than the year before. Counting playoff games, she calculated I'd make $13,000 less than the year before. And there were no guarantees I'd even work any playoff games. The year before I'd worked fewer by far than any of the other *HNIC* regulars.

I was thoroughly pissed off, but Joan said, "Hey, I don't want to make you feel worse than you do, but what have I been telling you for years? Why do you work for those people? You've allowed this to happen. You know the squeaking wheel gets the grease. And you've always been reluctant to complain. I'm not saying you should have been threatening or demanding, but you should have been looking for other jobs all along." She was right.

I slept badly that night and woke up determined to address the problem before leaving on the afternoon flight to Montreal. Joan and I checked our figures again. Sure enough, it looked like my "raise" would turn into a $10,000 loss—minimum.

I called Selke, and he was in a meeting. I told his secretary it was essential that I talk to him and he got right back to me.

"Frank," I began, "I want you to listen to me. I'm still in a state of shock after digesting your offer yesterday. Right now I don't know what I'm going to do. First you and Mellanby heap praise on me. You tell me I'm an excellent host. You tell me that Sam Pollock and others in Montreal want me to host their games.

"You know I'd like to get in my twenty years with *Hockey Night* but that doesn't seem possible because you want to change my role and take me away from a job that I enjoyed and was comfortable with. You are asking me to do more travel and take more time away from my other businesses. You want to deprive me of important exposure in the Toronto market. Your contract calls for fewer games and about half as many playoff assignments. I'm looking at a reduction of income of more than $10,000. I just don't understand it and I don't think I can live with it."

"Brian," he said, "I want you to know first off that the praise for your work, both from Ralph and myself, and from the young producers, was genuine. Second, when I got home last night I did some calculations of my own and I discovered you were destined to take quite a cut from last year. I reckoned about $8,000 but if you say it's ten then that's probably accurate. Now, obviously that doesn't seem to be fair.

"Meanwhile we have a major problem with Hodge and I'm not going to bend to his demands. So I'm asking you to help us out by going to Montreal, host the game there tomorrow night, then come to see us Monday and we'll attempt to straighten this out."

I smiled at Joan, who was sitting across the table pointing to a note she'd scrawled in block letters: CAN YOU AFFORD TO WORK FOR THEM? NO.

It was amazing how quickly Frank's words appeased me. He's very good with people.

So I packed my bags and went to Montreal.

I spent a pleasant Friday evening getting reacquainted with my old stomping grounds. I'd been away from Montreal so long that I'd almost forgotten what a fascinating city it was. I headed back to my hotel room and switched on the World Series game between the Detroit Tigers and San Diego Padres. I settled in to enjoy the silky-smooth play-by-play delivery of Vin Scully, a broadcaster whose eloquence and vast knowledge of the game I admired. Then I noticed the message light on my phone was lit.

"You have to call Toronto immediately," the operator said.

"Be prepared to come right back to Toronto," Mellanby said. "Hodge and Selke are battling over contracts and all I know is I have a show to produce. Hodge may not be available so you'll have to come back and be host in Toronto if these two guys don't work something out in the next half hour. Call me back at nine o'clock."

Bob Cole followed Foster Hewitt
and quickly established himself as
a superb play-by-play announcer.

Dave Hodge (left), Helen Hutchinson (centre), Darrel Sittler (right), and I (top).
Helen was one of the first female announcers to appear on a hockey broadcast.

"Here's another fine mess I'm in," I sighed. "Why can't *Hockey Night in Canada* ever get their contracts with us settled before the season starts?" I called back at nine. "Stay where you are," Ralph said. "Thank God, Selke and Hodge have reached an agreement. Hodge is going to work here after all." So it was settled. I relaxed and watched the Tigers wallop the Padres.

Mario Lemieux was a major disappointment in his Montreal debut the next night. He had played well in Boston two nights before, scoring a spectacular goal on his first shift, and everybody expected him to perform wonders before his hometown fans. As if he wasn't under enough pressure to rescue the failing Pittsburgh franchise. *Sports Illustrated* had done a piece on him, predictably taking him to the Pittsburgh zoo to look at the penguins.

Mario was my guest in the second intermission. I opened by saying, "Twenty years from now, folks, when Mario Lemieux is being ushered into the Hockey Hall of Fame, you'll be able to say 'I remember his first interview on *Hockey Night in Canada*.' But you may not recall his first game in Montreal because frankly, Mario, it's been a little disappointing, hasn't it?"

Mario, shy and soft-spoken, tentative in English, agreed with me. The interview was flat, unemotional, and mercifully short. Today, more than twenty-five years later, I wouldn't remember the interview at all if I hadn't taken notes. But since then my respect for Mario has soared.

A couple of years later *HNIC* executive producer Don Wallace called me in and asked me to make a long-term commitment to the show. "Great," I said, "I'll give you two years at least."

He asked, "If two become four and four becomes six—that's okay, too?"

"Sure."

That was after Dave Hodge announced he was leaving for Vancouver to work as the sports director at radio station CKNW at a rumoured $150,000 a year. Dave wanted security. (Don't we all?) He had impulsively thrown his pencil in the air one night, on camera, to show his disgust over a CBC decision to cut away from a game in progress. He had been suspended. The Toronto host's job was therefore open. Hodge's job as host of the midweek Leaf games on CHCH-TV in Hamilton was also vacant, and Wallace was also looking for a new play-by-play voice on the midweek games. When I suggested I might like to try the play-by-play assignment, Wallace just laughed. "I heard you in Buffalo a year ago," he said, his tone indicating he didn't like what he'd heard.

I thought that was unfair. I'd been called upon to do a playoff game between the Sabres and the Nordiques with little time to prepare, and from the worst possible location. Play-by-play isn't hard, but you have to do it on a regular basis to be successful. I've never had that chance.

Wallace really rubbed me the wrong way when he relayed a conversation he'd had with the CBC's Don McPherson. "How long has Brian been around now," McPherson said, "twenty-five years? Yeah, well, he's a good 'utility' announcer."

Utility announcer? Our bosses sure had a funny way of showing their appreciation for their talent. One thing that ticked a lot of us off was the business about whether the "A team" or the "B team" would be doing a broadcast. Do the viewers really care who does the play-by-play, whether it's Bob Cole, Dick Irvin, or Don Wittman? Whether I was the host or Hodge? Obviously the brass felt they did. It's hard to keep up your morale, to feel you're an integral part of the telecasts, when you're constantly made to feel you've been branded as a second-stringer, a "utility announcer."

Wallace asked what else I'd like to do. He gave me the impression he wanted me to become his number one guy.

I told him that I'd enjoyed doing "Inside Hockey"—a series of profiles and stories that ran during the intermission—but that I didn't much like hosting the Montreal games. "There's a lot of travel and the CBC staff in the studio at the Forum are lethargic and disinterested. Plus, French is their language and unfortunately it's not mine. And I don't smoke and they're all chain-smokers. They were really pissed off at me last season after I put a handwritten sign up on the studio wall: *'Defense de fumer s'il vous plaît.'* That wasn't my job but somebody had to tell those guys 'No smoking in the studio.' You could have done it."

"Well, we're never going to change that situation," Don said. "Anybody who works there just has to live with it."

"Why?"

"Because that's the way it is down there. It's Friday," he said. "These are big decisions for you to think about. Consider the options I've given you over the weekend and get back to me on Monday."

I called Don on Monday morning. I told Wallace I was really excited, that I wanted to do as much hosting as possible, especially in Toronto on CBC and on the midweek games.

"I thought that's what you might say," he replied.

"I'll help out if you need me on 'Inside Hockey,'" I offered. "I like doing that show, too, and would be reluctant to give it up."

He said he was glad I'd called and that he'd get back to me.

The next day I read in the *Toronto Sun* that Wallace had hired Ron MacLean from Calgary to be the new Leaf host. I was furious. I'm sure Wallace had already made up his mind before I called on Monday.

I tried to reach him to tell him I felt betrayed, that he'd led me down the old garden path, but I was told he was out of town. I called Frank Selke and told him of my bitter disappointment. "Frank, I'm really ticked off with Wallace."

Selke sounded sympathetic. "You may have good reason to be, the way it was handled. The TV people in Calgary are upset, too. They didn't expect to lose MacLean. Let me talk to Ted Hough about it."

Wallace called me the next day. He said he'd heard I was upset. I told him just how much, and repeated what I'd told Selke. "Well," he said, "I had to do what's right for the show. The CBC urged me to make changes, to bring some young people along, and we hope MacLean will be the next Dave Hodge."

That was too much. "If the CBC has so much influence over *Hockey Night in Canada*," I said, "why don't we announcers sign our contracts with them?"

After talking things over with Joan, I was almost ready to resign, but I had another talk with Wallace. I asked him for a reasonable raise to salve my hurt feelings. He said he couldn't do it, that the CBC was adamant: 3 per cent, take it or leave it. (Inflation in Toronto was running more than 5 per cent at the time.)

Joan and I agreed there wasn't much I could do. I would have to accept what was offered, she told me, but I should actively start seeking other employment.

"That's going to be hard to do," I said, "because I really enjoy being part of *Hockey Night in Canada*. I keep hoping they'll realize I have a lot more to offer."

"Face it," she said. "They've all but destroyed your career and that's a shame. You should have gone with a U.S. team years ago. Or stayed with NBC when you had the chance. Look how well Tim Ryan's done by going to the States. Now it may be too late." She was making a good point.

The Final Days at CBC

After Ballard banned me from the Gardens in 1981–82, I spent four years in Winnipeg, covering Jets games on a local TV station, CKND, working with two good fellows, Brian Swain and ex-NHLer Dave Richardson, and renewing acquaintances with old friend John Ferguson, the Jets' general manager. I would also work some CBC games with Don Wittman, whose professionalism I always admired. Occasionally, I would team up with Don Cherry and tape "Coach's Corner." Cherry and I worked well together in those days. "Geez, you set me up for some good lines," he said one night. "I wish they'd put us together more often. I'm going to ask them if they will. My brother Dick says we work great together. And my mother likes the way we get along." (Don always rushed to a phone after games to call his mother in Kingston. "How was it tonight, Mom? How'd I look?" Sometimes I could tell by the look on his face that she hadn't given him the response he expected.)

I switched to Montreal for four seasons, hosting Habs' games on the CBC and working with talented people like Mickey Redmond, Gary Dornhoefer, Scotty Bowman, Bob Cole, and, of course, Dick Irvin. During those latter seasons I also enjoyed working with producer Jim Hough on "Inside Hockey" features.

Dick and I were having a sandwich in the restaurant across from the Forum one morning when he nudged me. "See that kid in the booth across from us?" he whispered. I looked over. A scrawny teenager sat there. He looked like a busboy.

Dick said, "They tell me he might be the next great goaltender with the Canadiens."

I said, "You're kidding. What's his name?"

"His name is Patrick Roy."

I took another look and decided to remember the name. I thought it unlikely the kid would ever become an NHL star but looks can be deceiving. I thought of how Gretzky looked as a teenager. Not much different.

On December 11, 1988, I flew to New York to shoot an "Inside Hockey" feature at Central Park. It would become one of my favourite features, and it was one I had to work hard to convince Don Wallace to let us do.

Our assignment was to film some kids from Harlem skating and getting hockey tips from members of the Los Angeles Kings. The session had been organized by former NHLer Pat Hickey and a New Yorker named Dave Wilk. They'd approached the Rangers first, but they hemmed and hawed about showing up. The Kings, on the other hand, said they'd be happy to help out.

It was the coldest day of the year in Manhattan, but all of the Kings turned out, even owner Bruce McNall. We were told that the kids were so excited they couldn't sleep the night before.

The players went right to work, mingling with the kids on the ice. The youngsters borrowed Glenn Healy's goal stick and trapper and he flipped pucks at them and showed them the finer points of netminding. In another area, Luc Robitaille whooped it up in a game of keep-away. Wayne Gretzky wore a toque under his helmet. "It's the same toque I wore as a kid playing backyard hockey in Brantford," he told us. Bernie Nicholls wore a borrowed hat with earflaps, which made him look like a barnstorming

After an NHL Oldtimers' game at the Gardens. You may recognize Howie Menard (far left), Brian Conacher (dark helmet), Red Kelly, Peter Conacher, Carl Brewer, Ivan Irvin (in the toque), Sid Smith, and Frank Mahovlich (front row, far right).

pilot, as he showed how to win a faceoff. He talked about his own boyhood and the joys of playing pond hockey in Haliburton. "I haven't been this cold since those days," he said with a grin.

We were filming some kids at play when Marty McSorley skated over. "Would this big fellow be safe if he walked down your street tonight?" I asked them.

One of them laughed and replied, "No, everybody would chase him—to get his autograph."

When the hour was almost up, Gretzky called the kids toward him. A few skated over, then a few more. Within minutes all of them surrounded him. He was buried in kids. I saw one put his arm around Wayne's neck while others hugged him. A photographer from the *Toronto Star* snapped photos while tears spilled from his eyes, from the emotion, the extreme cold, or both.

"Brian," he said as he turned to me, "it was worth coming all this way just for that shot. This has been fantastic."

Gretzky threw his hockey stick to a youngster who kissed the stick over and over again. The Great One had tears in his eyes, too.

In the spring of 1991 I drove to Oshawa for an "Inside Hockey" feature about Eric Lindros. There was talk that the series wouldn't be brought back the next season—the bosses at Molstar, which was now putting together *Hockey Night in Canada*, felt it was too expensive to produce. And sometimes too controversial. On one occasion, I was the only media-type present at a meeting of former NHL stars in a Toronto hotel room, including Hull, Howe, Mahovlich, Shack, and many others, all invited by Carl Brewer. At the meeting, lawyers and players, angry and bitter over the way their pension benefits had been handled, hurled some shocking accusations at Alan Eagleson and the NHLPA, and decided to fight for millions of dollars they felt were owing them and other former players in court.

I had my tape recorder rolling throughout the meeting and typed the proceedings into my computer the following day. I called Ron Harrison to tell him I had one of the best features we'd ever have on "Inside Hockey." "We can get Brewer and others to comment and then have Eagleson on to rebut their charges, for the sake of balance. This is a huge story, Ron."

I was scheduled to go to Saskatoon for "Inside Hockey" that week. "Don't go to Saskatoon," Harrison ordered. "Stay put. I'll send MacLean in your place. And I'll get back to you."

He called back the following day and basically said the story was too hot, too controversial for "Inside Hockey." Somebody squashed it. It was a frustrating decision.

While we were editing the Lindros piece for "Inside Hockey," producer Jim Hough surprised me by saying the feature might not even make it to *HNIC*. Ed Milliken, who was producing the Saturday game from Maple Leaf Gardens, had suggested he might switch to game highlights from Winnipeg during the second intermission, since the Jets were battling the Vancouver Canucks for the last playoff spot in the Smythe Division.

Hough was angry. "Outside of fans in Winnipeg and Vancouver, who the hell cares about a snippet of a game from the Winnipeg Arena?" I agreed with him. I was certain that most fans would prefer to see a Lindros profile, especially one that included his parents, his agent, and the man everyone expected would be his general manager, Pierre Page of the Quebec Nordiques, the team with the first pick overall in the 1991 draft.

We were editing the piece on Thursday when executive producer Ron Harrison came into the suite and confronted Hough.

"I wanted to see the tapes of Lindros on Monday or Tuesday," he began. "I told you that. Then I could make a decision on whether to use it or not. Now it's Thursday afternoon and I haven't a clue how good this thing is."

Jim said that there'd been a misunderstanding. He'd been under the impression all along that Lindros would be slotted for Saturday night until earlier that day.

"Listen," Harrison said, "if this is just another run-of-the-mill puff piece on Lindros, then it's no go. By now everybody in the world has run features on Lindros. He's been covered to death. Don't you agree, Brian?"

"Well, not really, Ron," I said. "We've got stuff on him no one's seen before. I think fans are fascinated with Lindros and we've got shots of him figuring in all four Oshawa goals the other night—and getting involved in a fight. We've got his parents talking about the pressure they're under and we've got comments from his agent, Rick Curran, and Pierre Page, who'll have to sign him. Personally, I think it's much more interesting than switching to Winnipeg."

"Yeah, but if Winnipeg plans to jump to Seattle?" continued Harrison. "There are all kinds of rumours around that the team may leave Winnipeg. I was even thinking of sending you guys there to check it out."

"Then I agree that's a bigger story than Lindros," I told him. "But that's the first I've heard of the Jets moving to Seattle. There's been nothing in the papers about it. The last I heard, Winnipeg was moving to Milwaukee or even Hamilton."

"The point is," Harrison said, "I should have seen the tapes earlier this week. If the Lindros thing was only so-so and I cancelled it, I'm only out the cost of a cameraman and a sound man. Now I'm stuck for today's editing time and your fees if I dump it. That means I eat about five grand."

Jim interjected, repeating that there'd been a misunderstanding and offering to forgo his fee if that would help matters.

"No, no, no," said Harrison, "that's not the point. I should have seen it, is all. Go ahead and finish the edit. I'll look at it tomorrow and decide what I'm going to do then. At the worst, I'll have some archival stuff on Lindros that I may be able to use somewhere down the road."

So we finished the edit.

On Friday night I was in the studio at the Gardens for the Legends of Hockey game, a meeting of Montreal and Toronto Oldtimers. Harrison approached me before the game started. "What was your opinion of the Lindros feature after the edit?"

I answered that I hadn't seen the final edit, but I was sure it was all right.

"Well, the tape is in the truck," he said, "so I'll go out there and screen it."

When he rolled the tape it appeared on the video monitor in the studio, so I watched it with Ron MacLean. Harrison relies heavily on MacLean for his opinion, so I was pleased when MacLean said, "Hey, that was a great piece. I liked it."

I told him there might be a problem, that Harrison and Hough had had words and it might be dropped from Saturday's telecast.

The next evening I watched the second intermission. Where "Inside Hockey" would normally appear, Ron MacLean threw a cue and we saw game action from Winnipeg. "Shit," I thought, "there goes the Lindros piece."

Then the oddest thing happened. After a few seconds a Winnipeg player got smacked by the puck and down he went. The trainers rushed out onto the ice and it looked like play would not be resumed for quite a while.

The director cut back to Ron MacLean in the *Hockey Night* studio. "Let's go to Brian McFarlane now for a profile on Eric Lindros," he said, and the tape rolled. Thanks to the injured Winnipeg player, my Lindros story made it to air. Television is a funny business.

That marked the end of "Inside Hockey," and the end of my involvement with *Hockey Night in Canada*. During the off-season, Ron Harrison invited me to lunch. "This is hard for me to say," he began, "but Arthur Smith, the sports director at the CBC, wants to use his own people on *Hockey Night in Canada* and you're the odd man out."

"Well, Ron," I said, "I don't even know Smith, and I don't know how a guy gets to be head of CBC

Islander defenceman Gerry Hart gets some advice from the "poke-check professor" Peter Puck.

sports at age twenty-eight. But I know most guys in their twenties think anyone over forty is a has-been, has nothing more to offer. And I don't think it's true for a minute. Look at all the grey hair you see on the American golf and football telecasts. But if this is the end for me, so be it."

A few months later, Smith left CBC sports for a position with Dick Clark in Hollywood.

I walked away from *Hockey Night in Canada* that day. I must confess I thought there might be a call from time to time to do some research on a documentary, for some voice-over work, or to make use of my writing ability. I even expected there would be a little send-off party—a few beers, a few funny speeches from Cherry, Hodge, Cole, and the others. Lord knows I'd chipped in for enough retirement bashes, stags, and the like. But nothing. Not a word. That hurt. Bob Cole summed up my departure succinctly: "McFarlane got screwed," he said.

But life goes on. I decided to write more books. I completed the Original Six series of books. I sold the movie rights to a young adult novel, *The Youngest Goalie*, although the movie never reached the production stage. I've decided to revive Peter Puck after discovering there was a lot of enthusiasm for the character.

In Florida a few months ago, I took up painting again and found it very relaxing. Family members will be getting oil paintings this Christmas, and I won't mind if they decide to hang them in their closets.

In 1992, I opened the Brian McFarlane Hockey Museum at the Big Apple Theme Park in Colborne, Ontario. With support from Ron Ellis, Dave Taylor, Phil Pritchard, and Craig Campbell from the Hockey Hall of Fame, and all my NHL Oldtimer friends, the opening was quite successful. In time I took exhibits on the road, appearing at shopping malls in places like Sudbury, Belleville, Ogdensburg, New York, and the Canadian National Exhibition in Toronto.

When the rent at the Big Apple became exorbitant, I moved the museum to Niagara Falls, Ontario, and operated there until 1999, when someone decided to build a hotel on our site.

The Hockey Museum is now stored away, waiting for a buyer or a new home. Like some of my other ventures and schemes, this one didn't make us any money, but I like to think we broke even and met some nice people and appreciative fans. Our guest books were filled with compliments. "Even better than the Hockey Hall of Fame" surfaced from time to time.

I met and worked with some broadcasting greats along the way—the Hewitts, Danny Gallivan, Dan Kelly, Bob Cole, Dave Hodge, Don Cherry, Ron MacLean, Tim Ryan, and of course Dick Irvin. And I enjoyed working with ex-pros like Bob Goldham, Ted Lindsay, and Scotty Bowman.

Ron Harrison was my favourite director. I chuckle to think of the time he was starting out with the CBC and working the sidelines at a Grey Cup game. How he was told to delay the opening kickoff because the network was still in commercial. So Harrison whipped off his headset, streaked across the field and stole the football. The cops chased him right out of the stadium.

We had some outstanding young people helping us out on the telecasts over the years. Doug Beeforth, John Shannon, Rick Briggs-Jude—all Ryerson grads who went on to enjoy fine careers in sports television. Doug Stone, Ed Milliken, Joel Darling (Ted's son), and Paul Romanuk were other good ones. And Mark Askin, one of my favourites. I am so proud of these young men who started with us, working for a pittance, and who went on to become movers and shakers in the sports television industry.

Ralph Mellanby didn't forget me. He asked me to write and voice over a documentary series, not unlike A&E's *Biography*, called *Once Upon a Time in Hockey*. Wayne Gretzky has agreed to be the host. If it sells—and becomes my swan song—I'll know I'm going out with the greatest.

My World of Hockey 3

18

Loose Wires in the Broadcast Booth

Broadcasters and journalists have always been vital to hockey's success. They report and analyze the news and they inspire the fanfare that makes hockey so popular. I've always admired those, like Dave Hodge, who manage to express their opinions without being swayed by the influences of owners, managers, coaches, or PR officials. But over forty years in broadcasting I've encountered those who use devious methods to enhance a story at the expense of others—even their colleagues in the media.

Early in my career with *Hockey Night in Canada*, I was trapped in a situation that shocked me and might well have cost me my job. I had written a book, *Fifty Years of Hockey*, and was invited by CBC television to come to their studio and talk—I thought—about the book and the sport's history. The late Warren Davis was the interviewer and Ross McLean was the show's executive producer. Davis interviewed me (on videotape) for ten minutes but never mentioned my book or my research. "Doesn't this guy know why I'm here?" I thought to myself. Instead, he asked me questions about *Hockey Night in Canada*—in particular, whether I thought MacLaren Advertising had blackballed certain people from the show.

I denied it, but he pressed on. "But if they *were* blackballed, MacLaren would be involved, right?"

Figuring we were speaking hypothetically, I replied, "Yes, MacLaren would get involved if that's the situation," or words to that effect.

After the taping, I felt I'd been conned. I angrily demanded to see the producer, but was told he'd gone home. I marched up to Ross McLean's office and placed a handwritten note on his desk, denying the CBC permission to use my interview in whole or in part without my permission. I never heard back from him.

The next morning I phoned Bud Turner at MacLaren to explain the situation. He told me not to worry about it.

Weeks later, an old friend came to visit our home. "I saw you on TV last night with Scott Young," she said.

"No, you're mistaken. I've never been on TV with Scott Young."

"But you were. I saw you. You were talking about how people are blackballed from *Hockey Night in Canada*."

Uh-oh. I called ACTRA, my union, and someone there got a tape of the program for us to screen. Sure enough, Scott Young was on camera maintaining that certain individuals, notably himself, had been barred from the hockey telecasts. Then my image popped up on the screen and I said, "That's right, MacLaren Advertising would get involved if that's the situation." That was all I said, but it was enough. That sentence, taken completely out of context and edited so as to appear that Scott and I were sitting together in conversation, made it appear that I was in complete agreement with Young.

Fortunately, I had alerted my bosses at MacLaren to the situation and they were understanding. It was my first experience with the kind of journalism not unusual, I've been told, at the CBC in those days.

Danny Gallivan

We were flying back from Minnesota and I spotted an empty seat beside Danny Gallivan. This would be during the 1980–81 season, when Gallivan had replaced Bill Hewitt on the midweek Leaf games on CHCH-TV in Hamilton. I asked if I could join him and ask him a few questions. He said, "Sure." So I flipped on my tape recorder and Danny started talking. His booming responses soon caught the attention of the other passengers, who cocked their ears to hear what Danny was saying.

Brian: Who was your favourite player?

Danny: My favourite player, the greatest hockey player that I have every seen—and that's combining great ability with the gentlemanly aspect of play—would have to be Bobby Orr. Ah, but now we have another young man on the scene—a man about whom, half a dozen years from now, we'll say, "There is the greatest hockey player that has ever played the game." And this is in reference to Wayne Gretzky. Like Orr, he's blessed with incredible talent to play hockey, but more importantly, each is a real gentleman. As Bobby Orr is, so is Wayne Gretzky.

Brian: Do you like to invent new words like "spinarama" and "cannonading"?

Danny: Well, you know doing hockey for thirty years gets very boring at times. You know as well as I that some of the games get that way, and if it is boring to me, someone who's being paid well to cover it, what must it be like for the viewer? So sometimes I try to think of a way that I can get across to the viewer what is happening by making the best use of words.

I used a word one night and, at the time, I regretted having used it. Someone took a very hard shot, I thought of it as something being shot out of a cannon, and somehow I came up with the word "cannonading."

I got a couple of letters from people well-schooled in English and they said I had a lot of nerve to use a word like that, that there was no such word. I wrote back and said, "There is now." But after that I was determined not to overdo it.

Brian: How would you like to see hockey improved?

Danny: Oh, I'd like you to give me an hour on this. I think the game is just wonderful. But I think it could be improved even in this day and age. I would like to see, for instance, fewer teams than we have today. That would certainly enhance the calibre of play. I would like to see overtime. [Overtime was re-introduced to regular-season play a few years later, in 1983.] I would like to see some rule introduced to eliminate all these icings we have. I have always been an advocate that any team icing the puck deliberately—in the opinion of the official—would be assessed a two-minute penalty. You pay to see a talented, highly paid defenceman make the plays and do the things that make it possible for him to earn all that money. But far too often you see him go into the corner, get the puck, and whip it down the ice without looking. The overall picture of hockey as I see it can be improved in so many areas. It is too great a game to let slip.

Gary Dornhoefer

One night in Montreal, Gary Dornhoefer stopped me and said, "Hey, Mac, let's go out for a meal after the game. My treat. It'll give us a chance to get to know each other better."

I was flattered. I'd worked with Bill Hewitt for seventeen years and we never had more than two dinners together in all that time.

In the restaurant he asked me, "Who handles your investments?" I almost dropped my wine. I thought we were talking hockey.

"Gary, Whatever investments I have my wife takes care of," I said. "Perhaps you should ask her out to dinner some night." Gary became involved in the investment business and it wasn't long before he was asking NHL players about their investments at morning workouts, which annoyed his bosses on HNIC. I asked Dorny about his days as a Philadelphia Flyer:

When Fred Shero first took over the Flyers, he had a good reputation as a hockey man in the minors. After Vic Stasiuk, who was a hollering and screaming type, Fred was very quiet. Vic had taken the pop machine out of the dressing room, and one of the first things Freddie did was give it back. Vic would never let us have beer on the bus; Freddie made sure we always had three cases of it. All of a sudden Freddie was a nice guy and everybody responded to him.

His concentration was focused on the defence. He said, "First we look after the puck in our own end, and when we get that down pat"—which took about four years—"we are going to stop the teams from coming out of their own end. That is what we worked on every single day."

In Philadelphia, I gained a reputation of being very strong in front of the goaltender. I wasn't a good skater or quick. My game was contact, working the corners, and in front of the net. It was very successful for me, so it would have been silly for me to stop doing it. During my first year in pro hockey, when I was called up to Boston, every shot on goal hit me in the seat of the pants and bounced into the net, so I thought that this was a great way for me to make a living. That is why I kept doing it, kept parking myself in front of the goal. Once I established myself as an NHL player with Philadelphia, it was an easy thing to do.

With the Flyers, I played on a line with Ross Lonsberry and Rick MacLeish. We played together for about six years. Freddie was a firm believer in having the same line work together all the time, unlike a Scotty Bowman type.

It was a revelation for me to see Bobby Clarke emerge as a dominating personality on the team after coming right out of Junior hockey in Flin Flon. Because of his slight physique, the glasses he wore, and the fact he had diabetes, you didn't really expect it. But right from the first day of training camp, you knew that he was going to be a star—a superstar.

His work ethic alone told you that. He tried to outwork everyone on the team. The players decided they weren't going to let this little snot-nosed rookie outplay them, so we all responded to Clarke's example in a very positive way.

The first year, remember, Clarke had to play with Lew Morrison on one wing and Reggie Fleming on the other. You're not exactly going to fill the net playing with that pair. We had the rejects from other teams, from the Original Six, when they decided to double the size of the NHL.

When the Flyers drafted they were really looking for a defensive hockey club. Ed Van Impe, Joe Watson, and Bernie Parent and Doug Favell. They built the team from the goaltender out. So a lot of our games were 1–0, 2–1. We were very competitive because of that.

The Flyer fans were really hungry for a winner. Philadelphia had a reputation for being a city of losers. So they responded. They felt that there might be something building and they wanted to be part of a winner. Words cannot describe the final playoff game in 1974 when we won the first Cup. Unfortunately for me, I was sitting in the press box with a shoulder separation and I don't remember much of what happened. I had just gotten out of the hospital that day. I remember the traditional skate around the ice didn't happen, because there were so many people on the ice. They just leaped over the boards and streamed onto the ice.

I did not go in the parade the next day. The whole city just seemed to stop as millions turned out to salute the champs. It cost the city thousands of dollars to clean up. The fans would throw cans of beer to the players on the floats.

I was in the parade the following year when we won it again. I remember a guy caught me with a beer can and cut me open for a few stitches. I didn't see it coming. I was looking the other way and he was trying to throw it to one of the other players.

The worst thing was the brawls. As a player, on the ice, you really don't know how disgusting it looks. Now that I'm out of hockey and I see it, I have a much better perspective.

Of course Dave Schultz was involved in so many of them. Freddie never told Schultz or anyone else to go out and take care of an individual. And Davey, remember, was a totally different person off the ice. Very quiet and unassuming. You might even categorize him as a minister's son.

One thing that sticks out when I think of those days playing for Shero: He could be the centre of attention in the dressing room, but a minute later you would pass him in the hallway, he'd have his head down, lost in thought, and he wouldn't even acknowledge you.

Jim Hughson

The CBC's Jim Hughson hasn't always worked in the posh broadcast booths of the NHL. As a rookie announcer in northern Alberta and British Columbia, he called Intermediate games in places like Beaverlodge, Spirit River, and Dawson Creek.

"Geez, it got cold in some of those rinks," Hughson recalls. "One night, right in the middle of a game, the two of us in the booth couldn't stand it any more. It was just too bloody cold.

"In behind us, plugged into the wall, were two wires that represented our direct broadcast link to the radio station. This night, right in the middle of some action around the goal, we jerked the lines apart and cut off the broadcast. Then we raced down to the arena lobby to get warm. After a hot coffee and a lot of foot-stomping, we went back to the booth, hooked up the wires, and apologized to our listeners for the 'technical problems we'd been encountering.'"

Trent Frayne

Sportswriter Trent Frayne once told me about the winter of 1983–84, when everything seemed to go sour with the Maple Leafs—especially their relations with the media, and Frayne's paper, the Globe and Mail, *in particular.*

I knew the *Globe* wasn't kind to the Maple Leafs, but let's face it, they were a very bad hockey team. The role of a newspaper is not to be on the side of the home team. All kinds of people living in Toronto are not from Toronto, and the Leafs are not their favourite team. I think the adversarial role must be played by somebody. You just can't go around endlessly making excuses for Harold Ballard's shortcomings. I thought he was professional enough to recognize this. But most people know he banned the *Globe and Mail*'s reporters from the press box.

I encountered him only once. I don't go to the games too often—I don't think that is necessarily a failing. The *Globe* has two reporters who go to the games and I think the point of view of the fan who sits home watching television has merit. That has often been my role.

Anyway, I'd followed the Edmonton Oilers on a trip they made to Washington, Long Island, and Boston. Right after the Edmonton game in Boston, the Leafs came in, so I stayed around and covered that game.

It was one of those games where that young fellow, Allan Bester, played a marvellous game in goal. He had 52 shots and the Leafs won, 6–3. So I dashed to the dressing room, even though I knew it was a bad place for *Globe* people to be. I simply *had* to talk to Bester.

I went into the dressing room and had a few words with Bester, and as I turned away, my eyes happened to come directly into contact with Ballard's. He said, "You've got a lot of fucking nerve coming into this room. You're nothing but a leech."

At first I thought he might be kidding, because in the past he'd often talked that way. But on those occasions he'd always had a twinkle in his eye. I could tell that this time he was deadly earnest, so I just waved my hand at him to indicate that I didn't want any part of it. I started to walk away, and he shouted after me, "Why don't you get your fucking hair cut, you look like a violinist!"

Here was a man in charge of a major-league hockey team, one with the most unbelievable followers. They had to be crazy to be so loyal to the dismal team he moulded. I really lost an enormous amount of respect for him that day in Boston.

Don Wittman

Don Wittman, one of Canada's most versatile broadcasters, told me this story about his early days in television. There were a couple of occasions where he'd had a drink or two on the golf course during the day and then headed over to the CBC studios in the evening to do the late sports. When the camera's red light lit up, his cue to begin, Don leaned forward on the desk and said, "Good evening, fan sports."

A little later, he put his arms on the desk, and without realizing it began to push it forward—right off the 8-inch riser and onto the studio floor. The crew in the control room cut the feed, and Wit knew his sportscast—and possibly his career—was over.

When he awakened the next day, he felt sure that he'd be fired. To postpone the inevitable, he decided not to take any phone calls. Finally, his boss came looking for him and delivered a stern warning never to display such unprofessional conduct again.

"You mean I'm not fired?" Whit asked.

"Hell, no," the boss said. "We had about eighty calls today and almost all of them thought your act was hilarious. It's the best thing that's happened around here in a long time."

Harry Neale

Harry is a funny and interesting fellow who reminds me a bit of my late father—a much younger version, of course.

We were both at the airport in Montreal on a Sunday morning after a Buffalo Sabres victory at the Forum. I pointed out an article in the *Toronto Sun* about the $40,000 and $50,000 advances being paid to authors to write sports books. Incredible! I told Harry I thought he should write a book one day.

"If I ever do," he answered, "it would be called *I've Been Fired, Too*, and it would be about all the guys who've lost their jobs in the NHL.

"I remember when I was fired by Detroit. I was in my car, listening to the radio, on my way over to Windsor. I was just approaching the tunnel under the river when I heard the announcer say, 'The Red Wings have called a press conference for tomorrow morning. In all probability Harry Neale . . .' and I entered the tunnel and the radio faded.

"By the time I emerged at the other end, I knew it was all over for me."

I asked Harry about the night one of his players tried to beat the crap out of him in a hotel room.

"Well, Gordie Gallant was a tough Maritimer who played for me when I coached in the WHA. I was mad at him for breaking curfew. So Gallant calls me in my hotel room one night—it must have been midnight—and he says he wants a meeting. I told him to go to bed, and we'd discuss things in the morning. 'Nothing doing,' he says, 'We'll settle things tonight.' I told him to got to bed and I put the phone down. But it rings again and it was Gallant's roommate. He says, 'Be careful, Harry, Gallant's on his way up and he's pissed.'

"Moments later, there was a knock at the door. Now I open it a few inches and I see a huge fist coming straight at me. Gallant's punch knocks me bowlegged. I stagger back and Gallant storms in, saying he's going to beat the crap out of me. Just then, Jack McCartan, my assistant coach, races into the room and tackles Gallant. I'm a little stunned and I stagger into the hall naked, holding my eye, which is closing fast. Somehow the door slams shut behind me. Now I'm in the corridor, bare-ass naked and I hear one hell of a commotion in my room. McCartan, who tried to save my skin, is in there with Gallant the wild

Harry Neale went from junior hockey to coaching stints in college and NHL hockey and finally a long career with *Hockey Night in Canada.*

man. I hear them throwing punches and cursing and bouncing each other off the walls. Other players come running and some of the hotel guests are peeking out their doors. That room was an awful sight when we finally got the door open and got them apart.

"What did we do about Gallant? We got rid of him in a matter of hours."

Friar Nicholson

Friar Nicholson, the former voice of the Winnipeg Jets, once told me about that team's greatest star, Bobby Hull.

He was amazing. Often he was a one-man show. I remember one night the Jets played the Chicago Cougars—they had Reg Fleming, Ralph Backstrom, Pat Stapleton, and some others you'll know.

The Cougars were leading 3–2 with a couple of minutes to play, and Hull made rush after rush trying for the equalizer. There were twenty seconds left, and once again he raced up the ice—right into Reg Fleming. Fleming's stick came up and crashed into Hull's face. Blood started to pour out of his nose.

Hull turned, and I thought he was going to fight Fleming. Then he glanced up at the clock and thought better of it. He grabbed the loose puck and bulled his way in, taking one final shot on goal. The buzzer went and then Hull wheeled and chased after Fleming, blood streaming down his face.

By then, Fleming was over the boards and into the dressing room, while Hull stood there, frustrated.

Of course, the battles Hull had with his wife, Joanne, were as wild as some of those we saw on the ice.

One night Jets owner Ben Hatskin invited all the players and their wives to a fancy dinner at the Town and Country—his new restaurant. I was the MC, and sitting next to me at the head table were Ben, then Bobby, and next to him, Joanne. Well, the Hulls started a heated argument and suddenly Joanne stood up and threw a glass of wine at Bobby. But she missed and the wine flew all over Benny. He was soaked.

Bobby smiled all through this scene—that big grin on his face. But his lips were moving and I guess only Joanne heard what he had to say. And I'll bet she wouldn't have liked it.

Here's another bizarre story from the WHA years. The Cincinnati Stingers had a mascot—a guy who skated around in a bee costume. And one night the Stingers were at home against Indianapolis. Kim Clackson played for the Racers and he was always the first guy on the ice for his team. And he'd skate right into the opponents' zone—as if daring them to do anything about it.

He skated out this night and he picked up speed, nailed the Stinger bee, and flattened him into the boards. The mascot's head came flying off the costume, the stick went flying, and Clackson kept on motoring—right through the entire Cincinnati team. I think some of them pretended they didn't see what happened. Or maybe they said to themselves, 'Are we supposed to fight this bleepin' jerk over a bleepin' mascot?' Anyway, not one of them challenged Clackson. Talk about intimidation.

Gene Hart

The Flyers' late play-by-play announcer, Gene Hart, was always happy to talk about his team, especially the Stanley Cup years under coach Fred Shero.

Brian: Some people think that the Philadelphia team roster doesn't rank up there with other great Stanley Cup teams because they won a lot of their games on brute force.

Gene: You know what I think? You hear so much about how the Flyers bullied their way to the title, yet if you analyze that club, the first line was Bobby Clarke, Bill Barber, and Reggie Leach—not one fighter there. The second line: Rick MacLeish, Gary Dornhoefer, and Ross Lonsberry—not a fighter there. The third line was Orest Kindrachuk, who never fought; Don Saleski, who rarely did; and Dave Schultz, who fought often.

On defence, Bladon didn't fight, Jim Watson didn't fight, Joe Watson didn't fight, Barry Ashbee didn't fight.

So what it boiled down to was Bob Kelly, Moose Dupont, and Schultz doing all the fighting. Now I don't think three guys can intimidate their way to a Stanley Cup.

Let's consider the rest of the talent. You had an 80-goal scorer (counting playoffs) one season in Leach; a definite All-Star in Billy Barber; a Hall of Famer in Clarke; and a 50-goal scorer in MacLeish. And tenacious checking from Lonsberry and Dornhoefer. Very good players in Ashbee, Dupont, and Ed Van Impe.

I think that Flyer crowd has been maligned a bit, and I am sorry that it has happened. God, they were an exciting team. But there were too many people—and primarily people from Canada—who sneered at them. Dick Irvin, for example, who was a big fan of Montreal-style hockey, kept saying about the Flyers, "This is appalling, this is terrible, this is not hockey, it is ruining the game."

Brian: Now, Gene, don't knock my friend Dick. Do you have a favourite Fred Shero story?

Gene: Here's a funny one. In 1973–74, Bernie Parent had started about 73 games. It was a Sunday-afternoon game in Boston, and Tim Ryan, you, and Teddy Lindsay were drooling over the ratings you were about to get on NBC. Cheevers against Parent, Clarke against Esposito, the Broad Street Bullies against the hard-nosed Bruins.

Then, suddenly, everybody finds out Freddie is starting backup goalie Bob Taylor in place of Parent. Incredible. Taylor had played in about 8 games that season. So you guys go running around searching for Freddie. He's off in the corner by the Zamboni with his little notebook and one of you says, "Freddie, Freddie, how come you're starting Taylor?"

And Freddie peeked up and gave you that look, that pregnant pause, and he said, "Why? Because it's his turn."

Foster Hewitt

Foster Hewitt never tired of talking about his role in Team Canada's dramatic victory over the Soviets in 1972—and Paul Henderson's series-clinching goal. We were sitting around one day and he told me the story.

Well, we all got an awful shock when Team Canada lost the first game of that 8-game series in Montreal. Then the Canadian team came right back and won game two in Toronto. Then the teams went to Winnipeg and tied; by that time everybody was saying, "What is going on here?" Then there was another setback, another loss, this time in Vancouver.

That was the fourth game of the Canadian home series. Team Canada was really behind the eight ball and they still had another four games to play in Russia.

Nobody could believe what was happening. You'd watch the games and shake your head. We had great hockey players out there—the very best—and they were being beaten—at the time—by better players we'd never heard of. We blew the first game in Moscow, getting a lead and then blowing it. It was the old story of too many penalties, many of them questionable.

Then we started to click and we won the next three games. Team Canada was finally rolling. Still, they'd had so many ups and downs in the series, you didn't know what was going to happen next.

But the grand finale was the excitement and drama of game eight. It was the same story all over again: Canada got behind and they came back and tied it. We had about 3,500 fans there—all screaming their lungs out. I had never heard such cheering in my life. Never. They were marvellous. They out-yelled the Soviet crowd, and, in fact, were teaching the Soviets how to root. By the end, the Soviets were wildly excited about it, too.

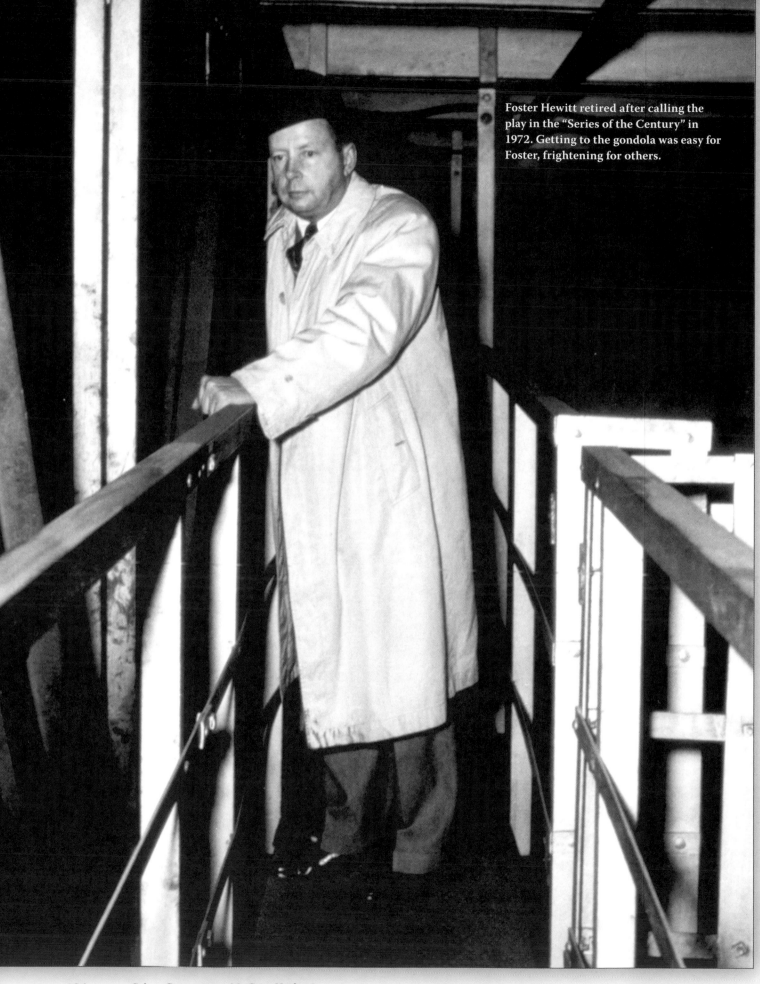

Foster Hewitt retired after calling the play in the "Series of the Century" in 1972. Getting to the gondola was easy for Foster, frightening for others.

Esposito just happened to get that puck and he cleared it out in front of the net and Henderson swept in from the side and broke the tie and that was it. Then the question was could they hold on for thirty-four seconds. The Soviets just tore up that ice in the final seconds. When it was all over, the excitement was just like an electric shock going all through your system.

I'll tell you that series and that final game had so much drama in it. It had everything. I think it gave Canada a tremendous lift. First of all it proved that hockey is our national sport and it is a huge part of our lives. And that series was perhaps the greatest series that we have ever seen. I doubt there'll ever be another one to equal it. When it is a first, it is always the best.

Ted Darling

Before he left Hockey Night in Canada *to become the longtime play-by-play voice of the Buffalo Sabres in 1970, Ted Darling commuted by train from Ottawa to Montreal. After he'd hosted several Habs games he began to wonder why he wasn't getting more recognition.*

I even began wearing my *HNIC* blazer on the train and I'd sit so that the logo stitched on my breast pocket would be quite visible to passersby. Still, nobody seemed to notice.

Then one day a man came staggering through the car, three sheets to the wind. He stopped in front of me, pointed a finger in my face and said, "Shay, I know you. Sure I do. You're that guy I shee on televishion, right?"

I grinned and nodded.

"Sure, I know you," said the stranger, beaming. "Why, you're the guy who comes on every Saturday night and says, 'Hello, everybody, from the Montreal Forum. This is *Hockey Night in Canada.*' Right?"

"That's me."

"Okay, now you wanna know who I am?" said the stranger.

I said, "Sure."

The drunk says, "Well, I'm the guy who sits at home and says, 'Yeah, well who gives a shit?'" And he walked away.

19

The Official View

I tried officiating at the college level when I lived in Schenectady. Coach Ned Harkness hired me to referee some games at Rensselaer Polytechnic Institute (RPI). I was surprised at how extremely difficult it was to call a game—to be a referee. Because I had played hockey all of my life, I assumed that I knew all the rules. I found out quickly that I didn't. Then, when I decided to make a call, even when I was sure that I was right, I'd sometimes hesitate a split second too long and the play would pass me by. I had to be accurate, impartial, intensely focused—and quick. Easier said than done. Darryl Sittler once told me that all players should have to referee a game or two during their careers. He insisted that the experience would undoubtedly curb a player's tendency to be too critical of the officials. Based on my own experiences officiating, I agree wholeheartedly.

Although their work is often overlooked, top-flight referees and linesmen are crucial. It takes a high level of training, dedication, conditioning, and knowledge to produce an NHL "zebra," and the NHL spends a great deal of time and money to scout and groom them.

It's easy to forget the sacrifices officials are expected to make to support their careers. Like players, they spend the majority of their time on the road. They risk injury and take abuse from fans, players, and coaches, on and off the ice. John McCauley, a fine official and a great man, lost his eye after an irate, cowardly fan attacked him in a restaurant.

I count many referees and linesmen among my friends. I admire them for the work they do and their ability to handle the vagaries and intense pressure that are part of life in the big leagues.

Bill Friday

Bill Friday was a no-nonsense type of referee in both the NHL and the WHA. Every game Friday worked in the latter league was an adventure. It was a league where Zambonis were known to fall through the ice; where a forty-five-year-old Gordie Howe would score 100 points and play with his two sons; where coloured pucks and post-game shootouts were introduced; where Bobby Hull would have his hair yanked off in a fight; and where a skinny seventeen-year-old by the name of Wayne Gretzky would make his professional debut. With all that going on, no wonder Friday's hair started turning gray after a season or two in the upstart league. Here's how he described those days.

In the WHA, we had the meanest, roughest, dirtiest hockey players that I have ever seen in my life. You worked hard every night for your money. You were at the rink for four hours we had so many bench clearings. So we put a rule in forcing the players to go into the neutral zone and get the hell out of the battle zone. Then the National league adopted it and a few of our other rules.

They had a guy by the name of Gilles Bilodeau playing in Birmingham. Look up Bilodeau's stats and you'll find he played two seasons with Birmingham and he had hundreds of penalty minutes and he hardly ever scored a goal. And this guy took a regular shift. One night he got a breakaway. He was going in on the goalie when he tripped, fell headfirst into the net, and the puck ended up in the corner. Typical.

The Minnesota Fighting Saints had the three Carlson brothers and a guy by the name of Dave Hanson. You'll remember them as the goons from the movie *Slap Shot*. If you saw *Slap Shot*, then you were looking at WHA hockey.

One night, Dave Hanson had a run-in with one of the greatest hockey players that God ever put skates on, Gordie Howe. Now Dave Hanson had a reputation of as a tough guy, so Gordie took a little bit of a run at him, like Gordie does. And in the nineteen years I refereed games involving Gordie Howe, I never saw him fight, not once. So he took a run at this Hanson kid and hit him pretty hard. Hanson turned around and was going to hit back. Then he saw it was Howe and he backed off. I couldn't figure out why, because this kid didn't have all his smarts. So I said to him, "Dave, why did you back off?"

He said, "Bill, I was in a no-win situation. Couldn't you see the papers? 'Young guy beats up old man'—or even worse, 'Old man beats the shit out of young guy.'" I think he was more worried about the latter.

I would also like to say that Gordie was probably one of the toughest, dirtiest hockey players that I ever saw. There is a little guy named Robbie Ftorek. He only came up to Gordie's belly button. Ftorek was playing for Cincy and the old man was playing with Hartford. About two or three weeks before this game, Ftorek had run young Mark Howe into the boards and separated his shoulder. I understand that it was not a dirty check. But this night Ftorek has the puck and Gordie goes after him. With one hand on his stick he stuck it under Ftorek's arm. I put my hand up and blew the whistle and Gordie headed straight for the penalty bench. But he nearly took the kid's eye out. That's how strong he was with one hand on the stick. Another time he dragged a player off his son Marty by sticking his fingers in the guy's nostrils and hauling him to his feet.

The Fighting Saints had some real gooneybirds. The Carlsons, Billy Butters on defence—another wacko—and John Arbour. And they had Glen Sonmor and Harry Neale coaching. Oh boy!

I go into Minnesota to do a game and the Winnipeg Jets are there. Winnipeg starts Hull, Nilsson, Hedberg—best line in the WHA—and Lars Sjoberg on defence and another guy back there I can't remember.

I drop the puck to start the game, and the damn thing doesn't move, no one touches it. The five Minnesota guys jump the five Winnipeg guys and there are five fights. And nobody bothers with the puck. So I pick it up and put it back in my pocket. When the battle is over I start dishing out the penalties—five majors for Minnesota and five minors to Winnipeg. By the time they finish serving the penalties it's 5–0 for the Jets. Harry Neale said to me, "You can't do that. Five majors to us and five minors to them."

I said, "I just did it."

He said, "But you can't do it."

And I said, "Harry, I did it."

We had another guy in Birmingham, you probably remember him, Steve Durbano. It was the only time in my life that I was ever scared. He came after me with blood in his eyes. Thank God saner heads prevailed and some guys grabbed him, and I threw him out of the game. I heard that the law caught up to him later on, and I really wasn't that surprised.

John D'Amico

Dick Irvin called me from Montreal on March 6, 1988. He said, "That was a great feature on last night's intermission, the one you did on John D'Amico." Dick was referring to an "Inside Hockey" segment about veteran linesman D'Amico working his final NHL game—Winnipeg versus Toronto at Maple Leaf Gardens. D'Amico worked more than 1,700 games in the NHL and officiated in the Stanley Cup finals twenty times. He was inducted into the Hockey Hall of Fame in 1993.

We started the segment before the game, in the officials' dressing room at Maple Leaf Gardens. The camera zoomed in on D'Amico's scarred leg. John told us, "I was at home shaving the edge off my skate with an X-Acto knife when the knife slipped and plunged into my leg. It missed an artery by a fraction. I rushed right down to the Gardens and Dr. Douglas stitched me up—inside and out. I was lucky. I could have killed myself."

I asked him if he could remember any other unusual accidents. "Yeah," he said. "I suffered a broken nose once when a stick got caught in the boards near one of the team benches. Just as I reached for it, one of the players leaned out and yanked on it. Then he released it and it snapped back and caught me right in the face."

While the camera was on D'Amico, I noticed a tear forming in the eye of his pal Ray Scapinello. "I'm really sad that it's John's last game," Ray said. "This man was so good to me when I broke in. That was seventeen years ago." The door burst open and Don Koharski, the big referee, walked in. He was stunned when we told him it was D'Amico's swan song.

"Why didn't somebody tell me? Really, John? This is really your last game? I can't believe it. And nobody told me." He turned to me. "Brian, does anybody realize what this man has done, what a great linesman he's been? Goddammit, he's a living legend. I'm all choked up. It's an honour to work the final game with him, a real honour. I'm telling you, I'm all choked up over this." He didn't have to tell me. It showed. Everybody would miss D'Amico.

When the game began, Ihor, my cameraman, trained his lens on D'Amico and followed him around the ice. D'Amico had agreed to wear a wireless microphone under his jersey so viewers could get a better idea of the official's perspective. At one point a puck ricocheted off the boards and flew over his head, just missing him by an inch or two. We heard John mutter, "Holy shit!" Moments later, he was caught in a traffic jam in front of the Winnipeg goal. And again we heard him say, "Holy shit!"

The game continued and several Jets stormed in on Ken Wregget in the Leaf goal and bowled him over. D'Amico was right there, pulling players off the pile, and from somewhere under the heap, we heard Wregget's voice, "Come on, guys. Let me get the fuck up."

D'Amico spotted a crack in the ice in Wregget's goal crease and spent a few seconds repairing it. We heard Wregget say, "Thanks, John." D'Amico responded, "You're welcome, Kenny. Hang in there, kid. You're doin' great."

Late in the game, Borje Salming started bitching about a Leaf goal that Koharski had called back. The referee relied on D'Amico for help. "It didn't go in, Donny. The puck hit one post, then the other, and it stayed out. Absolutely."

"All I saw was the red light go on," Koharski said.

"Don, it stayed out," D'Amico repeated.

Salming kept bitching, so D'Amico turned to him and said earnestly, "Borje, it didn't go in and that's it. And I don't lie."

In the dying moments of the game, Dale Hawerchuk moved in to take a faceoff. Before he put his stick down he said to D'Amico, "Congratulations, guy. You've had a great career."

After the game, a lot of people pumped John's hand and offered their congratulations. He appeared to be overwhelmed by all the attention and he was very slow to remove his equipment. I sat next to him for a few moments. He said, "You know, it's a player's game. I'm just happy to have played a small part in it. But it's been hard on the family life. I went straight from the OHA to the NHL. The first game I ever saw live at Maple Leaf Gardens was one I worked. I was the linesman."

Ray Scapinello
At the 2000 All-Star Game, I saw linesman Ray Scapinello skate out for the pregame warm-up. Kerry Fraser and Don Koharski were the referees for the match. As they circled the ice, I thought, all of these

Popular linesman Ray Scapinello—a Hall of Famer

fellows go back to my time on Hockey Night in Canada. *They help me maintain a connection to the game. Unfortunately, I know they can't stay around forever. Too soon, they'll all be gone.*

I remember talking to Scapinello and referee Bob Myers in Montreal in 1986, during a playoff series between the Hartford Whalers and the Habs.

Scapinello: Brian, just watch Claude Lemieux during the playoffs. If Montreal gets called for a penalty, you'll see Lemieux run in amongst the Hartford players and take a wild sprawl to the ice, hoping to attract the referee's eye and draw an offsetting penalty. The officials laugh at Lemieux's antics. One of them said to him, "Hey, Claude, don't be so stupid."

Brian: Can you think of any amusing comments made out there by certain players?

Scapinello: I had to laugh the other night during a game at the Forum. When the referee skated by the Montreal bench, someone yelled at him, "Wake up, you old fart!" And when he looked back, the guy said, "Pardon me, I said I just farted."

How about this one: Toronto was playing at Pittsburgh. Two guys came together, they had words, and the first thing you know Tiger Williams is mucking in there, protecting the Toronto player. So big Dave Schultz moves in and grabs Williams, and the linesmen are trying to get these two tough guys apart. I heard Williams say to Schultz, "Let's get out of here. You're the cementhead for your team and I'm the cementhead for the Leafs. That's all they pay us for. Let's fool 'em and go sit down on the bench."

Myers: Tiger is a very funny guy on the ice. Once he has his goal, he usually settles right down. I respect him for that. That's what he has to do.

Brian: Hockey players have idols growing up. Do you have other referees that you idolized or would like to emulate?

Myers: I think that we all do. Ever since I started I always respected any National League official and looked up to them all. When I did get to the NHL, I couldn't believe that I was on the ice with them and was actually working alongside them.

Brian: Darryl Sittler said an interesting thing the other day. He said that he used to referee games when he was about fourteen. He said that every NHL player should be forced to referee a few games, that it may cut down a lot of the bitching.

Myers: I think it would be a helluva idea. They would learn so much more about the game. When we are refereeing we can see such a different aspect of the game—the way it's going, the flow of the game, the passes, and so on. I just think it would help the game.

Most of the officials have played organized hockey at one time or another; we have a feel for the game. We understand what the players are going through, the pressure that they are under. We know that they don't want to make mistakes, and we certainly don't want to make mistakes. It could mean our jobs.

I personally wish that the players could referee a game or two. They'd soon appreciate what we have to go through. It would be interesting to get their views on that.

John Ashley

On a flight from Montreal to Toronto in 1987–88 I sit next to referee John Ashley. I make a faux pas by asking, "Where's your brother George these days?"

He gives me a dark look. "George Ashley is not my brother. Haven't seen him in years. But don't feel bad. Even the league got us mixed up. His name was George John and my name is John George. One time I even got his pension cheque and he got mine. And I'll say this, his was horseshit."

I ask him if he remembers the time Forbes Kennedy smacked George Ashley during a playoff game in Boston.

"Remember it well," he replied. "Clarence Campbell, King Clancy, and I looked at that tape about a million times. Finally Mr. Campbell says, 'Well, King, what do you think?' And Clancy says, 'Gee, Clarence, I haven't seen our guy hit him yet.'"

Referee John Ashley supported me in the Forbes Kennedy controversy.

Referee King Clancy chats with Ranger manager Lester Patrick.

I tell John that I called that game, and Kennedy really smacked the linesman.

"Sure he did. Belted him good. But Clancy refused to see it. They tell me Imlach wanted you fired over that incident. Is that true?"

"Sure did," I confirm. "When he saw the tape he told our *Hockey Night in Canada* people, 'That fucking McFarlane has to go.' But I got lucky. Before he could nail me to the wall his Leafs lost the series and Imlach was dumped right after the loss."

Wally Harris

I met former NHL referee Wally Harris in the press box at Maple Leaf Gardens one night and we got talking about the old six-team league.

One of the funniest things I remember took place in a game between Detroit and Montreal. Gary Bergman of the Wings got hit in the face with a shot and fell to the ice. He's bleeding from a bad cut and Gordie Howe, linesman Neil Armstrong, and I gather around the fallen defenceman.

Gordie says to us, "How many stitches will he get?"

Armstrong says "Oh, less than five," and I say, "No, more than that, I think about seven." And Gordie says, "I'll bet you a couple of beers it'll be more than eight." So we make the bet.

And when Bergman comes back later in the game Gordie happens to be on the ice and so the three of us gather around him. "How many stitches did you take?" we ask, almost in unison. Bergman thinks we're being sympathetic, I guess. Anyway, he says, "Nine," and Gordie laughs. "You guys owe me some beer," skating away.

And Bergman's indignant: "Nice guys. I'm lying in the infirmary—I could be dead, for all you care—and you're out here betting on how many stitches I'm getting."

I asked Harris about the strangest game he could remember.

I'll never forget, the Rangers were playing the Sabres one night. It was really early in the game and I got knocked flat. I'm unconscious for a few seconds and the trainer rushes out to administer smelling salts. In a few seconds I convince everybody I'm all right. Back on my feet, I get the game under way again.

I'm up and down the ice and I've got things in hand and then, late in the period, I give [Gilbert] Perreault a strange tripping penalty—strange because Perreault must have been 20 feet away from the nearest opponent. He couldn't have tripped anybody. But Perreault doesn't even question the call. He goes straight to the penalty box.

Buffalo coach Scotty Bowman is furious. He's up on the boards yelling at me, but I just ignore him. During the intermission, referee-in-chief Scotty Morrison comes into our dressing room and says, "Why in the world did you call that last penalty on Perreault?"

I say, "What penalty?"

He says, "The one you just gave Perreault."

I say, "Perreault who?"

He says, "You know where you are, don't you?" I look around and say, "Yeah, I'm in a dressing room."

He says, "Who's playing?"

"Darned if I know."

He says, "You know you're refereeing a hockey game?"

I say, "No."

Scotty says, "Better get him out of here. Take him to the hospital."

The only thing I could remember was having a cup of coffee before the game. Even today I have no recollection of what happened during the time I refereed that game. Well, they took me to hospital, and of course I had a concussion.

I heard later that, when Scotty Bowman got wind of what had happened, he pleaded with Scotty Morrison to cancel the penalty to Perreault. But Scotty said no, the penalty would stick, even if the referee couldn't remember why he called it.

Ron Wicks

Coming back to Toronto from Winnipeg on an early morning flight in 1983, I had the privilege of sitting next to referee Ron Wicks. Wicks told me about a time when Montreal had too many men on the ice during a 12–2 rout of the Jets.

Bill Sutherland, the Jets' assistant coach, yells at me, "Hell, they've got eight players on the ice!" I yelled back, "Do you think they need eight?" Suds laughed and said, "Not tonight. They only need three or four."

I heard the ultimate insult in Vancouver the other night. Someone called me a fucking Liberal! They don't like me in Vancouver. I gave the Canucks five straight penalties in a game there a while ago. Boy, did they boo me. Then, when I'm back in Vancouver a few nights later, they started booing me as soon as I stepped on the ice. So just for fun, I skated over to the PA announcer and said, "Tonight, when you introduce the officials, I want you to say, 'Tonight, back by popular demand, referee Ron Wicks.'" Well, he did it. When the crowd heard that "back by popular demand" boom over the arena, they roared. They booed and then they laughed and some of them applauded. It was good fun, although both the PA announcer and I got a note from the League office about it.

Wicks and I got around to talking about Tiger Williams, then with Vancouver:

You know, Gretzky told me a funny story about Williams. Tiger was involved in a scuffle with one of the Oiler rookies early in the season. Gretzky was skating past when he heard Tiger say to the kid, "Listen, kid, get the hell out of here. Do you know you're pushing around a $200,000 hockey player? Just fuck off." Gretzky told me he burst out laughing.

A few days later, linesman Bob Hodges told me this anecdote about Wicks:

When Ron was a rookie official, he took the train to his first NHL assignment. Naively he asked one of the veteran officials on board where he'd be sleeping. Wicks was told, "Go down to that little room at the end of the car and put on your pajamas, brush your teeth, and then come back here. After that, I'll help you put the seat back and you can settle in for the night."

Wicks followed the instructions to the letter. On his way back to reclaim his seat, he wondered why all the other passengers were nudging each other and chuckling as he made his way down the aisle. Of course, he looked ridiculous, standing there in his pajamas.

Bruce Hood

Bruce is the only official who ever angered me—not in a hockey game, but in lacrosse. He refereed a game involving my Montreal Canadiens lacrosse team one day, and for some reason his calls infuriated me. But I got over it. And it made me so much more aware that people with a vested interest in the outcome of a game, be it players, coaches, or owners, get much more emotionally involved than most others. Here's Bruce:

They used to say when I refereed the Leafs games that I hated them and caused them to lose a lot of hockey games. The last seven years they've had a terrible record, but I don't think it was because of me.

Montreal team captain Bob Gainey was a player I admired and respected. The Soviets once called him "the best in the world."

People often ask me why I became a referee, and how did I get to be one? I like to tell the story of how I started out as a hockey player with a pocket full of marbles, and as the season progressed I lost some of those marbles. After I lost all my marbles, I became a referee.

I retired after twenty-one years. I remember the first night I came into Pittsburgh. I'm in the airport and two police officers come and tell me to drop my bags and get up against the wall. They frisked me and asked me if I had a gun. Of course I didn't have a gun. I was asked if I had ever made a mistake. I always use the term the late Bill Clemens used: "I'm never wrong, but I can think of a thousand times that I wished my arm was cut off at the shoulder."

Ron Asselstine

Ron Asselstine is on the Montreal–Toronto flight with me in January 1984 and we talk about the previous night's game at the Forum:

After the second period last night, Frank Udvari [the NHL's supervisor of officials] came into our room. He said to Don Koharski, who's a fine young referee starting his first full season, "Hey, those guys have been running at you and yapping all night. If you're going to show them who's in charge out there, you've got to let them know you're not going to take any more shit. You can't let guys call you an asshole and all those things. You've got to show your authority."

So Koharski calls Bob Gainey over before the third period begins and tells him, "Bob, you tell your guys that I'm not taking any more of this shit. Especially you tell Nilan and Carbonneau. But I'm warning all of you. I'm not taking any more crap from your guys."

Gainey, a good guy, says, "Okay, Don."

Now [Pat] Boutette and the Montreal kid [Petr] Svoboda are mixing it up in the corner, and Svoboda gets cut on the finger. He goes off and Chris Nilan starts reaming out Koharski. So Koharski says, "Listen, Nilan, I've warned you not to get on me anymore. Now get out of here!" And Nilan keeps on yapping: "You lowlife! You asshole!" So Koharski nails him with a penalty, and he's no sooner in the box than the puck is in the Montreal net. Pittsburgh wins the game, 6–5.

You should have seen the old guys on the Montreal bench when Nilan came out of the box. What dirty looks they gave him! And he skates over with his head down. What a dumb penalty! Yet off the ice he's the nicest guy you'd ever want to meet.

Art Skov

Another of my favourite officials was referee Art Skov. I was talking to him one day and I said to him that he'd seen a lot of hockey players come and go, and some of them would get hot under the collar and abuse him verbally. I asked him who comes to mind when he thinks about players who always kept their cool and treated him with respect:

One of the guys who is at the top of my list is Jean Beliveau. Jean never got excited. He was the captain of the team. He asked questions, whether it was a penalty against him or one of his teammates, but he never raised his voice. He is one of many I can think of.

A guy like Gilles Tremblay was another. All he wanted to do was go up and down that wing and score goals, which he could do very well. If he got a penalty he never said a word, went straight to the box. I respected that. Gilles was a real pro.

There are very few that have acted up, and those who have often were rookies. After the game is over you may bump into them at an airport or in a hotel and they don't talk hockey—they don't say boo to you. That very night you may have given them three, four penalties, or even thrown them out, but no, they never mention it. But the next game back on the ice they give it to you all over again.

Later I asked him about managers and owners. Sometimes they get very verbal in their criticism of game officials. Did he have any memories of that?:

I had a run-in with Mr. Staff Smythe one night. I had given Shack a penalty and I was going over to report him. You know where Staff used to sit at Maple Leaf Gardens—right back of the penalty box—and this night he threw his program at me. I thought it was very, very small of him. Then again, I blame myself for not reacting faster, because the rules state that no manager, coach, or general manager—anyone like that—can throw anything from the bench, and I could have given the Toronto Maple Leafs a bench minor penalty for this infraction. I didn't give it, but Scotty Morrison pointed it out to me later.

Bowman and the Other Bench Bosses

As a lifelong hockey fan, I've seen coaches of all shapes, sizes, and styles break into the NHL. Sometimes they last and sometimes they don't. It's difficult to define what makes a good coach. Simply put, a good coach is someone who gets the best out of his players. Does he have to be popular, well liked by his charges? Lord, no. Coaches like Scotty Bowman and Mike Keenan were often the least popular men in their dressing rooms. But both knew how to win.

In a way, those two are throwbacks to old-time coaches like Toe Blake, Jack Adams, and Punch Imlach: hard-nosed, dictatorial types who achieved results through intimidation and fear of demotion. They ruled without worrying about losing stars to free agency, the interference of agents, cliques of foreign players, overpaid prima donnas, or clubhouse lawyers. Adams, it's said, kept a number of train tickets to the minors in his pocket, ready to distribute to any malcontent or underachiever.

During the 1970s, a new generation revolutionized the role of coaches. Roger Neilson believed strongly in watching, learning, and correcting miscues through the use of videotape. He was ahead of his time on the latter front, and his detractors nicknamed him "Captain Video." He never played in the NHL, he didn't profess to be an expert, and he relied on his best players for input.

Colourful coaches like Don Cherry, Pat Burns, Pat Quinn, Glen Sather, and Mike Keenan elevated coaching to celebrity status—and they've been reimbursed accordingly.

Scotty Bowman

Scotty Bowman, who came along with expansion in 1967, is often cited for his unique, unpredictable coaching style. He's always challenged his players, kept them off balance by rearranging his lines and occasionally knocking his superstars off their pedestals. Bowman didn't care how much a player was earning or how beloved he was by the paying public. He would bench a star in a heartbeat, or even force a trade, if he felt the man wasn't producing.

In his splendid bestselling book *The Game*, Ken Dryden speaks often of Bowman. He writes:

Bowman is not someone who is easy to like. He has no coach's con about him. He does not slap backs, punch arms, or grab elbows. He doesn't search eyes, spew out ingratiating blarney or disarm with faint, enervating praise. He is shy and not very friendly.

Abrupt, straightforward, without flair or charm, he seems cold and abrasive, sometimes obnoxious, controversial, but never colourful. He is not Vince Lombardi, tough and gruff with a heart of gold. He plays favourites. His favourites, while rarely feeling favoured, are those who work and produce for him. He is complex, misunderstood, unclear in every way but one. He is a brilliant coach, the best of his time.

Scotty Bowman, hockey's winningest coach, was fun to work with on *Hockey Night in Canada*. Ken Dryden calls him "a brilliant coach, the best of his time."

St. Lawrence University grad Mike Keenan was always an engaging guest on TV. He coached the Rangers to a Cup win in 1994.

I really enjoyed working with Scotty Bowman when he was an analyst on *Hockey Night in Canada*, particularly our conversations after the telecasts. We worked together often on the Montreal broadcasts after Scotty had been fired by the Buffalo Sabres in December 1986.

One thing about Scotty, it was hockey before anything else. One Saturday morning I rushed from the airport to the Forum in time for the morning skate. Scotty was the first person I encountered. I said to him, "Geez, Scotty, I had a rough flight in. Turbulence you wouldn't believe, rain and sleet. It was scary."

He looked at me as if he hadn't heard and said, "The Montreal power play has been pretty shitty."

That's Scotty—deaf to anything outside hockey, especially trivial things like turbulence. But he was a fascinating guy. And of course, a coaching legend. And he always sends a card at Christmas—with the Bowman family photo on it. I like that.

I asked Scotty about Doug Jarvis and his streak of 964 consecutive games—a remarkable record for durability:

When I was with the Canadiens years ago, I was talking with Roger Neilson one day about some of the kids he was coaching in Peterborough. And he said to me, "Scotty, I've got a kid who's the best face-off man in hockey." I said to Roger, "You mean in Junior hockey?" And he said, "No, in *all* of hockey. I'd stack him up against any centre in the NHL. His name is Doug Jarvis."

So I mentioned Jarvis to [Montreal GM Sam Pollock] and Sam said, "Well, I'm not interested in the kid. He's small and our scouts aren't too high on him." But Sam did promise to take another look at him and he did—but he decided not to waste a draft choice on him.

The Leafs grabbed Jarvis in the second round that year, twenty-fourth overall. In Montreal, Scotty still felt his centres were inconsistent on faceoffs and he kept bringing the name Doug Jarvis to Pollock's attention. Wasn't there some way the Habs could acquire him?

As it turned out, Pollock was talking with the Leafs anyway about a trade that would send goalie Wayne Thomas to Toronto for the Leafs' first-round draft choice. He was also thinking about dangling minor-leaguer Greg Hubick in front of the Leafs to see what they'd offer in return. "I'll try to get Jarvis for you," he told Scotty, "but the Leafs are going to try to foist Jim McKenny or Brian Glennie or one of their old guys on me."

When Pollock called the Leafs a week or so after the Thomas deal, general manager Jim Gregory was out of town. Owner Harold Ballard took the call. Pollock said he was willing to give up Hubick, but he still needed a body in return. "Give me one of your throwaway players, somebody you're not too high on. But make it a young player, will you? I don't want McKenny or Glennie."

"Well, who did you have in mind?" asked Ballard.

Sam said, "I dunno. How about that kid Jarvis, the religious kid from Peterborough?"

Sam knew well that Harold was suspicious of any player with strong religious beliefs, especially born-again Christians. Right on cue, Ballard said, "Okay, Sam, you've got him."

Jarvis reported to the Habs' training camp and immediately looked like he was ready for the NHL. But Pollock kept asking Scotty, "When are you going to send the kid to Halifax? He's not ready for the NHL."

"Sam, he's holding his own," Scotty would say. "Let's keep him around for a few more days. I'd like to see what he does against Chicago in a preseason game."

Well, we went on the road and played Chicago, and Jarvis had to go head-to-head with Stan Mikita, one of the all-time great face-off men. Jarvis stole the puck from Mikita on almost every face-off. I phoned Sam after the game and told him how well Jarvis had played, and Sam kept saying, "Yeah, well, we should send him down. We can't keep him with the big club. He's not ready."

Jarvis got a huge break when Jacques Lemaire was injured and couldn't play. I persuaded Sam to keep Jarvis with the big club, and he was in the lineup for the opening game in 1975. After that he played so well we just couldn't send him down. And that was the start of his consecutive-game streak. Twelve years later it was still intact.

I asked Scotty if there were one or two players, out of all those he coached in Montreal, who stood out from the others in terms of dedication, discipline, and reliability:

Yeah, I thought [Bob] Gainey and Jarvis were those kind of guys. And Jacques Lemaire. You could always count on Lemaire, especially in a big game. And Serge Savard. They knew the game, Savard and Lemaire. I didn't always have to come and tell them you should be doing this, you should be doing that. They knew how to play the game.

One day I talked to my friend and occasional broadcast partner Dan Kelly about Scotty Bowman. Both Kelly and Bowman were legends in St. Louis. Kelly says:

I remember I was sitting in a press lounge—it was in '69 or '70—when he was coaching St. Louis. Scotty came in and he said, "Can I see you for a minute?" I said sure and he took me aside. He said, "St. Marseille, Sabourin, and Ecclestone are benched tonight. Benched. Do you understand me? It's not that they're not dressing, it's not that they're injured, they're benched." End of conversation.

I could see that he was playing mind games with them. He wanted the world to know that his players were benched and he didn't want any misconceptions about it. Why? Because the next game he knew they'd come back and they'd be going 150 miles an hour. And they did.

Kelly tells me about his first year in St. Louis, when he lived for a time with Bowman:

I remember moving to St. Louis in '68. My family stayed in Ottawa because I didn't have a house built yet, so for the first month I was there, I lived with Scotty. I learned more about hockey from October 1 to October 30 than I had in the previous thirty-one years, because it was hockey night and day. What an education he gave me!

He was the first coach I ever saw with a videotape machine, and that was in '68. We would meet for dinner at six o'clock and then go back to the arena and watch tapes all night. He would say, "Look at this guy over here, look at him!" And I would look and say, "Well, what's wrong with him? Why shouldn't he be there?" And he would point to the screen and say, "Look at him, Dan. He should be over here."

At the 1993 Legends of Hockey game at Maple Leaf Gardens, I sat with Scotty Bowman throughout the game and we appeared on the telecast intermissions. In the stands, I asked him how his hockey-card collection was coming along and he said, "I've got fifty Brett Hull rookie cards and they're worth a bundle—something like fifty bucks apiece."

He told me he'd been interviewed by the Ottawa Senators, who were just joining the NHL, a few months earlier, but the job description there was that of a consultant, not a general manager. Scotty lost interest when Jim Durrell and Randy Sexton said they would be signing the players. He also disagreed with Ottawa management when they talked about signing the toughest, meanest players available.

Scotty said he'd been insulted by the Ottawa offer. At one point they even said, "Of course, we'll pay your moving expenses if you come to Ottawa." Scotty said it had never entered his mind that they wouldn't.

He stayed in Pittsburgh instead. When Penguin coach Bob Johnson died, Scotty took over and helped the Penguins win two Stanley Cups. Then he moved behind the Detroit bench and captured two more. Both were pretty good career decisions, I'd say.

Chicago superstar Stan Mikita was quick on the ice and quick-witted on camera.
In two seasons (1966–67 and 1967–68) he captured six major individual trophies

Tom McVie

Tom McVie coached Washington from 1975 to 1978, Winnipeg in 1979–81, and New Jersey in 1983–84. He enjoyed a second stint with the Devils in 1991–92.

I interviewed him in Winnipeg on a Jets-Devils telecast during the 1991–92 season.

Brian: Coach, I'm pleased you haven't lost your sense of humour. At practice today, you placed some chairs on the ice and had your players skating around them. When someone called you to rinkside, pointed at one of the chairs and said, "What's that?" what did you reply?

McVie (*laughs*): I said, "Sssh, that's my best defenceman." I told the guy we came up a little short in the draft last year so we'll take anything we can get.

Brian: Tommy, when you left Winnipeg in 1980, I remember you saying, "Don't worry about Tom McVie because I'll be back in the NHL."

McVie: The thing is, when I left Winnipeg and was driving west my eyes were a little moist, and I reflected on my hockey career, which appeared to be behind me. I'd had some tough times in Winnipeg, and in Washington before that. But then Cliff Fletcher gave me a job. I did a pretty good job for him. Then Keith Allen gave me another job and my team went to the Calder Cup in the American league. I'd underestimated my ability and my enthusiasm. So I simply worked my way back to the NHL, three times now, and I don't think you guys know anybody who's ever done that. And if they send me out again I'll simply work my way back again.

Brian: Tommy, a guy told me that someone named Duke should have had the job ahead of you because Duke knows more about the game than you do.

McVie (*chuckles*): Well, Duke's my wife and she's been a hockey wife for twenty-seven years so, sure, she knows as much about hockey as I do. The thing is, she's not with me at present, she's out in Oregon, but she does send me plays to use. I wish she'd sent me a couple before tonight's game. I haven't seen her since August, but when she joins me we're going to work on some new plays.

Brian: Tommy, you could have used some of those plays when you were with the Jets back in 1980.

McVie: You're right. And the reason I left was because [general manager John Ferguson] had a five-year plan and I had a two-year contract. And it didn't help that my team won only 1 of 28 games. But now I'm back with the Devils and I'm enjoying my best season ever.

During our interview, McVie talked about his family. I noticed that he has been surrounded by people with unusual names. His wife's name is Duke, and his kids are named Dallas and Denver, after two of the cities where he played minor-league hockey. "Thank God you never played in Albuquerque," I said.

"Yeah. Or Muskegon."

McVie's Devils would tie a team record for wins during the 1991–92 season, with 38. Despite his fine effort, he would be replaced by Herb Brooks the following season.

Roger Neilson

When it comes to innovations on the ice, nobody tops coach Roger Neilson. He's been a trend-setter ever since Junior hockey. During his Junior days he was also one of the best practical jokers around.

Looking ahead to a playoff game between his Peterborough Petes and the London Knights, Roger

Montreal coach Toe Blake was blessed with great talent—superstars like Rocket Richard (left) and Jean Beliveau (right). Blake's teams set a record with five consecutive Stanley Cup victories from 1956–1960.

Roger Neilson's first of many NHL coaching stints was in Toronto.
He was a breath of fresh air around Maple Leaf Gardens.

anticipated that he'd need a few delays during the game, some "breathers" to give his top players a moment's rest. So he handed some eggs to the Peterborough Junior B players, who were seated in the stands, to throw on the ice when he gave the signal.

Whenever Roger tugged on his ear, three or four eggs were to be tossed on the ice, the referee would blow his whistle, and there'd be a nice long pause while the gooey mess was cleaned up.

But Roger overlooked one important factor: He forgot to let the Junior B coach in on his plan. When the "B" coach arrived at the game midway through the contest and caught his players throwing eggs over the boards, he was so angry that he rounded them up and turfed them out of the arena.

"Go home! Learn to behave yourselves!" he thundered.

It wasn't long before Roger's first-liners needed another breather. Roger tugged on his ear, but no eggs flew overhead. He tugged again, harder. Still no eggs. Roger looked over his shoulder to discover a row of empty seats. His egg throwers had disappeared.

Roger came up with what he thought was an improved plan for the next game. This time he handed the team trainer the eggs and ordered him to hide behind the boards at rinkside. When Roger tugged on his ear, the trainer was to lob an egg or two onto the ice. But when the referee made a call that went against the Petes, the trainer let emotion get the better of him. He stood up and fired a couple of eggs right at the ref, was caught red-handed, and was thrown out of the rink. Again, Roger was left with no eggs and no one to throw them.

Michel Bergeron

During the 1987–88 season, the youthful Michel Bergeron made his first trip to Maple Leaf Gardens as coach of the New York Rangers. Manager Phil Esposito had given up a first-round draft choice, plus a lot of cash, to acquire his rights from the Quebec Nordiques. He spent some time with our crew and we were all impressed with his energy and his enthusiasm.

Brian: Michel, you are a very emotional coach—we have all seen that in the past, when you'd jump up onto the boards and scream and shout. Phil Esposito is an emotional manager. Are you guys on a collision course?

Michel: So far, there is no problem with Phil and myself. I don't see any problems. Phil is a good hockey man, he knows what we need here to win. He is a good man for the players. Maybe he is too nice to the players. He gives them everything and I am really impressed. Last year Phil made so many trades that when I came here I said Phil must be a really tough manager. But he's not, he is a nice man. I remember at training camp we cut the young players, and I remember one guy, a young guy, broke down and cried. And Phil gave him money and said to him, "Kid, it is all part of the game." I was really impressed with the way he handled it.

Brian: I remember you came into the studio in Toronto when you were a rookie coach with Quebec. None of us knew you very well and you told us the story about what happened when you applied for the coaching job in Buffalo. During the interview they asked you about yourself and you said, "Well, I'm pretty good. I was a good Junior coach and I can be a good pro coach." And they asked you, "Michel, who do you think is the best coach around?"

Michel (laughs): Yeah. And I told them the best coach is Scotty Bowman. So what did they do? They hired Scotty Bowman. Then Scotty gave me that shot three years ago—remember when we beat them in the playoffs? We beat Buffalo in the fifth game and Scotty didn't come across the rink to shake my hand. He said that he got beat by a "goon" coach. I couldn't believe it. I mean, Scotty was my idol. It was one of the very sad moments for me when Scotty said that.

Grapes Is in a Class by Himself

Don Cherry is unique to the game of hockey. He's never afraid to express an opinion, embrace a controversy, or say exactly what he thinks and feels. People either love him or abhor him.

He is much more complex than people assume. He has made a lifelong commitment to hockey as a player, coach, owner and, above all, a broadcaster. He enjoys and embraces the limelight. What I like about Cherry is his loyalty. He is always supportive of his friends and family. If he likes you, he'll stand up for you when it counts.

He is now a captive of his fame, unable to move a mile in any direction without having to surrender a batch of autographs or kibitz with the crowd—especially his legion of blue-collar fans.

One day in the studio at the Gardens, early in his career with *Hockey Night in Canada*, he told me about a flight from Edmonton to Toronto the night before. He said he was napping on the plane when a big bruiser moved clown the aisle and stood next to him. The stranger grabbed a full bottle of wine from the flight attendant's cart, then pushed the cart aside. He was inhaling on a cigarette—despite the no-smoking regulations—and waved the butt in Cherry's eyes. He said, "Are you Don Cherry?"

When Don just nodded, the stranger turned nasty.

"Who's the greatest player you ever seen?"

Don said, "Bobby Orr."

The bruiser said, "Oh, yeah? Piece of shit, Bobby Orr."

"Then Gordie Howe."

"Piece of shit, Gordie Howe."

The guy was really getting out of control, Don said. It looked like a dangerous situation. Nobody around was willing to get involved, to help him out of his predicament. The flight attendant was up front, and the copilot wouldn't come back. Finally he told the bruiser he had to go to the washroom, and the guy let him up. When Don came back, two big cops who happened to be on the plane had the guy in handcuffs. They had broken his nose and there was blood all over him. And when the plane landed in Toronto they hauled him away.

I told Don that I always enjoyed attending the Bruins' morning workouts when he was coach. They looked like fun. Here's what Don said:

What the Bruins used to do in a practice, they would gather at centre ice and start mock fighting. It would be unbelievable. They'd rip up the practice sweaters. Every practice, there'd be two or three sweaters torn apart. They would fight at centre ice all the time. Not fist fighting, but wrestling and horsing around. A lot of the guys got hurt. In fact, [Brad] Park was out for three games.

We would have an optional practice and nineteen guys would show up because they had so much fun. One time it backfired on me. We were in first place by about 20 points and we were having a bad March. I mean, we were the worst team in the league that month. We were on a ten-day road trip, and our final game of the trip was in Montreal. We got in about four o'clock in the afternoon and the guys said, "Okay, we want to practice." I think they just wanted to skate around and work up a thirst.

Grapes is a fascinating guy, a unique fixture on our show. Who'd have thought he'd become one of the most famous Canadians in history?

That did it. Then Cherry goes into his Redd Foxx heart-attack routine. He clutches his chest and his eyes start to roll and he starts to cough with his tongue hanging out. Then he yells at the trainer, "Toby, get in here, I don't believe this guy! He's worried about his girlfriend. Can you believe this shit?" Oh, he went on for half an hour having his heart attack while Berry sat there squirming. We died laughing, but the poor guy should have known better.

So finally Grapes says, "All right, you can go downtown, but you better think twice about ever comin' back." Ray Miron told Grapes he should play Berry a lot more because Glen Sather liked Berry a lot and Edmonton might give up a good player to get him. Grapes would say, "Sather wants Berry? In a million years he wouldn't make a deal for the guy."

Grapes wasn't big on girlfriends. His attitude was what the hell did they have to do with anything? And he may have had a point there.

Grapes used to bring Blue down to the rink every once in a while. In the dressing room he'd be all right. But if you stared at Blue for a long time he'd get mad and start growling. He'd think you were confronting him.

We were playing Hartford one day and Blue was running around and getting excited. We went out for a skate and Grapes said to Toby, the trainer, "Put Blue in my office while we're on the ice." So the trainer fired Blue in there. A Hartford reporter came around looking for Grapes and the trainer said, "I don't know where he is. Check the office."

So the reporter opened the office door and yelled, "Cherry, are you there?" The damn dog attacked the guy. *Yar, yar, yar, yar, yar.* Really went after him and grabbed him by the pant leg. Cherry had to come running in from the ice to tear his mad dog off the reporter.

We got thumped pretty good that night, something like 7–2, and the next morning the headlines on the sports page are all about Blue. "I wish my players had the heart of Blue," Grapes was quoted as saying. And Cherry goes on to tell the story, or his version of it, how Blue kicked the shit out of a reporter, but the Whalers belted the Rockies all around on the ice.

In 1985, the year the All-Star game was played in Calgary, I was on "Coach's Corner" with Don Cherry. I thought we had a hell of an act going, and so did Don. He told me we worked perfectly together. But obviously others disagreed because we were split up a few months later. I have a tape of one of our shows and the conversation went like this:

Brian: Grapes, what is this thing you've got going with Mike McEwen, who said this week, "I played for Grapes in Colorado and he was the pits as a coach?"

Grapes: Well, I'm glad he did. Mike didn't like me coaching and I didn't like him playing. But can I tell you a little story about Mike?

Brian: That's why we're here.

Grapes: Mike, after a loss in Colorado—and we had a lot of them—if the owners weren't there, whoosh, he's gone. Ten minutes and he's outta there. Now if the owners were there he'd sit there with all his equipment on, head down, you know, real dejected. "Geez, we've lost another one." And the owners would come over and say, "Mike, don't be so hard on yourself. We know you're in the game." Then they'd come over to me and say, "Poor Mike takes a loss awful hard." And the other players would be across the room giggling.

But I don't mind that he doesn't like me, Attila the Hun here. That's okay. But he doesn't like Al Arbour and he's a saint! So I'm in pretty good company.

Brian: Is that when you grabbed him by the throat?

Grapes: Yeah, I grabbed him by the throat. Gave him a little choke. Why? Because he wouldn't do what he was told.

Wearing fifties-style attire, Grapes and I head for Montreal by train to help celebrate the NHL's seventy-fifth anniversary in 1992.

Brian: Well, how did the other players respond to that? And what did the Players Association have to say about it?

Grapes: The Players Association usually do somethin'. Not this time. And one of my players, Rene Robert, my captain, came up to me and said, "You know, Don, when you had him by the throat, why didn't you squeeze a little harder?"

Brian: Oh, oh, oh. Let's turn to another subject. What about Orval Tessier getting fired in Chicago? You must have felt some sympathy for somebody in your profession to lose his job.

Grapes: If there was ever a guy who deserved to get fired, it was Orval Tessier. That business about sayin' his players needed heart transplants in the playoffs and all that stuff. The players played for him and then he turned on them when they were losing. Not only that, he had strange ideas. Former players couldn't go in the dressing room and all that. Jimmy Pappin, who scouts for the team, couldn't even go in the room. Orval deserved what he got.

Brian: Let's try to end on a positive note. What about the All-Star game coming up in Calgary? But then, you don't like All-Star games either, do you?

Grapes: Nah, I don't like the All-Stars. But I understand this one is really going to be spectacular. The players are going to give away hats and all that. And it's going to be great. But there's one thing you gotta tune in for, folks. Our president, John Ziegler, is goin' to get all dressed up as a cowboy, with the chaps and everything, and I hope they give him a great big ten-gallon hat. And it should be good. So tune in for that.

Brian: And he'll have a great big horse as well.

Grapes: Well, a great big horse's somethin'.

Brian: Thanks for those kind words, Coach. And to Mike McEwen, Happy Valentine's Day.

McEwen would be quoted in the *Globe and Mail* a few days later:

I think Cherry is perfect for TV. It's much more suited to his personality. He sure couldn't coach. He badgered me for four months in Colorado before I finally walked off the team. Mostly there were his put-downs in the dressing room in front of the other players. He was always bugging me. My frustrations ended when I was traded to the Islanders and won three Stanley Cups.

During the 1991 All-Star break, I went to Chicago to interview Mike Keenan and John Candy for two "Inside Hockey" features. Don asked me to call his daughter Cindy. He wanted to introduce her to Candy if I got the chance.

While we waited for Candy to arrive, I asked Cindy about her famous father:

Dad raised us—and no one ever asked me this before—exactly like he coached his hockey teams. He never had curfews on his hockey teams, and my brother Tim and I never had curfews. He gave us all the freedom that we wanted. But we knew, and his teams knew, that you can only push him so far. And if you take advantage of him you are really going to pay the price.

I've seen what he did to a few hockey players. I remember one time in Rochester, he declared a certain bar—the Orange Monkey—off-limits to his players. He said, "I don't care if you stay up all night—don't go in that bar."

Some of his boys sneaked in there and one of them was Herman Karp, his leading scorer—and Dad found out about it. Well, Dad got rid of Herman so fast. I don't know where he sent him, but poor Herman was never seen again, just because he went into the wrong bar. It ruined his career.

I remember I stayed out late one night. It was getting two, then three, then it was three-thirty. All Dad said to me the next day was, "You know, Cindy, remember what happened to Herman Karp when he pushed me too far." I said, "Yep, Dad, okay." And I came in earlier from then on.

I used to tend bar at Dad's Hamilton bar and Herman came in there several times. I recognized him and we talked about the good old days in Rochester. He still speaks highly of Dad. Of course, he wouldn't badmouth him to me.

My brother Timothy didn't have to worry much growing up because he was always the perfect angel. Not like me. Tim was a really good hockey player when he was five, six, and seven. But then he got a disease called vasculitis, some form of arthritis. So what they did was give him strong steroids to combat this disease and that ruined his kidneys. They didn't know this, unfortunately, until he reached puberty. He was always getting bruised and we thought perhaps he wasn't tough enough. It was hard on Tim because nobody knew how sick he was.

Tim had all the moves. He skated with his legs wide apart and he had good balance. He was a Ricky Middleton type, with good hockey sense—my dad says you can't teach that—and he anticipated very well. He wasn't big but he had talent. Now he uses that knowledge to advantage in business, in the film and video world.

Finally, Tim's health got so bad he needed a kidney transplant. I was in my last year of college in Kingston. All that last year in school, I didn't realize how sick Tim was because he was in Boston. He had to go on dialysis about three times a week and I didn't know it. He was really in bad shape. When I came down to Boston from college, I would go and see Tim with my mom. And it came down to the fact he was going to die if somebody didn't help him. So we all took tests and I was a perfect match to make the donation. So we did it. We set a record. I was out in seven days and Tim was out in ten days.

I remember it was like one big happy family at the Massachusetts General that October. Brad Park was in there for his knee, Wayne Cashman was in for his back, and people came every day to see us. One afternoon the referee and the linesmen came to see us. They brought us tapes for our tape recorder and they said, "Is your dad coming over to see you after the game tonight?" We said, "Oh, I don't think so. Visiting hours are over at ten o'clock and the hockey game doesn't start until 7:30." They winked and said, "Aw, he'll make it all right."

So we're watching the game that night and there were hardly any whistles. The linesmen let off-sides go by 2 feet and there couldn't have been more than two penalties all night. And right after the game, my dad showed up, just a few minutes before visiting hours were over. I said, "Pretty quick game, eh, Dad?" And he said, "Yeah, those referees are getting better. They really hustled us through that one tonight." Of course, my brother and I knew why.

One day I got Don started about his bull terrier, Blue:

You know, beauty is in the eye of the beholder, and I happen to think she's absolutely beautiful. One time when I was in Denver, some people called me up. They wanted Blue and me to be part of an "Ugliest Dog in Denver" contest. Well, I thought they wanted me to enter Blue in the contest and I was really hot. I had smoke comin' out my ears. Then I found out they wanted us to be judges at the contest. Well, that's different, that's okay. So we did it and Blue was the most beautiful dog there by far. I think that any boy or girl who gets a dog should love them just as much as I love Blue.

Before the games in Boston I used to rely on Blue. I'd ask her who I should start in goal, Gerry Cheevers or Gilles Gilbert? And she liked Cheevers a lot so she always told me to put Cheevers in there. If I said, "Cheevers?" she'd give me the nod. When I went to Colorado and asked her about the goalies, she'd say, "Are you kidding me? None of them are any good. That's like asking me do I want the cold or the flu?"

When Blue died at age fifteen I swear Rose and I cried for a month. Rose is not an emotional woman, but we'd be sitting at home and the tears kept falling. I'd say, "Rose, you've got to stop that." And my eyes would fill up, too. And I'd grab a tissue.

So one day I said, "That's enough." I called this guy and I said, "Have you got any bull terriers?" He said, "Yeah, I've got one, but he's the pick of the litter and I'm saving him for myself." I said, "I'll be right over. I've got $500 cash for you." Click. So I went over and bought Baby Blue even though the guy didn't want to part with him.

When the Winnipeg Jets hired a Finnish coach, Alpo Suhonen, for their American League farm club, Cherry snorted, "A Finn coaching pros? And what's his name—Alpo? Sounds like a dog food." According to Montreal sports columnist Red Fisher, the appropriate response might have been, "Cherry? Sounds like a fruit."

Cherry tells me about going from Boston to Colorado in 1979:

Al Eagleson was my agent back then. Al came to me and said, "Don, it is time for you to leave Boston."

"Okay, Al, you're the boss. Where are we going?"

"You are going to Colorado."

"Now, Al," I say, "do they have a good team out there? We only played them a couple of times and they didn't look like world-beaters to me."

"Don, you are going to love them. Great team."

I said, "But, Al, I am used to players like Orr, Esposito, Cashman, and Cheevers. Guys like that. What kind of hockey players will I get in Colorado?"

He says, "Don, you are going to love them. They have great guys—like Merlin Malinowski. They call him the Magician."

I said, "Now wait, Al, I'm used to good goaltenders. Gilbert, Cheevers, and others. What kind of goaltenders will I have?"

"You're going to love them. Especially Hardy Astrom."

"I've never heard of him, Al."

"But you are going to love him."

So I promise the owner I'll sign with Colorado. Then Al calls back.

"Don, great news. Ballard wants you to coach the Leafs. You're coming to Toronto. And for a lot more money."

"I can't do that, Al. I made a promise to Colorado."

"Fuck Colorado. I didn't make any promise."

"No, but I did. And I can't break it. I'm not that kind of guy."

So I went to Colorado. Later, Ballard said he didn't really want me anyways. Didn't want a comedian coaching his team. Who knows?

I got to Colorado and right away I know why they called Malinowski the Magician. Every time the game started he disappeared.

Then I find out Astrom's nickname is the Swedish Sieve. Or maybe I gave him that name. Anyways, that's when I learned to hate Swedes. The only problem with this guy Astrom was pucks.

I'll tell you one thing. We had the breakout play—everyone knows the breakout play. The breakout play is when the coach gets the puck at centre ice and the goaltender is in the net—no problem, he's ready and waiting there. The coach shoots the puck at the net, the goalie catches it or blocks it, then puts it over to his defenceman, who sends it up to the winger. Out they go.

But on my first two shots on Hardy—I scored! I said to Rose after practice, "Rose, pack the bags. We'll soon be outta here."

I'm telling you. The Edmonton Oilers came in for a game. Gretzky was smoking; it was unbelievable. Suddenly we have a big snowstorm. I'll tell you how bad my team was—because of the snowstorm, they cancelled the game. I was so happy I called for a victory party.

Here's another one Don told me:

> When I was coaching the Rockies, we travelled so much we had to have a little fun on the trips. We'd be waiting in an airport somewhere, waiting for the customs, and Lanny McDonald would go into his act. He can make like a ventriloquist. He'd lay his bag down and Schmautzie would say, "Shut up in there," and Lanny would go, "Ruff, ruff."
>
> "Shut up!"
>
> "Ruff!"
>
> "Shut up!"
>
> "Ruff!"
>
> So Schmautzie is kicking the bag and you'd swear there was a dog inside. This time they did it and the kids waiting there started to cry. So the customs agent came running over and grabbed Schmautzie. The kids were all crying, "Mommy, he's kicking the dog in that bag." God, it was funny. You'd never see Lanny's mouth move with that mustache he has. You'd swear there was a dog in the bag.

In April of 1988, I was flattered when Cherry changed his flight plans so that he could come down to Montreal with me for a game at the Forum. It's really fun travelling with him and it's seldom dull when Don is around.

And he was kind to me on the telecast. My alma mater, St. Lawrence University, was going for the NCAA hockey championship at Lake Placid, and Dick Irvin was talking about goaltender Darren Puppa having played for RPI (Rensselaer Polytechnic Institute). Don interrupted and said, "Hey, since yer talkin' college hockey, you know who owns all the records down at St. Lawrence? Brian McFarlane, that's who. He owns four or five scoring records there. The only guy there to score over 100 goals. Set them thirty years ago."

And Dick came right back with, "I thought the only records Brian collected down there were Benny Goodman, Sammy Kaye, and Guy Lombardo." I have often said that Dick is very fast on the comeback, very good with the quips.

After the game, Don talked about his first (and only) game in the NHL and how proud his mother was that he finally got his chance. "I remember she'd made cookies and cakes for me and I felt like a real greenhorn after the game, coming through the crowd with a bagful of baked goods. My teammates all kidded me about it, but you know who ate them all—they did!"

That was the season (1987–88) Don found himself in the middle of a confrontation with Molstar and the CBC. It happened when his "Coach's Corner" acquired a sponsor—Tremco. Cherry went to Don Wallace and the CBC guys and said, "Hey, they're obviously buying me, not just 'Coach's Corner.'"

The brass argued with him and said, "No, no. They just bought the show."

"No way, guys," Don said. "You think they'd have bought the show if I wasn't on it? I've got to get more money. They're buying Don Cherry. This happened to me once before and they ended up putting out posters of me and everything."

Don gave them forty-eight hours to straighten things out, or he wouldn't be working the playoffs. They straightened it out. Good for Cherry. He's a ram. The rest of us are sheep. If any of the rest of us tried to fight the establishment we'd be gone in a minute.

I remember early in my career suggesting to the rest of the announcers that we retain an agent to look out for us. Bill Hewitt and some of the others were reluctant to go along with me. I got answers like, "Gee, Brian, I don't want to make them mad," and "Isn't that a little risky?" and this from Bill:

"Well, I just take what they offer me each year and I'm okay with that."

"Listen," I said to Bill, "if you never ask for a raise or fair treatment, how can the rest of us? You're the senior guy here." It was also rumoured that Bill had no financial worries because his father looked after him very well. I felt like Ted Lindsay must have felt when he tried to enlist members for his Players Association back in 1957.

After our game at the Forum, Grapes and I went for a beer. He said to me, "You're a nice guy and Dick Irvin's a nice guy and I like working with nice guys. The only ones who wouldn't like the telecast we did last night would be guys like Wallace and the CBC guys—simply because we kibitzed and had some fun."

He told me once, after he had been on the job a year or two, that he was as happy as hell, but his boss, Don Wallace, took him aside one day and said, "I'm a little concerned about you, Don."

Don said, "Oh yeah? What's the problem?"

Wallace said, "You don't pronounce the players' names right. You say Holemgram, instead of Holmgren. Things like that."

So Cherry got upset and phoned Ralph Mellanby, the executive producer, and Mellanby said, "Oh, for Christ sakes, forget Wallace. Don't ever change the way you talk. People like you just the way you are."

Mellanby was absolutely right. Screwing up the language and mispronouncing names are all part of Cherry's charm. He's a master at that—he's right up there with Archie Bunker.

The Players I've Known

Wayne Gretzky

The NHL Oldtimers originally recruited me for just a game or two when they were short a couple of wingers. I was the only amateur on the team. I stayed around for the next seventeen years and what a thrill it was to be on the same ice as such former NHLers as Andy Bathgate, Bob Goldham, Danny Lewicki, Cal Gardner, Harry Watson, Murray Henderson, Pete Conacher, and many others.

One night in about 1971 we played a fundraising game in Hamilton against some media types. Our opponents had added a fresh face to their lineup—a ten-year-old kid whose little legs churned nonstop as he skated during the warm-up.

"Hey, guys," I told the others, "that's the Gretzky kid from Brantford. He was a big star at the Quebec Peewee tournament. Already they're saying he's going to be in the NHL someday."

A couple of the guys shrugged as if they'd heard the same line about other young phenoms. And of course they had. But I was impressed. I watched as Gretzky controlled the puck and closed in on our defence. He went wide on Bathgate, zipped around him, and scored. Did Bathgate let the youngster sift by? Did our goalie move too late on purpose? Perhaps. But who knows? He scored another goal and the fans applauded his efforts enthusiastically.

The Oldtimers won easily—in seventeen years I only remember us losing two or three times—but after the game I sought out Gretzky's parents, Walter and Phyllis, and met his coach, Ron St. Amand. Later, I wrote a story about Gretzky and his astonishing minor-hockey career for my Scotiabank Hockey College bulletin. From that day on I followed his career with great interest.

Recently, I sat with Walter Gretzky at our annual Oldtimers dinner. He was our guest speaker and he spoke from the heart, captivating his audience with his stories, which he told with humour and humility. I related my memories of that long-ago game in Hamilton to him.

"But you played hundreds of games with the Oldtimers," he said. "Why would you remember that one so clearly—even the name of Wayne's coach?"

"Don't know," I answered. "Perhaps instinctively I knew I was watching someone special that night. Someone who would make a real impact on hockey some day in the future."

I was in Winnipeg early in the 1983–84 season, the Jets against Gretzky's Oilers. At the morning skate, I talked with Wayne about his Christmas memories for another story I was doing for Scotiabank. Wayne, who'd just been named captain of the Oilers (veteran Lee Fogolin had gladly given up the *C*, a generous and classy act), told me about a Christmas he'll never forget.

Wayne: When I was about four I got a Red Wing sweater with the number 9 on the back. My hero was Gordie Howe and I wanted his sweater more than anything. I remember playing hockey all the next day in the backyard with that sweater on. I never wanted to take it off.

Brian: What memories do you have of your backyard rink?

Wayne: Well, what I remember most about it is that it was my place to relax and unwind and do what I wanted to do, and that was play hockey. I used to go out there and nobody would bother me. I used to enjoy it an awful lot.

Our Oldtimers played against Wayne Gretzky when he was a Pee Wee. We watched him grow up to become the most prolific scorer of all time .

On November 21, 1999, the night before he was to be inducted into the Hockey Hall of Fame, Wayne Gretzky invited about two hundred of his friends to join him at his downtown restaurant in Toronto for a pre-induction party. Joan and I were thrilled to be invited, although we have no idea how our names made the guest list. It was a real honour. I remember the looks of envy on the faces of the autograph hunters who gathered outside as we made our way to the entrance.

Wayne and Janet made certain they spent a few moments with everyone who attended. Late in the evening, Joan and I had an opportunity to chat with Wayne. He has that marvellous ability to make everyone around him feel they are very important to him. It's both a gift and a skill he's developed; one that comes as easily to him as setting up a teammate for a goal, making them look good and feel good. He talked about his first two trips to Maple Leaf Gardens.

It was my grandmother who took me to my first game at the Gardens. I must have been about six. And we sat up in the last row of the greys, as far away from the ice as it was possible to be. A lot of steps to climb to get there. And when the game was over, my grandmother got up to leave. But I refused to go. She says I sat there while all the other seats emptied. And finally an elderly usher hobbled up the stairs and said, 'Folks, you're gonna have to leave now. We'll soon be turning out the lights.' My grandmother said I probably would have stayed the night if they'd let me.

Brian, you may not remember this but I remember it clearly. It was my second trip to the Gardens and I was about thirteen years old. That was the night you took me aside and told me where to stand so they could put a camera on me during the game. When that happened, you said some nice things about me on TV and predicted a bright future for the kid from Brantford—that sort of thing.

But the place you had me stand before the game was right near the Leaf dressing room, outside the *Hockey Night in Canada* studio. And just then Tiger Williams came out of the room wearing a big white robe—like some heavyweight boxers do. Tiger was scowling for some reason and looking very fierce. And I remember saying to myself, "Geez, am I going to have to play against guys like him when I get older?"

Mario Lemieux

In the summer of 1988, at the Concord Hotel resort north of New York in the Catskills, I get the chance of a lifetime—to play right wing for Mario Lemieux. There I am, in my mid-fifties, pot-bellied, weak-eyed, weak-wristed, awkward, nervous, and slow afoot, trying to keep pace with one of the greatest players who ever lived.

Thanks to *Hockey Night in Canada* producer Mark Askin, we were there to film Mario, Steve Duchesne, Larry Robinson, Dan Quinn, and others, all of them guests of the hotel management. In return for a free week-long vacation, they'd agreed to spend a couple of hours a day instructing the children of hotel guests in the fundamentals of hockey. Their arena was almost laughable, one of the smallest ice surfaces I've ever seen—about 100 feet long by 50 feet wide. The day we arrived, the players had completed their teaching chores and were about to engage in an old-fashioned game of shinny.

"Got your skates with you?" someone asked.

"Yes, as a matter of fact, I have."

"Get 'em on. You can play wing for Mario."

Moments later, I was out on the ice and the guys were flying. *Click, click, click*—the puck danced from one stick to another. Players were bobbing and weaving and faking and deking. They laughed and whooped it up as if they were kids again, sliding around some frozen pond. The goals piled up but I still hadn't touched the damn puck. The guys changed direction so fast that by the time I could pivot and turn they were already at the other end of the rink. A couple of hard passes were sent my way and I lunged for them. They bounced off the blade of my stick and spun away.

Playing hockey and golf with Mario one summer was one of my all-time thrills. Mario was an incredible player on and off the ice—a perfect gentleman.

"Sorry, Mario." There was no reply. He was too polite to laugh.

I could almost hear his thoughts: "Did this guy *ever* play the game?" And I wanted to say, "Geez, Mario, I'm fifty-five years old. Thirty years ago I might almost have been able to keep pace with you guys. Now I'm out of gas, with two bricks for hands."

After a few minutes I relaxed and began to enjoy myself. And when Mario set me up again, I scored. Oh my, that felt good. Mario looked over and grinned. Thanks, Mario. Thank you. You made my day.

The next day, the players switched hockey sticks for golf clubs. Poor Mario drew my wife, Joan, and me as partners.

We teed up. I had heard all about Mario's golfing skills. He hits the ball a ton. He has really incredible drives off the tee. And he was so patient with the McFarlanes as we played like Tiger—Williams, not Woods. We dribbled balls off the tee, plunked balls into every creek, and bounced balls off trees. Squirrels, birds, and fish ran for cover when we approached. The harder we tried, the worse it got.

On the ninth hole, Mario was teeing up his ball when a film crew from Madison Square Garden Sports came running up the fairway. They were shouting and waving their arms.

"Mario, Mario! Wait a minute! We want to get shots of you driving off the tee."

So Mario stepped back and waited patiently while they set up their camera. When they waved him on, he teed up and drove a ball 300 yards straight down the fairway. Joan and I caught up to him after splitting a dozen shots. Mario drilled his next shot 180 yards to the very centre of the green. His ball rolled to within 5 feet of the cup. Then he calmly dropped his putt for a birdie, despite the presence of a cameraman, a director, a sound man, and the heavy-breathing McFarlanes. Mario plucked his ball from the cup, gave the grateful film crew a grin and a wave, and walked off the green.

Here's part of an interview I did with Mario:

Brian: Mario, some of the criticism you received early in your career must have hurt. Don Cherry calling you a floater and that sort of thing. Did some inner voice say, "I'm going to show those people. I'll show them the real Mario Lemieux"?

Mario: No, not really. I didn't worry too much about Don Cherry because he makes a living out of being outspoken. He likes controversy. But now he is my buddy, he has turned around quite a bit when he talks about me.

For myself, it was a tough adjustment to make at first. I was only eighteen years old when I broke in. I was told that I was not very fast and I think in the last three years I have worked hard on my skating and shooting ability. I think that people have a different view of me now. You know, I just go on the ice and try to do the best that I can, game after game, and get better.

Brian: Most people recognize you as one of the two best hockey players in the world—the other being Wayne Gretzky, of course. Tell me about your friendship with Gretzky, and your rivalry with him.

Mario: Well, my friendship comes first. Every time we play together on the Canada Cup team or in an All-Star game, we talk as much as we can. We are both so busy at those times, so busy with the press, that we can't talk very much, but he is a very nice guy. I have seen him a number of times in the summer, at golf tournaments and other activities and he is a great guy to be with, very nice to talk to. As for the rivalry, every time I step on the ice with Wayne, it is a great honour, whether it's to play against him or with him, makes no difference. I certainly give a little extra when he's around.

Brian: You had an incredible 70-goal season, Mario. But what about 92 goals—Gretzky's record? Does that seem out of reach, or is it your next objective?

Mario: That is unbelievable, 92 goals in a season. That is something that is going to stay around for a while, maybe forever. I thought that I had a good season this year with 70 goals. When you take a look at Gretzky's numbers, like 92 goals and 215 points in a season, it is simply amazing what he has done in the past.

Mario came close to Gretzky's marks the following season, scoring 85 goals and 199 points, both career highs. His 199 points is the fifth-best mark in NHL history—Gretzky topped 200 points four times, with a high of 215.

Bobby Hull

I ask Bobby about the night he hit Harold Ballard in the face with one of his blazing slapshots during a warm-up at Maple Leaf Gardens.

> I used to sign a lot of autographs during the warm-up—dozens of them—until there were only a couple of minutes left to warm up. Then I'd take a few dashes around the rink and whip a couple of shots on the goal.
>
> This night I cut over the blue line and drove a shot at the net, but the puck hit the crossbar and flew up into the crowd.
>
> Ballard and King Clancy were standing up in their private bunker at the north end of the Gardens and they didn't see the deflected missile coming. As soon as that puck hit the crossbar I knew it was headed right for Ballard. Sure enough, it caught the Leaf owner right between the eyes. I felt terrible.
>
> When I came out of the Hawk dressing room to go back on the ice for the start of the game, Harold intercepted me. He grabbed me and yanked me into the room next door. By then his cut was all stitched up, and his eyes were starting to turn black. I said, "Gee, Harold, I'm sorry. I didn't mean to do that." And he said, "Don't worry about it, Bobby. These things happen. I just want to get a photo of the two of us together." He had a photographer standing by.
>
> So we were posing for the photo when my coach, Billy Reay, came along and yanked me out of the room by the back of my shirt. He said to me, "You're not getting your picture taken with that son of a bitch." Reay had been fired by the Leafs a few years earlier and he was still hot about it.

Glen Hanlon

On a warm July day in the late sixties, I was at the fairgrounds in Brandon, Manitoba. *Hockey Night in Canada* had invited me to be host/interviewer for a series of hockey shows in front of live audiences. Stops on the tour included Brandon, Regina, and Calgary. The highlight of the trip was riding in an open convertible in the famous Calgary Stampede parade.

But back to Brandon for a moment. After our little show, Jim McKenny (who was just breaking in with the Leafs) and I were invited back to the farm of Rudy Pilous. Pilous, who'd once coached the Chicago Blackhawks to the Stanley Cup, was heading up the Brandon Wheat Kings that year. It was a treat to dine with him in his rambling farmhouse, where we laughed away the evening. Nobody could tell hockey stories like Rudy Pilous.

During the evening, a couple of youngsters were introduced to the visitors. McKenny signed autographs and we chatted with the boys. One lad of about twelve said he wanted to be a big-league goalie someday. Jim said to look him up if he ever got to Toronto; he might be able to get him a ticket for a Leaf game. I offered a tour of the television studio and Foster Hewitt's famous gondola.

Of course we never really expected to see this young lad from Brandon again. And we were right: he never did show up—not for a long, long time, anyway.

During the 1978–79 hockey season, I received a letter from a Mr. John Hanlon and it was postmarked Brandon, Manitoba:

Dear Brian,

I am writing to remind you of an incident that happened several years ago when you and Jim McKenny attended the summer fair in Brandon.

Bobby Hull had charisma and charm. And a great nickname—the Golden Jet. His blistering slapshot during a warm-up at Maple Leaf Gardens caught Harold Ballard between the eyes.

King Clancy with two Leaf greats—Ted Kennedy and Sid Smith. In the sixties, Clancy allowed me to write his autobiography. It remains one of my favourite books.

One evening you were at the home of Rudy Pilous and there was a young fellow there who wanted to meet you. I believe you and Jim even promised him some tickets for a Leafs game if he was ever in Toronto.

That red-haired boy was Glen Hanlon, now the goalie with the Vancouver Canucks. Glen will be in Toronto on December 13th. Glen has enjoyed a fair amount of success in hockey since you met him in Brandon. He played junior hockey with the Brandon Wheat Kings for three seasons. The last two years he was the Western Canada All-Star Goalie. He was drafted by Vancouver and spent his first year of pro hockey with Tulsa of the Central League. There he was named all-star goalie, rookie of the year and runner up for the most valuable player award. This year he is playing for the Canucks and he has played most of their games so far.

It is a small world, isn't it? Have a Merry Christmas and wish the Leafs good luck for me—except when they play the Canucks.

Kindest Regards,
John Hanlon

What a pleasant surprise it was to receive Mr. Hanlon's letter! Trouble was, it arrived two days *after* the Vancouver Canucks had played in Toronto. As a result, I didn't get a chance to renew acquaintance.

I finally managed to catch up to Hanlon in the early 1980s, when he was with the New York Rangers, and we both enjoyed reminiscing about that long-ago meeting in Brandon.

Garry Unger

Former NHL ironman Garry Unger told me a couple of stories one day in a hotel lobby in Calgary. Neither had a happy ending.

When I was with Detroit I had a friend who owned some horses. Being from Calgary, I always thought I might like to own a little horse farm someday, so I stayed involved with this fellow. There was a doctor there who'd bought a really high-spirited horse. I don't know why, because he was about sixty-five and he couldn't ride a horse, anyway. It seemed like nobody else could ride that horse, either, so I said, "Sure, I can stay on that horse." So I got on—this was a week before training camp—and I rode him around for about twenty minutes. He was jumping around a lot, but it was all right.

I went back a few days later and I rode this same horse on a little trail ride. About five or six of us went along and we rode through this big field. The horse started jumping around pretty good, so I yanked hard on his reins and suddenly they broke. He took off and raced across the field and into the woods. I didn't have time to jump off before we were in among the trees and right in front of me was a mean-looking barbed-wire fence. That's when I bailed out. I went flying one way and the horse went the other. I slammed into a tree, back first.

I reported to training camp in a wheelchair because of this horseback-riding injury. It wasn't a broken vertebrae (or I might have been paralyzed), but it was a fracture of three small bones inside my back. For a couple of weeks I was in the chair and after that I was on crutches.

That was the year Ned Harkness had taken over the Red Wings, and one of the first things he did at training camp was invite me to lunch. I usually let my hair grow long over the summer—when training camp rolled around I'd cut it off. For one reason or another, this time I'd decided not to cut my hair, maybe because I knew I wouldn't be suiting up for a while yet.

At lunch, I waited for Ned to ask me about my back—maybe I expected a lecture about taking part in dangerous off-season sports—but he never mentioned it. I was amazed. All he wanted to talk about was the length of my hair.

I missed all of training camp that year, then my back started feeling better and about two days before the season opened I was able to skate a little. They asked me if I could play on opening night

I first met Glen Hanlon when he was a youngster in Brandon. He grew up to be an outstanding goaltender.

and I said sure. I remember I scored a goal on my first shift. After that game I immediately went into a slump. I was really dying, really hurting out there.

No one would have guessed it, but Garry was just starting a streak of 914 consecutive NHL games. Fast-forward to the 1979–80 season, when Unger was with the Atlanta Flames.

The last game of the streak happened to be in St. Louis, where I'd played for so many years. Two weeks before that game, I'd pulled some cartilage in my shoulder really bad in Winnipeg. We had a game in Edmonton the next night and then we had a week off.

Al MacNeil came to me and said, "Can you play tonight?"

I said, "It's going to be awful tough but I'll give it a try."

"Well, we can't get anybody up from our farm club in time to replace you, so take a few shifts and see how it goes." I played but I was really in pain, hurting bad.

We went back to Atlanta the next day and I had about three days of sitting in the whirlpool. I asked the team doctor, "Is this thing going to affect me later on in life?" I wanted to play tennis and golf when I retired. And the doc said, "No, it should be okay. If you can live with the pain, you can play." So I took therapy hour after hour to get ready for our next home game, which was against the Blues.

It was an important game. We needed some points and I played regularly. After the game, I thought, "Boy, I'm glad I'm over the worst of it." I thought I'd played decent hockey against the Blues, even though we got beat 5–1. We flew back to St. Louis for a return game, and when I came to the arena that night, Al never said a word to me, he just walked right by me. That was unusual.

In the dressing room, I was getting dressed and I had this strange feeling that something weird was going on. I skated in the warm-up and took my practice shots and I was feeling good. The arm and shoulder were fine.

The game started and right away Al put Curt Bennett in for me. I knew for sure something strange was going on. After the first period, general manager Cliff Fletcher came up to me. He'd noticed I hadn't touched the ice so he said, "What's wrong, is your shoulder sore?" And I said, "No, it's fine." Now I knew Cliff and Al hadn't talked about not playing me. It was Al's decision alone.

As the game progressed, I could see he'd made up his mind not to play me. Now, with about three minutes to play in the game, my teammates were coming up to me and saying, "Hey, have you been on yet?" Bobby MacMillan came off the ice and said, "Go on for me, go on for me." Ivan Boldirev nudged me and said, "Jump on for me." I kept saying, "No, no. If I do that there'll be a war. It would be outright defiance." So I wouldn't go over the boards.

With about a minute left in the game, the puck came flying over toward our bench and it got there in the middle of a line change. Both teams fought for it by the bench and the sticks were flying high, so I jumped up to get out of the way. That's when Al grabbed me by the back of the jersey. He thought I was going to jump over the boards. He had a grip on the back of my shirt like you wouldn't believe.

I'm really embarrassed because the score is 7–3 for us—the game is in the bag—and here's my coach hanging all over me on the bench. By then, the St. Louis crowd had figured out what was going on and they were yelling, "We want Unger! We want Unger!" We even played for about thirty seconds with only three guys in the play because the other two were standing by the bench trying to haul me on the ice and keep the streak alive.

I never talked to Al about it, never asked him why he deliberately kept me out, because it was too emotional. [Blues broadcaster] Dan Kelly asked him about it afterward and he said something about wanting to win the game. And I guess he told other reporters that the streak was getting to be more important than the team. Maybe in a way it was, then maybe it wasn't. Still, I was hoping to extend it to a thousand games.

I was more disappointed for the people around me, like my sister, who is crippled. She had given me a lot of incentive to play as hard as I could as long as I could. The streak was a big thing to her and my family and I know they felt badly when it ended.

The next day, two days before Christmas, I got up really early. I couldn't sleep that night. It was a beautiful morning. So I got my horse saddled up and went riding through the fields—all by myself. I thought about what had really changed in my life because I didn't play that game last night. Nothing, really. If someone had come to me and said, "Your house burned down and your family is gone" or "You can't walk anymore," then I'd have had something to feel badly about, to be depressed about. It was still a record, and I decided it really didn't mean all that much.

The day after Christmas, I was back in Atlanta playing another game, against the tough Boston Bruins, and I didn't miss a shift. The streak was history, something Doug Jarvis, then with Montreal, was already pointing toward. [Jarvis wound up playing a record 964 consecutive games.]

As far as hockey is concerned, I learned more about the game in my final three seasons—as a bench warmer, as a fourteenth, fifteenth, or sixteenth player on the team—than I did in the rest of my fifteen years playing as a star. What you do as a star is forget about everything else that's going on and figure everybody else is having a good time like you are.

Jack Valiquette, Claire Alexander, Dave Hutchison, and Bob Lorimer
In July of 1990, I was in Kitchener, Ontario, taping the *Stars of Hockey* TV series. Dozens of former NHL players were involved. At breakfast one morning I reminisced about the 1970s with Jack Valiquette, Claire Alexander, Dave Hutchison, and Bob Lorimer.

Claire: I'll never forget some of the battles between Tiger [Williams] and Lanny [McDonald]. They were always getting into it. We'd be playing cards on the plane and Tiger would get roaring mad when he'd lose, and he'd rip up all the cards. Then Lanny would leap on him. When they were done scuffling and wrestling there'd be enough hair left on the table for Jack to make himself a new wig. Oh, there were some good old times.

Hutch: One day Alan Eagleson calls me in the morning and tells me that I've been traded to Chicago. So I get down to the rink and I'm tellin' the guys I've been dealt and they say, "Go on. Nah, you haven't been traded." Even the trainer says to me, "Geez, I haven't heard anything about you bein' traded." Nobody from the team is there to tell me I'm no longer a Leaf. Typical, eh?

After practice I'm still hangin' around, and still no word about a trade. So we all go down to Delaney's to have lunch and the guys are sayin', "Sure you've been traded, Hutch. Sure you've been traded." And I'm sayin', "I'm tellin' you, boys. It's a done deal. I've been traded."

So then the phone rings and it's Punch [Imlach] on the line. The guy at the bar brings the phone over and sure enough Punch says, "Congratulations, Mr. Hutchison, you've been traded to Chicago." And I'm holdin' the phone out like this [demonstrates], and there were about ten of us there—Salming, Turnbull, and a bunch of guys. And they're leanin' into the phone and goin', "Fuck you, you fuckin' asshole!" I don't know whether Punch heard them or not, but anyway, he tells me I'm goin' to Chicago. And the guys just get louder.

Just about then, Jim Kernaghan, the sportswriter, is comin' down the street and he's holdin' a newspaper under his arm with Punch's picture in it. He comes in to say hello and Walt McKechnie spots the photo of Imlach. So he grabs it and tears it out and puts it up on the dartboard. And we start heavin' darts at Punch's photo. Kernaghan wrote about it but he wouldn't say who the Leafs were who were throwin' darts. Well, Punch wanted to find out who they were, but Kernaghan never would tell, even though some of his newspaper pals got on his ass for it. Turnbull was one guy there and Tiger was another. Hell, we were all there tossin' darts.

In the seventies, Garry Unger reigned as the NHL's "iron man," compiling a streak of 914 consecutive games. The streak might have continued but for a mean-spirited coach.

On the day the Leafs traded Dave Hutchison to Chicago, the Toronto players used coach Punch Imlach's photo as a dart board.

One of the guys brings up Lanny McDonald's name again. "He loved to shoot that puck. And when he'd line up a shot and he'd fan on one—Christ, he'd throw his back out, he put so much effort into it. In the warm-up, we'd all be lined up along the blue line, leaning forward, waiting for a puck, and Mac would come up behind us and whack us on the ass with his stick. Christ, it would hurt! You could hear that stick smack an ass right across the rink. You were ready for a game after Mac smacked you. It would bring tears to your eyes."

I ask Jack Valiquette to tell me about "Olympic sit-ups."

Jack: Oh, geez, should I? How in hell did you hear about that? Well, okay. This little deal required a two-day set-up. You know, to suck a guy in. The first day we did little things, like squats and leg lifts, meaningless contests that involved all of us. It was just to set up the rookies. Ron Ellis was in his comeback year and he had that strong body, so we challenged him to do the Olympic sit-ups. He says—like he's never heard of them before—"What the hell are Olympic sit-ups?" And we say, "Well, it's just like regular sit-ups, but you have a weight on your chest and a towel on your forehead. But since we don't have a weight just give it a try."

"Okay," he says, and gets down on the floor. We put the towel over his head and he does maybe three or four, but he pretends it's really tough. He's grunting and straining, like he's really out of shape. Tiger sees this and he jumps in and says, "For Chrissake, get out of the way. Let a man in here. I can do this shit. I'm in great shape."

So Ellis jumps up and Tiger replaces him and we get the towel on his forehead and it slips off. He says, "Put that damn thing on right," so we put it right over his eyes so he can't see anything—which is just what we wanted.

Now he's ready. And when he begins the sit-ups someone slips in and drops his drawers right over Tiger's face. The guy squats there and Tiger lifts up and puts his nose right up this guy's ass. Then we whip the towel away and Tiger goes berserk.

Was he livid! We scatter like hell and there are tables flying and curses and threats like you wouldn't believe. Geez, we got him good! He went off like a Tasmanian devil.

Brian: Tiger was in the penalty box at Maple Leaf Gardens one night and he was jawing away with Joe Lamantia, the timekeeper. After a big ruckus on the ice, more players started filing into the box. Lamantia was punching in the penalties on the timekeeper's console when Tiger lunged forward, said, "Hey, Joe, let me help you out there," and reached for the machine.

Lamantia grabbed his hand and pushed it away, saying angrily, "Damn you, Tiger, you just sit there and shut up!"

So Tiger gave him a hurt look and he said, "All right, Joe, that's it, if you're going to talk to me like that I'm never coming back in here again!"

Jack: That's Tiger. The Leafs were in Colorado and between games we re guests of the Broadmoor Hotel, a posh hotel with a beautiful golf course up in the mountains. So the four of us go out to golf. I've got to take Tiger as my partner because we're both lefties, and we're playing Claire and Lanny. We were always together, the four of us. So we're playing the game and Tiger is duffing shots everywhere. Now we come to a short par 3—only about 100 yards. But if you duff your drive you're right smack in a deep ravine. So Tiger duffs his drive, naturally, and dribbles the ball out of sight in this ravine. Down he goes after it and we're waiting on the green. We hear him yell, "Look out! I'm bringing it up!"

Claire: I couldn't believe what happened next.

Jack: Tiger hit an unbelievable shot. Landed right on the green about 2 feet from the pin. So I'm jumping around yelling "Attaboy, partner, attaboy, Tige!" and Tiger comes up grinning and I say, "Now you've got an easy putt for your par." Then he misses the putt and the smile falls off his face. Misses it and the ball rolls past the hole about a foot. I say, "Tiger, don't worry about it. So you get a bogie, so what." But then he misses the next putt coming back and is he pissed. He takes his putter, lifts it high, and buries it 6 inches into the damn green. Just drills it in there, cursing and muttering. And he has a hell of a time getting it out. He's yanking on it and twisting it and then Lanny lets him have it. Over comes Mac and barrels into him. Down they go and they're wrestling each other and throwing punches and Mac is yelling something about being guests of the management and what a stupid thing that was to do. The grass is flying and clods of dirt are bouncing around. I'm telling you, by the time we broke up the fight it looked like someone had run a plough through there.

Then on the next tee, Tiger starts yapping and they go at it again. Now there's more grass flying and the tee is all torn up. I didn't think we'd ever finish that golf game.

Claire: I didn't think we'd ever finish our card game, either. It was nothing for us to roll into a hotel at 3 a.m. and just get to bed when the phone would ring. Tiger would say, "Yeah?" "It's Lanny. Come on down here. We gotta finish this game." And down we'd go to Lanny's room. We played every damn night and on all the plane trips. We were always together, playing cards.

Jack: The damn game went on for two years. It was the longest game of cards I ever played.

Claire: But I've never seen two guys go at it like those two, Lanny and Tiger. Never in my life. And if we were playing hearts and you gave Tiger the queen of spades, look out. He'd go wild. We'd be playing and Tiger would go, like, "Should I lead this card or the other one?" He could never remember what cards had been played so he'd make his lead. And me or Lanny would throw the queen on it and he'd go ape.

Jack (*laughing*): And then I'd slip a lower card under his and he'd be stuck with the bitch. That's when he was apt to rip the deck of cards in two. He'd explode and jump up and down with pieces of cards flying everywhere. "Get another fuckin' deck!" he'd scream. We had to bring about five decks with us or we'd be caught short. One night he tore up the last deck we had on a charter coming back from Vancouver, so Lanny tackled him and the hair started flying. We were glad Lanny did it because we had no cards to play with on a long flight like that.

Remember the time I gave Lanny the clamp?

Claire: Yeah. Jack had this remarkable ability to use his two toes, his big toe and the one next to it. I'm telling you, he can spread them wide and then put them together like a vise. You've never seen anything like it. Those toes are like a pair of pliers. What a grip!

One night we're in Montreal and we called a card game at two or three in the morning and Lanny comes in and he's got a towel wrapped around him. That's all he had on. So he pulls up a chair across from Jack. Jack peeked under the table and saw that Lanny's nuts were hanging down. Jack never said a word, but up goes his foot and he gets the toes apart and he clamps down onto Lanny's left nut. Lanny leaped about 4 feet in the air. He went up like an astronaut.

Jack (*laughing*): And I didn't let go until he was about 3 feet in the air.

Islander defenseman Bob Lorimer was among a group of entertaining story tellers in Kitchener in 1990.

Derek Sanderson

In the press room at the Montreal Forum I have a snack before the game with Derek Sanderson. He worked as colour man on the Boston Bruins telecasts and we've always had a good rapport. I slap a tape recorder in front of him and ask him about his famous contract with the Philadelphia Blazers of the World Hockey Association, the pact that made him the highest paid athlete in the world.

Now this is an unbelievable story. For five months I'm fightin' to get a five-grand raise from the Bruins. This is in 1972 when I'm makin' $75,000 and I'm holding out for $80,000. And Mulcahy, who was a VP or something, tells Harry Sinden not to pay it. So Pie [Johnny McKenzie] comes to me and he says, "Listen, Turk, I'm jumpin' to the WHA for big bucks. Come on with me." And I go, "Nah, nah, nah," and he says, "Well, hear them out," and I say, "Okay, tell them to meet me at my lawyer's."

So I go to Bob Woolf's office and I say, "Bobby, you sit down over there. I'll sit behind your desk and negotiate this deal." So I sit down at Bobby's desk and I'm half lit. I don't know where I was the night before, but I must've had fun. Now this joker comes in the room and right away he says, "Derek, I'm prepared to offer you $2.3 million." And I go, "Aw, I dunno. I got a girlfriend in Boston, the cops are nice to me here, I own part of four nightclubs. Why would I wanna move to Philly?" And he says, "All right, I'm prepared to go as high as $2,650,000."

He came up $350,000 in fifteen seconds! I figure these Philadelphia people are crazy. I ask him to write the figures down and it looks like a long-distance telephone number. Now I'm beginnin' to wake up a bit. He's definitely got my attention.

So I say, "Aw, I know you guys. You'll probably sell the team and I'll have to move somewhere else, like they did in Miami." [The Miami Screaming Eagles folded before they played a single game. The Blazers franchise was quickly organized to take their place in the WHA.] He says, "Derek, we won't sell the team without your approval. I'll even write it in the contract." I say, "Hey, that's all right. But you'll probably trade all my buddies on the club." And he comes right back with, "We won't trade anybody if you don't say it's all right."

Now I'm wide awake. I'm thinkin', "What else can I ask for?" So I say to him, "I gotta tell you somethin' else. I hate to fly." And he says, "Okay, just play home games then." Can you believe this guy? He's writin' all these extra clauses in the contract and I'm tryin' to sober up, tryin' to focus on what's goin' on. He says, "You wanna sign it?" and I say, "Hell, no—not right now, anyway. I wanna show it to the Bruins. I'll get back to you."

So now I can't wait to go to the Bruins—but not to Mulcahy. I go to see Mr. Adams [Weston Adams Sr.], who was always very good to me. He had faith in me as a player from the time I was fourteen years old. If it hadn't been for him I'd never have made it to the NHL, and I feel I owe him something. I've got no intention of going to Philadelphia. I showed him the crazy contract I'd been offered. He looks it over and says, "Is this any good?" I say, "Bob Woolf says it's good." So he laughs and says, "All right, we'll give you the $80,000 you've been holding out for."

Well, at the time that sounded okay to me so I said I'd sign on one condition—I didn't want to deal with Mulcahy. Mr. Adams said, "Take the contract down the hall and sign with my son Westy [Weston Adams Jr.]."

So I go to see Westy and I've got an $80,000 contract in one hand and a $2,650,000 contract in the other. Westy's getting a pen out so I can sign again with the Bruins when Mulcahy comes along. He must have got wind of what was happening and he couldn't resist sticking his nose in the door and givin' me a shot. He says, "Derek, I still don't think you're worth $80,000 a year." So I get mad and grab the Philadelphia contract and I say, "Okay, screw you then. I'm off to Philadelphia." And I got the hell out of there and went to the Blazers, even though it was the farthest thing from my mind when I went to the Boston Garden that day.

It's the most amazing contract story I've ever heard. And I tell Sanderson so. "But you didn't stay in Philadelphia long," I remind him. "You got hurt and didn't play much. And then there was the story about the million dollars they paid you not to play in Philadelphia."

He grins and says, "Yeah, I don't know what happened to that money."

"You mean they never paid it? You never got it?"

He says, "I dunno. Can't remember what happened with that money. Then, I can't remember a lot of things about those days."

Sanderson continued:

Geez, what a team we had in Philly! We get all these hotshots—me, Andre Lacroix, Pie McKenzie, [Bryan] Soupy Campbell—and we all get hurt in training camp. All of us. We lose about 20 games in a row. [Actually, the Blazers were 4–16, a stretch during which two GMs and a coach resigned.] We needed a goalie because all of our goalies were hurt—Bernie Parent, Marcel Paille, and a guy named Yves. So I called a buddy of mine, Tommy Cottringer, a Senior B goalie with the Welland Merchants. Weighed 235 pounds. I say, "Can you get to Philadelphia?" and he says, "Sure." Stopped something like 47 shots in his first game and we won.

Now the team gets straightened out and the Blazers have a tremendous second half. They make it to the quarterfinals. And the team's most important player, Bernie Parent, goes to the bank to get his money—$650,000 in escrow—and it isn't there. So he quit on them—went on strike, call it what you want, the fact is he wouldn't play.

Parent was suspended, then traded to the New York Raiders, but he would never play another game in the WHA. During the summer of 1973 the Philadelphia Flyers traded goalie Doug Favell to the Toronto Maple Leafs in exchange for Parent's NHL rights, and with Bernie in net they won the Stanley Cup in each of the next two years.

I remind Derek that Ted Lindsay castigated him on one of our NBC games in 1974 for his behaviour in those days. Even though Ted ripped into him, Derek refused to fight fire with fire. On a national telecast, he told me, "I'm not going to attack Lindsay, not after all what he's given to the game."

A dozen years later, Derek tells me another story about Lindsay.

Ted Lindsay did me a great favour when I made my comeback after I was burned in a fire in '77. By then Ted was general manager in Detroit, and I was trying to get back on my feet, trying to stay sober, so I called Ted and said, "Will you give me a chance?" And he said, "I don't know if I should, but I will. But if you break one rule, open your mouth once, argue back, or have a drink, then you're gone."

Teddy sent me to Windsor to get in shape. I worked out with the Windsor Juniors. Toughest thing I ever had to do. Here I am back in Junior hockey, eleven years later, saying, "What am I doin' here?"

After six weeks, Lindsay said, "You've passed the test. Here's a ticket to Kansas City [the Wings' farm team in the Central Hockey League]." I went there and in my first game I got 3 goals and 2 assists. Ted called and said, "Well, that league is kinda easy for you, eh?"

Now one thing Lindsay asked of me was loyalty. He told me if somebody tried to grab me I was to tell him, so he'd have a chance to make me an offer. He told me to respect what I'd done, coming back from a hospital bed after a fire, getting sober, and making it all the way back in such a short span of time. He wanted me to go on a summer fitness program so that I could join the Red Wings in the fall.

But then Pittsburgh called my agent, Bob Woolf, and offered us $75,000 just to play the last fourteen games of the season. Woolf told me to grab it and I did—it was instant gratification, you know? My ego was telling me I was still an NHLer, that I deserved to be up there. And Woolf said

Derek "Turk" Sanderson wanted a $5,000 raise from the Bruins in 1972. Then he got a surprise offer from the WHA and became the highest paid athlete in the world.

he had already talked to Ted, so I was surprised when I read the headlines in a Los Angeles paper: "Lindsay Calls Sanderson a Disloyal So-and-so"—that sort of thing. I felt terrible about it and it took me a long time to get up the nerve to call Ted and apologize. I told him I'd got bad advice and I was sorry I'd let him down. He was awfully good about it, but he did say, "Why'd you pick me, Derek? Why me?" Yeah, Teddy was good to me, he was one guy who had some faith in me.

Andre Lacroix

Did you know that diminutive Andre Lacroix, the slick centreman, finished his career with more games, more assists, and more points to his credit than any player in the history of the WHA? His 798 points lead Bobby Hull by 160 and Mark Tardif by 132.

In Hartford—where he'd played his final season with the NHL Whalers in 1979–80—I sit in the stands and chat with this amazing fellow. Two hours later I walk away convinced that he's one of the smartest hockey players I've ever met—on or off the ice.

Andre begins by saying, "You know why Bernie Parent was traded by the Philadelphia Flyers, don't you?" I say that I don't. Andre told me the story:

Well, we had the worst coach in hockey in Vic Stasiuk. He was a dumb coach as well as being obnoxious. One day he orders all the French-speaking players on the team—Jean-Guy Gendron, Serge Bernier, Parent, Lacroix, and one or two others—not to speak French anymore. It was English only. Bernie Parent mentioned this to some friends in Montreal and first thing you know it's in all the papers in Montreal—not on the sports page, but on the front page. Big headlines: "Stasiuk Orders Flyers Not to Speak French."

Clarence Campbell called Stasiuk in and he denied it. Well, the Flyer management was upset about the headlines and Stasiuk was furious. They vowed to find out who spilled the beans to the press and when they discovered it was Parent they decided to get rid of him.

When we jumped to the WHA we all jumped for the money. I was with the Chicago Blackhawks, making $30,000 a year, and the WHA guys came to me and said, "We'll double your salary and give you a five-year contract."

Pie McKenzie jumped for a different reason—the money, sure, but he also got a chance to coach in Philadelphia. Pie was a good guy. He made the right move because his days were numbered in Boston. [McKenzie was thirty-four years old when he jumped to the WHA. He played in all seven WHA seasons.]

One thing I have to say, the money was always there—at least for me. I played throughout the history of the WHA and I always got the money that was coming to me. And I was never traded even though I changed teams something like seven times because I was always a free agent. I never lost a penny.

I started with the Blazers in Philadelphia and it was the only time I had an agent. The Blazers had called a press conference to announce the new coach, Fred Creighton. The night before the press conference, Creighton decided he didn't want to coach in Philadelphia after all. So I got a call at home and the team owners said, "We'd like to negotiate with you because we have to announce something at the press conference tomorrow." So I went to a hotel in Philly and negotiated a five-year contract. I signed for $65,000 a year with a raise every year.

If the team was sold or moved I became a free agent—I always had that clause in my WHA contracts. [When the Blazers moved to Vancouver, Lacroix became a member of the New York Raiders.] In New York I said I wanted to drive a Cadillac, so they gave me one and the first thing you know I get a call from the sheriff telling me to give the car back. The team couldn't make the payments on it. So I return the car and the team tells me they're moving to New Jersey. So now I'm a free agent again.

Ann: No, even though they were only 30 air miles from home. Mind you, they did search that area, but because of the high tree density and the muskeg it was impossible to see any traces of the plane. It just happened to be a bit of luck that they found the crash site. It was in June 1962 and two bush pilots happened to be fishing in that area. They came back and told their supervisor that they had seen something while flying over the muskeg that looked yellow. The supervisor said, "Do you think you could find that area if you went back the next day?" They said, "Yes, we think we could."

The pilots took rolls of toilet paper with them so that when they spotted the yellow wreckage they would throw these rolls of toilet paper out the window and they would land in the trees and act as markers. Then they could go back directly to the spot. And that is exactly what happened.

They flew back the next day and there was all the toilet tissue in the trees. That is when they finally verified the serial number of the plane. They could even see the skeletal remains of Bill and Dr. Hudson still sitting in the seats of the aircraft.

There's an ironic postscript to the Bill Barilko story. The Leafs won the Stanley Cup in 1951 on Barilko's goal, and they didn't win again until 1961–62—the spring after the Leaf's plane was found.

Hall of Fame defenceman Allan Stanley says, "I was supposed to go with Bill Barilko on that trip, but somehow there was a misunderstanding and Lou Hudson, Henry's brother, showed up in my place. Then, when the plane tried to take off from Timmins, there was a dead calm on the lake and the plane wouldn't lift off the water. So Lou said he'd hop out and go another time."

There's also a rumour that the pontoons of the plane were filled with high-grade ore, not fish.

Ted Lindsay

I ask Ted Lindsay, my old NBC broadcast partner, in which arena in the old six-team league the fans gave him the worst reception.

Ted: The Boston Garden was a tough rink to play in, and the Bruins always played well at home against Detroit. In the stands there were all those loudmouth people, and they always got on Gordie because Gordie was big and he had some of his greatest nights against Boston.

I remember that long corridor from the dressing room to the ice. There was a little bit of linoleum to walk on, about a foot wide, and the fans used to line up on each side of this strip and give us a lot of lip. Howe and I were always the last ones out of the dressing room and we'd hold our sticks very close to our bodies—with about 8 inches of butt end sticking out. We always expected somebody to take a swing at us, and when they did we'd take a quick swing back at them. Just a little jab with the stick—with the butt end. After we did that a couple of times, the fans would jump back. They learned their lessons quickly, and even though their ribs might be hurt their tongues kept wagging.

Brian: Another great Bruin was Johnny Bucyk. Did you see Bucyk in Detroit before he went to Boston? Do you think it was a big mistake to let him go?

Ted: It was a major mistake. It was unbelievable. I was in Detroit at the time, I was team captain. The big thing about Bucyk, the big rap, was that he couldn't check. If you were a player going behind your net, John would try and time it so he hit you just after you cleared the net. Usually he would turn his ass to the guy, and the guys would get to know John and they would take two quick strides, and John's rear end would hit the boards and he'd fall down. By the time he got up the other players would be gone.

So Jack Adams traded him because he didn't know how to check. He goes to Boston, learns how to check guys right out of their skates, plays for twenty-one years, scores over 500 goals, and was regarded as one of the best left wingers in the game for fifteen of those twenty-one years.

Yeah, it was a major mistake letting him get away from Detroit.

Brian: What did you think about [Terry] Sawchuk?

The Barilkos—Alex, Anne, and Bill. In Timmins one night, Anne gave me a gripping behind-the-scenes account of Bill's untimely death in 1951.

Joe Klukay with Ted Lindsay. Bitter rivals on the ice, good friends when the game was over.

Ted: Sawchuk, for the first five years he played in the league, was the best there ever was. There will never be a better goaltender. He weighed 205 pounds and he was so fast and so quick.

We won the Stanley Cup one year [1952], and we beat Toronto and Montreal in 8 straight games—and neither team scored a goal at the Olympia. I'd say that's pretty outstanding—4 shutouts in 8 playoff games. They couldn't put a pea by him.

Brian: Didn't you once say that Adams could have traded Sawchuk to Montreal for Doug Harvey, and you would have won a couple of more Stanley Cups in Detroit?

Ted: Well, more than a couple. When we won in '55, Adams traded nine players away from our championship team. The five Stanley Cups that Montreal won after that would have been ours. We only had one weakness on our team and that was defence. Not because of lack of ability, because of age. Bob Goldham was getting older, so if we could have gotten Harvey for Sawchuk, who had not established himself yet, or even Tom Johnson, we would have won those five Stanley Cups. If we had gotten Doug Harvey, we would have won seven!

There will never be a better defenceman than Doug Harvey. I have always said that the only thing Bobby Orr did better than Doug was skate. Harvey controlled games and power plays. They went as fast or as slow as Harvey wanted them to go.

Ace Bailey

Irvine "Ace" Bailey had his brilliant hockey career terminated by Boston defenceman Eddie Shore on December 12, 1933. Shore hit Bailey from behind, sent him flying through the air, and saw him crash to the ice headfirst. Bailey suffered a fractured skull, was at death's door for several days, and never played hockey again. In December 1990, I visited with Ace, then eighty-seven, in his small but neat room in a nursing home in Willowdale, Ontario.

Brian, I kept 164 scrapbooks. In one of them is my obituary. It appeared in all the papers in the early sixties. I think you and a lot of other sportscasters put it on the radio and TV that I'd died. But it was another Ace Bailey who passed away that day. And people almost fainted when I walked into Maple Leaf Gardens that night.

You ask me about my early days in hockey. Well, I remember I used to play street hockey with wooden pucks, made out of oak, made by my father. I played Junior hockey for the Marlboros when the team was run by Frank Selke. I had many offers to play Senior hockey and chose to play in Peterborough.

Later, in Toronto, when I joined the St. Pats, we played in the Mutual Street Arena. Conn Smythe and some others bought the team shortly after that for $225,000 and changed the name to the Maple Leafs. I and the others were very pleased and felt proud on opening night at the Gardens.

Of course, everybody wants to know about the incident in Boston, when Eddie Shore checked me from behind and almost killed me. In Boston it was Dr. Monroe who saved my life. He drilled holes on either side of my head to get the blood clot to come out. A little brandy may have come out with it.

I laid charges against Eddie Shore and the Boston club. The nurses would not let Shore into my room, although he tried. My surgeon, Dr. Ross, told me to withdraw the charges and Smythe would put on a benefit game for me. He said I'd be lucky to get $5,000 from a Boston court. We got $20,000 from the benefit game.

I shook hands with Shore at the game—there's a famous picture of it—and he said, "It's nice to shake your hand, Ace." We gave him a dark-blue Maple Leaf jacket. The gate from a Maroons game in Boston was sent to me, and that was worth $7,800. With that money we built a house on a piece of property on Hillhurst Boulevard in Toronto. You can't do that today. Clancy lived one street over on Cortleigh.

Ace Bailey was eighty-seven when I visited with him in a Toronto nursing home. Ace was the last Leaf to win the NHL individual scoring title— back in 1929. He tallied 32 points in 44 games. Heck, Gretzky used to score that many in a weekend.

"Ace" Bailey

After hockey, Smythe got me a job coaching at U of T. Some of my players became doctors, lawyers, and one was on the Supreme Court of Canada. We won three championships. Then I worked for forty-seven years for Harold Ballard and not even a thank you when I left. I told him to take the job and stick it up his keester.

Who was the greatest player? Howie Morenz was the best—you couldn't skate with him unless you picked him up in his end. Smythe told me once to knock his baseball cap off so he'd get mad and get a penalty. He told me off in French and I didn't even know it. He was smart—he would give you a nickel and low change, he was so smart.

I remember the organist in Chicago playing "Three Blind Mice" when Bill Chadwick and the linesmen came on the ice. So Chadwick jumped the boards to crucify the organist, but some maintenance man got to Chadwick first and put him out. Then they brought in a rule not allowing that song to be played.

Cyclone Taylor

A player who might well be called a turn-of-the-century Wayne Gretzky or Mario Lemieux was Fred "Cyclone" Taylor. Taylor was the most sought-after star of his era and in 1909 he signed with the Renfrew Millionaires for a reported $5,250 to play 12 games. Taylor's baseball counterpart, Ty Cobb, earned $6,500 with the Detroit Tigers that year, but he performed in 154 games.

Brian: Cyclone, I would like you to go back a few years—many years—to your earliest recollection of hockey.

Cyclone: I go back to playing hockey as far back as 1896. I was a teenager, even older than the Stanley Cup.

Brian: What was hockey like in those days?

Cyclone: I don't know that it was any different so far as the excitement and the will to play than it is today. It was a seven-man game, you know, and was a seven-man game until 1911–12. But the desire to play was always with me and the spectators who watched were just as eager and excited as they are today. In fact, I think the spectators in our day were closer to the game. Remember there was no picture show, no radios, no automobiles, nothing to distract your attention from sports. Lacrosse and football in the fall, baseball in summer, and hockey in winter.

I pay the highest compliment to fans of that day. They suffered through long winter drives in horse-drawn cutters, they sat in frozen seats to watch us play. You cannot believe all the hardships and trials that they went through to come to our games. I can tell you, when the Stanley Cup was being played for in Winnipeg by a Montreal or Ottawa club, every telegraph office between Montreal and Winnipeg would be crowded. Fans in every small town would be standing out in the cold with two coats on listening for the scores. All we would get was word from the telegrapher: Winnipeg scores! And later—Ottawa scores!

We get hockey now over the radio and television and if we don't like it we just turn it off. People in those days walked miles to come to games and stayed right through to the end despite frozen fingers or faces. They were determined to get their money's worth, they didn't want to miss a minute.

Brian: You were a defenceman in the NHA and I understand you didn't stay long in Renfrew.

Cyclone: Well, Renfrew dropped out of hockey after the 1911–12 season, and I sat out a few months while Ottawa and Montreal Wanderers fought over my rights. Finally, I decided to go to Vancouver, where I signed on with my friend Frank Patrick and the Vancouver Millionaires of the Pacific Coast League. I played forward out there and led the league in scoring five times.

Brian: How about a story regarding yourself, like how you got the name Cyclone?

Cyclone: That was given to me by the late Malcolm T. Bright, who, when I went to Ottawa in the summer of 1907, was the sports editor of the *Ottawa Free Press*. We played our first game in a new arena, which was built in Ottawa during the summer of 1907, and we were playing the Wanderers, who were the Stanley Cup winners of the year before. The Governor General, Lord Grey, and his household were all at the game. It was a packed house.

Although I was started on the forward line of Ottawa, it seems that my skating was too speedy for the rest of the forwards, and we couldn't get a combination going. Our trainer, the late Pete Green, said, "No, we will try this young man on the defence."

Ottawa won the game 8–4 and I scored 4 goals from cover point, which made my entry into the Ottawa hockey club secure for the next four years. It was a tremendous opening for me.

I will always have a kindly feeling towards Malcolm T. Bright, who said in his column the next day: "This boy Taylor, we understand, when he played in Portage La Prairie, was called 'Tornado.' When he went down into the International Professional league, which was the first professional hockey in North America, they called him 'Thunderbolt.' Today I am christening him 'Cyclone.'" And that name has stuck with me ever since. That is the origin of "Cyclone."

Marcel Dionne

When I met with Marcel Dionne at his home in Los Angeles in 1986 he had completed fifteen seasons of NHL play and had proven himself to be one of the greatest scorers in history. A few months later he would be traded to the New York Rangers, and his career would wind down quickly after that. In Los Angeles, he was taking good care of two Kings rookies, Jimmy Carson and Luc Robitaille.

Marcel: Because they are new, I tell the kids a lot. I probably tell them a lot more than I should, but why not? I tell them about the movie stars. I tell them about the famous stars I have met and been with. Then I might say, "But listen, where are they now?"

I just don't socialize very much with the Hollywood people. A lot of youngsters are impressed by who they see out here. They see a $4-million dollar house, they see Rolls-Royces. There was a guy I knew who had $178 million, going around buying this, buying that. Now this was a smart guy. But the oil business went bad in Texas, he happened to own a bank, so what do you do when you lose millions fast? It just shows you that money is nothing. What you see out here means nothing.

The big difference here is the hockey mentality. With other NHL teams, you can't have anybody in the dressing room. In Montreal, nobody would walk into the dressing room before the game, but here it's different. The movie stars wander into the room and soon you learn to accept it. Some of those people are legitimate hockey fans, like Michael J. Fox. They love the game and they love the guys. When a new coach comes in and says, "Well, I don't want anybody in the room but the players," we laugh and say, "Hey, you have to understand what is going on out here."

Brian: Are you are going to stay here in L.A. when you retire? You've been here a long time.

Marcel: I don't know, Brian. There is an adjustment that has to be made because it is very, very demanding on the kids. You can't walk to school here. You have to take your kids to a school. The kids have cars when they are fifteen or sixteen years old. The drugs are always out there. We go to Niagara Falls, where my in-laws live, during the summer. We go to Quebec for a couple of weeks. It's so much better for my kids then, because you have the time, you know, to watch them. They leave the house and you don't worry about them. Here, if they leave the house, you wonder where are they? We try never to allow the kids out of our sight.

But here the climate is so great. You do things all year round. You do the same thing in December that you do in August. It is amazing. So now you go home for a while, it rains for a week, you think, "Geez, I want to go back to California."

You don't get depressed here. If you live by the beach and it gets foggy, you move inland, you go to Palm Springs. You go where the sun is going to be. It is guaranteed—incredible.

Leaf owner Conn Smythe
arranged a benefit game for
Bailey and raised $20,000. King
Clancy and Red Horner took
part.

Marcel Dionne enjoyed a fabulous career with the Kings—and hardly anybody noticed.

Pierre Larouche

In New York, Pierre Larouche, who liked to call himself Peter Puck when he played with Pittsburgh, tells me about growing up in Amos, Quebec.

Gordie Howe was always my idol. When I first played against Howe in the NHL, during the warm-up before the game, I got up enough nerve to skate over to him. I said, "Mr. Howe, may I have your stick after the game? You've always been my idol."

He kinda grunted, didn't say much. But with four minutes to play he gave me his stick all right—right across the eye for about six stitches. He said to me, "Here, rookie, you can have the stick now, it will mean more to you now," or words to that effect.

John Tonelli

When the New York Islanders traded John Tonelli to Calgary in 1986, we rushed to Long Island to cover the story for "Inside Hockey." When our crew arrived at the Nassau County Coliseum, we were told that Tonelli was very upset about the deal and that he was not talking to the media, not giving any interviews.

I asked the Islanders' PR person to plead with John to make an exception, since we'd come all the way from Toronto. She returned and said, "He said all right, he'll do it for you, Mr. McFarlane." John gave me an exclusive, excellent interview, then packed and left for Calgary.

John had a long and productive career in hockey, starting in Junior with the Toronto Marlboros, where he scored 49 goals in his final season. He played three seasons with the Houston Aeros of the WHA, and in the NHL he played in more than 1,000 games and scored 325 goals. He was the MVP of the 1984 Canada Cup and played on four Stanley Cup–winning teams—all of them with the Islanders.

John: Near the end of my second season in Junior hockey, just before I turned eighteen, I retained an agent named Gus Badali. He had been talking to Houston of the WHA, because Houston wanted me. So it looked like the following season [1975–76] I would be turning pro and playing with the Houston Aeros.

But at the start of the [1974–75] Junior season, the Marlies came out with a new contract that bound some players for three years, plus an option year. Reluctantly, and later to my regret, I'd signed such a contract at the beginning of the year. I didn't know back then that I would have a chance to play pro with Houston. Once I turned eighteen I repudiated [the Marlie contract]—I wanted it revoked. I went to Marlie management, to Frank Bonello, and I tried to convince him I should be allowed to leave the Marlies after that season.

He said, "No way! You are here for four years."

We tried to settle with them, but they wanted an enormous amount of money, so we ended up in court. I didn't play another game in Junior after my eighteenth birthday. I missed all the playoffs and the team went on to win the Memorial Cup that year—that part made me happy, because if they hadn't won they could have blamed it on me.

Brian: But you missed the thrill of being part of it.

John: Oh yeah. That would have been a thrill, too.

Brian: That's unfortunate. You only get that one chance.

John: Well, that's life. So we went to court. I couldn't believe that something like this was happening. They were trying to stop me from playing professional hockey, something I always wanted to do.

Brian: What was it like in Houston the first year?

John: Houston was great. Fantastic. I had trouble at the beginning. I didn't have that much confidence, so they switched me around a lot. As soon as I started to play with Terry Ruskowski and Don Larway, things began to roll.

My first shift, I played centre between Gordie Howe and Mark Howe. We came back to the bench

Ed Westfall went from the Stanley Cup champion Bruins to the expansion
Islanders. He organized a season-ending party that lasted a week.

something like $2,200 of fine money collected over the season, for a party at my house. But first we had a couple of games to play. We went into Philly and lost 10–2. We went down to Atlanta to play the Flames and emerged with a 4–4 tie.

We caught a flight out of Atlanta at 2 a.m. and we're the only passengers on the plane, a bunch of grubby hockey players being catered to by seven lovely stewardesses. They were all adorable. Before the flight was over I had all seven of them lined up to come to the party. Then our coach, Earl Ingarfield, said, "Let them come on the bus from the airport."

We arrived at the Coliseum, a raunchy bunch of guys, half drunk, accompanied by seven beautiful flight attendants with their overnight bags. We pull into the Coliseum parking lot and the wives of the married guys are standing around gawking when the seven beauties walk off the bus.

Everybody—the coach, the general manager, the trainers, the wives—headed straight for my house. The guys were trying to convince their wives that the flight attendants were only interested in the single guys. With the wives, I was the most unpopular captain ever in the history of the New York Islanders, but the girls were great. They were so funny. Some of them couldn't stay long because they had other flights. Some of them stayed overnight. It was like a steady procession from my house to Kennedy Airport. I was driving them back and forth. Do you know that party went on for one full week? I don't think a Stanley Cup–winning team ever had such a party. The story of that party even made *Sports Illustrated*.

Tiger Williams (22) gave me a great line on TV in a playoff series versus Pittsburgh: "Them Penguins are done like dinner!"

in the briefcase. Some guys would have made fun of me if I had carried my comics out in the open.

Brian: Seriously, though, you had an interest in business that you pursued on the road trips, did you not?

Tiger: I did what I had to do on the road. You know what it's like. You've been on road trips. There is a lot of sitting around and I wanted to be able to come home off the road and not have to catch up on everything that had to be done. I wanted it all done so that when I got home I had time for my two kids and my wife. Plus, when I first started playing, when I first ran into you, I didn't think I would be sitting here thirteen years later thinking that it was all over. I still don't think that it's all over.

But the reason that I stayed on top and wanted to learn everything in business, as much as I could, is that I didn't think that I was going to be in the game that long. And when you only have four or five years' earnings, which the average guy does, I wanted to be able to make it work.

Brian: How do you feel about bowing out as hockey's most penalized player?

Tiger: Well now, Brian, don't bow me out till I am bowed out. I am not out of this yet. I can't answer that question because it is a little premature right now.

Brian: When you do go, you are going to be hockey's most penalized player, right?

Tiger: Somebody else will break it. That's what records are for. There is about six or seven refs in the league whose name should be right behind mine, because out of all those sin-bin occurrences I don't think I deserved half of them.

Brian: You're probably right. Tell me about being charged with assault a few years ago and having to appear in court in Toronto. Was that a bitter memory for you?

Tiger: I wasn't too pleased about it. Roy McMurtry [at the time, the Attorney General of Ontario], he used me as a political pawn. I always understood by other people who went to school with the McMurtrys that they were a pretty rough group themselves. But I don't think you should use an individual to try to, you know, to step on. He tried to step right on my face to improve his position and it backfired on him.

Brian: Tiger, there seems to be a trend among the clubs this year to get the tough guys on the roster. Do you think that fighting is the "in" thing again in the NHL?

Tiger: What do you mean by the "in" thing?

Brian: Well, there was a movement in recent months to get rid of violence or fighting in hockey, and it seems to be that the coaches are loading up with the tough guys again.

Tiger: This is the thing in hockey. The whole league has never got together. The owners have never got together with the managers, the managers have never got together with the coaches, and the coaches have never got together with the players. They never had a plan of where they wanted this game to go. It's just scatterbrained.

The latitude on rules is just incredible. There is a rule for the first period, there is a rule for the third period, and there is a rule for the playoffs. Look at the NFL and the NBA. They call a penalty no matter what time it is in the game or what the score is. We don't have that in our sport. I said a year ago [1986] that fighting would be out of the game by 1990.

Brian: That's a good answer, Tiger.

Tiger: You mean that's the only good answer I gave you?

Brian (*laughs*): No, they've all been good. Remember a few years ago when you gave me your famous quote before a playoff game in Pittsburgh? You said, "Them Penguins is done like dinner!" Do you remember that?

Tiger: Yeah! Hey, that's the name of my cookbook! *Done Like Dinner.* It's gonna be a bestseller.

Brian: Surely you have a Harold Ballard story?

Tiger: Harold? You know, if I could adopt a grandfather—because I don't have one—I would adopt Harold. In my own dream world Harold is my granddad, as far as I'm concerned, and Harold is a tremendous guy. I can remember when [my son] Ben was being born and I was in Pittsburgh. Harold says to me, "Just come down. If you don't want to play, that's fine. If you want to go home, I'll fly you home. I'll rent a plane. You make the decision." I'll never forget that. I love Harold Ballard.

I used to enjoy going to practices and getting there early and arguing with Harold about nothing. Just sit there and argue with him. If he took one side, I'd take the other side. I enjoyed those times. He is a tremendous guy. Nobody ever will convince me that Harold is not a great person. He is a character. In the country of Canada, I don't think there is anybody like him.

Brian: But you didn't like Imlach?

Tiger: No, I didn't like Punch. Punch was there on a spiteful campaign. He took it out on us. The game had passed Punch by. He didn't know the game anymore. He never kept up with it. There was a big generation gap there in how the players thought. Punch blew his brains out in '67 when they last won the Cup and there was nothing left. It is unfortunate the hockey fans suffered for his spite. That happened in Toronto.

In October 1987, Tiger joined the Hartford Whalers, scored 6 goals in 26 games, and called it a career after being released again.

Phil Esposito

Shortly after Phil Esposito was named president of the Tampa Bay Lightning in 1992, he appeared as guest speaker at a huge sports celebrities dinner in Saskatoon. There were about eight hundred people in the hall. It was quite a classy affair. As master of ceremonies for the evening, I remember looking out over the audience and thinking, be careful about what you say tonight, this isn't the time or place for bad language or off-colour jokes. Somehow, I don't think Phil Esposito read the audience the same way I did. I gave him a grand introduction and here's part of what he said when he stepped to the microphone:

Folks, I remember my first NHL game. It was in Montreal and the Canadiens were whipping us 7–2. I've always been an outspoken individual, as Billy Reay, who was coaching Chicago at that time, soon found out. Now there are about two minutes to play in the game and I hadn't touched the ice all night. Suddenly Reay barks, "Esposito, get out there!"

I turned to him and said, "Coach, do you want me to win it or tie it?" And he says, "You can sit back down, you smart ass!"

In my second game, we're in Detroit and Billy Reay says to me, "Esposito, go out there with Bobby Hull and Reg Fleming and let Hull take the draw." So Bobby goes into the faceoff circle and who do I find myself standing next to but Gordie Howe, my boyhood idol. I'm looking at Gordie and I'm saying to myself 'Holy shit! That's Gordie Howe.' I'm sayin' to myself, 'What the hell am I doing out here?'

Bobby Hull nods toward Gordie and says to me, "Watch that old son of a bitch!" With that, Howe gets this little grin on his face and his eyes are blinkin' at me and that's when the puck is dropped. I'm still lookin' at him, thinkin' this is unbelievable and suddenly, bam! He gives me an elbow in the mouth. Well, I stagger back and I say, "Why, you old son of a bitch!" And I speared him a good one and we both get penalties.

In those days, in the penalty box, an usher or a cop would sit between the two penalized players. So I'm sitting there with a towel to my split lip and I'm upset with big Howe. I leaned across the cop and said to him, "And to think you used to be my fuckin' idol."

He snarled back, "What'd you say, Woppo?"

And I said, "Nothin', Mr. Howe, not a word."

He was something, boy. The toughest son of a bitch I ever played against. I played an old-timers game on the same side with Gordie and some guy was flying down the ice. Gordie leaned over to

Colourful, controversial Phil Esposito was never at a loss for words,
whether it be with Team Canada '72 or on our telecasts.

me and said, "You know, Phil, I think it's time we cut that guy down to size." Two minutes later, the guy was lying on the ice and Gordie's leaning over him saying innocently, "Are you all right?" He just speared the guy, right in the balls. It was unbelievable.

I remember one time watching *The Dick Cavett Show*. Gordie was on with his sons, Mark and Marty. He was sittin' there and Cavett says, "What kind of equipment did you wear?"

Gordie says, "I wore skates, shin pads, elbow pads, pants and shoulder pads, and a cup."

Cavett says to the boys, "Did you wear the same things?"

They say, "Yeah, but we also wore helmets."

And Cavett turns back to Gordie and says, "You never wore a helmet?"

Gordie says, "Nah, I never wore a helmet."

Cavett says, "But you wore a cup? Why would you wear a cup but not a helmet?"

And Gordie says, "Hey, you can always get someone to do your thinking for you." Geez, I fell right out of bed when he said that.

John Candy

I didn't know him well, but actor John Candy was one of my favourite people. In Edmonton one night, when he was starring on *SCTV*, I had the pleasure of having him as an intermission guest. I was fortunate enough to have Rick Moranis, his co-star, join us. I was surprised at their nervousness.

"Are you kidding me?" John said. "This is such a big deal for both of us—being on *Hockey Night in Canada*. We're so nervous, we're both in a sweat."

If they were, it didn't show on the air. John and Rick were excellent guests. Later, at the 1991 All-Star game in Chicago, I asked Candy if he'd join me on "Inside Hockey." He said, "Of course I will."

Brian: John, tell me about your love for the game.

John: Well, I guess my love for hockey goes back many years, almost to my birth. Don't all Canadians come out with a blanket and a hockey stick? I've always enjoyed the game.

Brian: Were you a player?

John: Yeah, in East York [Toronto], Ontario, and then through high school and in the intermediate league. So I had a lot of fun playing.

Brian: Tell me about some of your favourite players.

John: My favourite players growing up. Geez, well I grew up during the era of Dave Keon, Frank Mahovlich, Johnny Bower, Tim Horton, and Allan Stanley. Those men were legends for me. I can't recall anybody I didn't like. I mean, there were the Original Six teams. It was a time when you knew every player on every team. You even knew the farm teams. I had it all—you know, the cards and everything. I just had a passion for the game.

Brian: What about your current loyalties? You still a Leaf fan?

John: Bleed blue, that's me. But I live in Los Angeles now, and follow the Kings, and when I'm in Chicago I follow the Blackhawks.

Brian: John, I told Don Cherry I was going to be talking to you today and he said, "Tell John I loved *Trains, Planes, and Automobiles*." There's a scene in the movie where you wash your socks and underwear in the sink. Cherry says to tell you he had roommates like that in the American League.

John: Well, in that scene, Steve Martin and I had taken all the towels and soaked out the socks and underwear in the small bathroom that we both shared. Yeah, he has soap in his eyes from the shower and when he went to dry his face he pulled out my big shorts. He freaked out. But the final straw was Steve having to sleep with me. That scene drew a lot of laughs.

Brian: Perhaps I was misinformed, but I heard you had a great career with Mellonville in some obscure league.

John: Well, that's true. The Mellonville Mexicans were my team later on in life—when I was with

SCTV. They had a goalie there by the name of Eddie Lumley. He was a wonderful fellow, really, but a rotten goalie. The owner of the Mellonville Mexicans, Chief Stoner, was arrested and thrown in jail for a number of crimes he had committed in Mellonville. So he took this fourth-string goalie, Eddie Lumley, and made him president of the club and captain of the team—and, of course, goaltender. Eddie had never played goal before and had a rough year. I think he had 2 ties, 1 win and 700 losses. It was just a sad, sad thing to see.

Eddie never played with a mask or a cup and it was a shame. I think he learned later on that he should have. I think in his book, *The Lumley Years, the Lonely Years*, he mentions that. It was a good book—sold seven copies, all of them in Mellonville.

Brian: Are you aware of a former hockey player named Jim Ralph in Toronto doing impressions of you?

John: Wait a minute! What?

Brian: This guy Jim Ralph does impressions of you.

John: Oh God! Is he good?

Brian: Terrific.

John: I'll be seeing him when I go to Toronto, I guess I'll check him out.

John passed away before he got to see Jim Ralph's act. We all miss you, big guy.

Anne Murray

In February 1991, producer Jim Hough and I travelled to Atlantic City to interview longtime hockey fan Anne Murray.

I met her guitarist, Steve Sexton, and he reminded me that he had a letter from me that I'd written many years before.

"I played on a good Pee Wee team in Richmond Hill, Ontario, when I was twelve," he said. "We won the Quebec Peewee tournament that year and then I got badly hurt. I remember you sent me a get-well letter, which I still have at home. Because of my injury I took up the guitar and I've had a pretty good career in music."

Anne was extremely friendly and easy to talk to. After she gave me a dandy interview, she invited us to see her show in the casino. She even gave us a front row booth at the show and sent us over drinks. She invited us back to her dressing room afterwards, popped open a beer and drank from the bottle, kicked off her shoes, and put her feet up on the table. Then she said, "Let's talk hockey."

Brian: With all the brothers in your family, tell us about your early interest in hockey.

Anne: I was kind of weaned on it. There were five brothers and my father and we watched hockey every Saturday night. My father was a Montreal fan, my brothers were Toronto fans, and I was a Detroit Red Wings fan. That's because I was a big Gordie Howe fan. So there was some dissension in the house on hockey nights. I also liked Toronto. I liked anyone but Montreal, that's what it boiled down to. I'm not too sure why, because I was a big fan of Jean Beliveau, who, as it turns out, is a distant cousin of mine.

Brian: A few years ago we heard that Anne Murray was going to buy the Toronto Maple Leafs. How serious was that?

Anne: Very serious at the time. I had some people who were interested in backing me. Some people who had a lot more money than I have, who were seriously interested in buying them. Of course, Harold Ballard was not interested in selling. His selling price was just out of this world.

Brian: You say that your band members are avid hockey fans—do you have a hockey pool?

Anne: We have had it every year for the past five years and I have won three of the pools so now they all hate me. They think that I have some inside information but, really, I just pay close attention to what's going on.

Brian: Do you think that women should play a more active role in hockey?

In Atlantic City with hockey fan Anne Murray. Too bad she didn't buy the Leafs in the early 1980s, as rumoured. She might have spared us all those dismal Ballard years.

Anne: I think hockey would be a little too rough for me, but there are lots of women's teams around and all the more power to them. I think that women can play the game too. Women can play any game.

Brian: Anne, how would you like to replace Ron MacLean one night and go up against Don Cherry on "Coach's Corner"?

Anne: I am a big fan of Don Cherry and Ron MacLean. I talked to them at the CBC's big gala, where they announce what is coming up in the next year. Those two guys are great together.

Brian: Have you any advice to our *HNIC* announcers? You watch our shows regularly. Where do we go wrong, what would you like to see improved?

Anne: My biggest complaint about commentators is that they never paid any attention to Danny Gallivan or any of the greats.

Brian: Is there one moment in hockey that really registered with you?

Anne: There were a couple. I remember when Gordie Howe broke Lou Fontinato's nose. I didn't think that Gordie was much of a fighter, I knew he was good with his elbows in corners and good with his stick. I also remember Lou Fontinato going into the boards, headfirst and breaking his neck. It was a horrible moment in hockey. Another game that I remember was the game between the Red Army and the Canadiens, a New Year's Eve game which ended in a 3–3 tie. I think that it was the best hockey game that I have ever seen.

Brian: Is this unusual for you to give us this time an hour before you have to go in front of a huge audience?

Anne: It used to be that I wouldn't do interviews before I did a show, because I would be so nervous, but now I am more relaxed. I really don't have to prove myself anymore. Since I turned forty, I say, "What the hell, just go do it," and I think you do relax a little more. You stop pushing a bit. Everything is a little easier for you. Audiences know who I am now and I don't have to go out and explain myself to anybody. It's all very relaxing and a lot of fun.

Mike Myers

On "Inside Hockey" one night we profiled actor and comedian Mike Myers. This was before his hugely successful movie career, when he was just rising to prominence on *Saturday Night Live*. He knew his hockey. What is it they say? You can take the boy out of Canada, but you can't take the Canada out of the boy.

My strongest memory of my childhood is playing hockey on the street. And when a car came in sight we'd all yell *"Car!"* and we'd have to move the goal nets. Then we'd put 'em back again when the car passed by. *"Game on!"*

"Hey, no slappers from 2 feet out, eh. No slaps."

"You hacker!"

And if somebody fell down, we'd say, "Oh, you're a faker. You faker."

I had two older bothers so I was always the goalie. I never played organized hockey. You see, my parents were English immigrants. They were afraid of hockey. To them it was soccer with an attitude. They couldn't handle the fighting and stuff like that.

And they couldn't handle the Canadian hockey parents. You know, always yelling. "Come on, you little bastard! Skate, skate, skate! Okay, yer walkin' home, yer walkin' home! No Life Savers after the game for you!"

My parents would have been soft-spoken and reserved, like, "Come on, Michael, please skate. I know you can." And the other parents would be looking over and saying, "Get a load of them."

Myers then proclaims his love for the Leafs.

Growing up I loved Dave Keon and Darryl Sittler. And Ron Ellis. Ellis used to skate very quickly and then run right into the end boards. Like he never learned how to stop. I liked Yvan Cournoyer. I like the little guys like Theo Fleury. He's great.

Of course, Wayne Gretzky is my ultimate favourite player. He's a genius. When I heard he was going to be a host on *Saturday Night Live* I couldn't believe it. I immediately called my brother. I was so excited. And Wayne turned out to be just the nicest guy in the world. It's such a cliché to say he's nice. It's like saying Niagara Falls is neat. I was really proud as a Canadian that they had Wayne Gretzky on. And he did a great job as host.

We did a little skit on "Wayne's World" where we had to simulate slow motion on the ice. We didn't have the budget for real slow motion, so we skated very slowly. I had to slowly check Wayne into the boards and he had to slowly fall. But he fell kinda funny and he said, "Oh, my leg."

Oh, God, I'd ruined Wayne Gretzky's career. For a couple of seconds there I thought, "Oh Jesus, I creamed him."

I like the Rangers, but I love the Leafs. I love Maple Leaf Gardens. Every day I live and die with whether they win or not. Tom Hanks was on the show, and he went to see a game there. He said, "The building had such character. It reeked of hockey history."

One night Wayne Gretzky got me tickets to a game—'cause he was on the show, eh. It was the Rangers versus L.A., and I've still got the ticket sub in my wallet. And I got invited into the dressing room after and John Candy was there. I met him that night for the first time. And who should show up but Liza Minelli! Oh, it was fabulous, really exciting.

I was in London for a few months, early in my career, and Canada House was able to broadcast the Stanley Cup games over there. They showed the game to a lot of Canadians and it was great. Then Don Cherry came on. I felt so homesick I almost started to cry. I wanted to go home so much. And I'm saying after a few beers, in a wimpy voice, "I wonder if Blue's still alive. If I ever have a dog I'm going to name him Blue. I love Blue. I love Don Cherry. I'd even wear collars that high if I could be with Don Cherry right now."

And when Cherry came on, the whole room leapt to its feet and gave him a standing ovation. They were all as homesick as I was.

Michael J. Fox

When I interviewed Michael J. Fox in New York for "Inside Hockey," we arrived at his posh apartment for the shoot and he quickly charmed us with his friendliness and his enthusiasm for hockey. He was genuinely excited about being on *Hockey Night in Canada*. Just before we started he asked, "Can you hang on a minute? I've gotta call my mom in Vancouver and tell her about this."

He called home and said, "Mom, you won't believe this but a crew from *Hockey Night in Canada* is here in my apartment. They're doing something on me for Saturday night's show. You better be watching. And hey, Brian McFarlane's here. I'm gonna put him on for a minute." He handed me the phone. "Say hello to my mom. She's been watching you for years."

Michael's mother and I had a wonderful chat, then it was down to business. He told me about playing in charity games all over the country for the Hollywood All-Stars.

"I even played against Bobby Orr one day and I think I may have ended his career—once and for all. We got tangled up and he went down and hurt his knee. And I'm thinking, 'Geez, what a villain I'll be if he can't play again. I'll be known as the guy who ended Bobby's hockey career.'"

I had heard that Michael was a friend of Boston Bruins star Cam Neely, so I asked him about it.

Yeah, he's a great guy. And Lyndon Byers, too. They came to see me when I was shooting a film in Thailand a few years ago and, oh yeah, I've gotta tell you about a little joke I played on them.

Mike Myers teams up with Peter Puck in a Second City skit, doing a Danny Gallivan imitation for "Inside Hockey." Myers went on to much greater things. At the time my boss didn't think he was very funny.

The day before they arrived, I went for a walk down a street in Bangkok. Along the way I saw a man, a snake charmer, sitting in a pit full of cobras. I watched, fascinated, while the man played his flute and these deadly cobras, swaying gracefully, reacted to the music. I quickly realized that the cobras posed no real threat to me or the other passersby. So I talked with the snake charmer, gave him some money, and told him I'd be back the next day with some friends.

The following day, after Neely and Byers arrived, I said, "Guys, let's go for a walk. I've got something neat to show you."

I took them to the snake pit where the piper played and the cobras swayed, their cold, unblinking eyes sizing up the newcomers. Neely and Byers jumped back from the edge of the pit.

"Come on, guys, don't be chicken. They're just cobras. You two tough hockey players aren't afraid, are you? Well, I'm half your size and I'm not afraid of them. Watch this!"

I slipped over the edge and into the pit. Well, Neely and Byers flipped out. They screamed and shouted at me, telling me to get the heck out of the pit. Was I crazy or what? They didn't know the snake charmer had told me I'd be perfectly safe if I followed his instructions. And of course I did—and I was.

But Neely and Byers thought I was a goner. They thought I was nuts. They almost had simultaneous heart attacks while I was down in that pit. They said it scared the hell out of them.

And I said, "Guys, that was the whole idea."

24

Confessions from the Rubber Chicken Circuit

Once a broadcaster gets established on *Hockey Night in Canada*, the invitations to appear at sports celebrity dinners or roasts, to ride in parades, or to appear on talk shows, start rolling in. Now, speaking is what we do for a living, of course, but describing a game into a microphone on *HNIC* is far removed from entertaining an auditorium or ballroom full of fans. We're always in demand, and sometimes for quite significant fees. A popular speaker, like Dick Irvin, Ron MacLean, Dennis Hull, Red Storey, or Jim Ralph, can command anywhere from $1,000 to $5,000 per appearance.

I started speaking in 1955, in Schenectady, New York, where I began my broadcasting career. I earned about $25 per engagement, which I thought was exorbitant for someone as inexperienced as I was at the time. I still have rough drafts of my material from those days, and it was abominable—corny jokes that I actually thought were funny, told in a manner that would make any storyteller cringe.

But I was determined to improve. I sought funnier jokes, told true stories I considered to be humorous, and learned the secret of timing—when to pause, when to add punch to a line. I bought a tape recorder and recorded all of my speeches, then I'd play each one back later and make notes of the parts where the audience laughed and what they seemed to enjoy.

I learned to anticipate the unexpected: the microphone that doesn't work; the program that begins far too late; the presence of another speaker on thedais who is drunk or boring—or both; the presence of little children in the audience, which forces you to edit your presentation, deleting the more mature comments.

Sometimes you have to be ready to throw out an entire presentation and wing it. That happened to me one year when I MCd the biggest sports celebrity dinner in Canada, the Conn Smythe Dinner in Toronto. I nearly made a major gaffe that would have been televised coast to coast.

I'd been told that Paul Henderson would be a featured guest and that the CBC would provide a thirty-second clip of Paul's famous goal in Moscow in 1972. I was to introduce Paul while the film was screened.

Minutes before the guests were to march in and take their places at the two-tiered head table, something didn't seem right. I sought out the dinner chairman.

"I don't see Paul Henderson among the guests," I said. "It is possible that the committee has booked the other Paul Henderson—you know, the guy trying to get the Olympics for Toronto?"

As it turned out, my hunch was right. The video clip was scrapped, of course, and we threw out Paul's bio. I was told to introduce the other Henderson "as best I could." (Paul's bio wasn't the only one that went missing. I went from guest to guest, jotting down names and accomplishments.)

Yes, you have to be ready for anything. Recently I was sitting at home alone one night when the phone rang.

"Brian, where are you? We're all waiting for you here in Bolton. You're our guest speaker tonight."

I was shocked. "I have that dinner on my calendar for tomorrow night," I protested.

"Oh, sorry. Didn't someone call and tell you we moved it up a day?"

"No, they didn't. But if you can hang on for an hour, I'll be there." I scrambled into some clothes, grabbed an old speech from my files, and drove like a maniac through the rainy night. I arrived, as promised, within the hour, and made an excellent presentation, if I do say so. Then I downed a cold beer and went home.

One year I travelled across the country to Vancouver Island for the Howie Meeker Roast. I'd been asked to MC the event and it looked like it was pretty badly organized. But the problems started before the event.

A bunch of us—Bob Goldham, Bob Nevin, Jim McKenny, Steve Vickers, Bobby Baun, Gaye Stewart, Eddie Shack, Bill White, Pierre Pilote, and a few others—had flown out together the day before. It didn't take long for me to get involved in a confrontation with my old nemesis, Eddie Shack. Just when I was beginning to conclude the guy had mellowed or matured, he did something to really piss me off.

The plane to Vancouver was a wide-bodied jumbo with a hundred or more people up in our section. And Eddie had been into the wine.

"Hey, McFarlane!" he hollered. "You cheap son of a bitch! How much money did you make out of that 'Clear the Track' record you wrote about me? Whatcha gonna do with all the dough you made?"

Heads turned in front of me, and unfortunately I took the bait. "Not much," I replied. "You can't do much with $1.98, Eddie." I immediately wished I'd just ignored him.

"Yeah," he roared, laughing like a hyena, "well, whatcha gonna do about that rug you got on? All the glue running down yer face and into yer eyes in this hot weather. That must be awful! Har, har, har."

Well, I couldn't believe he'd said such an ignorant thing in front of all those people. I was speechless. Later, we were all standing around the carousel waiting for our bags. Eddie waltzed by, guffawing and drawing attention to himself.

When he drew near I called him over.

"Yeah, whaddaya want?"

"I want you to know, now that we're eye to eye, exactly what I think of you. I think you're an absolute prick, Eddie, a big fucking prick. I don't mind you making fun of me in front of all these old-timers—they're our friends and they all know about our feud. But you embarrassed me in front of a hundred strangers on a plane. So I'm telling you right to your face what I think of you. I think you're a prick, and I'm going to cut you a new asshole when I introduce you at Meeker's dinner tomorrow night. You watch me."

At first I didn't think my verbal ambush had fazed Eddie. But I know it surprised the old-timers who were gathered around. Hell, I'd even surprised myself!

My old friend Bob Goldham came over to me and said quietly, "Good for you. I guess he knows how you feel about him now."

That was just the start of my weekend.

When we arrived in Parksville, I discovered my pal Red Storey had already checked into the hotel. He'd flown in from Montreal on an earlier flight, and he didn't look too happy. For starters, he'd been told he had a roommate—me. Red hadn't roomed with anyone in years, and he preferred it that way.

"Aw, I'm glad it's you," he said. "We get along. But I wish someone had told me we were doubling up. Another thing, this dinner tomorrow is being televised on TSN. I didn't know anything about that. I don't like this set-up at all."

I didn't like the television idea, either. I felt I had to rein in my material whenever I knew I'd be on TV. I'd complained to my union, ACTRA, about it, and they said they'd contact all the guys who speak at these events and tell them not to get involved if the banquets were televised, but it was never dealt with to my satisfaction. I'd also asked ACTRA to intercede several times over the years whenever we had contract problems with *Hockey Night*. One time they said, "Gee, we thought you fellows were happy working for *Hockey Night in Canada.*" Another time they said, "*Hockey Night in Canada* just ignores us or sloughs us off when we request information." I guess if you want a cushy, high-paying job in broadcasting, you should work for the union.

Later, in the hotel lobby, I ran into Ross Brewitt, the organizer of the roast. Brewitt looks like Don Rickles and sometimes at banquets he tries to emulate Rickles' act. One night in Milton, Ontario, he got up at a Don Cherry roast and peppered Grapes with some one-liners that infuriated Cherry.

Cherry came into the *Hockey Night in Canada* studio the next day and soon had Hodge and me chuckling with his description of the roast.

"So this asshole gets up and starts throwing darts at me," he roared. "I couldn't believe it! I don't even know this clown and he's puttin' me down, makin' all these jokes about me."

"Don, that's what happens at a roast," Hodge said. "It's all about poking fun at the guest of honour."

"I know that. But I'm tellin' ya. I almost jumped up and grabbed the guy by the throat. Insultin' me like that. They'll never get me back in Milton again."

In the hotel lobby in Parksville, Brewitt asked me, "How's your roommate?"

"Red Storey? He's just fine. I guess we were both surprised to find out we were rooming together."

"Yeah. Well, Red gave me a hard time about it today. He was a bit of an asshole this afternoon about the room situation and this television stuff."

"Wait a minute, Ross," I said, "this problem with the telecast has to be addressed. The TV really limits what we can say when we get up in front of a crowd. I spoke at a banquet in Newmarket one night, but nobody told us they were putting it on cable TV. On Sunday morning I turn on my TV at home and there I am, telling Harold Ballard jokes. Jim McKenny's saying things like, 'I watch *The 20-Minute Workout* until my arm gets tired.' Kids could've been watching and listening to this stuff.

"When these things are televised, those of us who perform have to edit our remarks, and the people who pay good money to attend the event are the losers. Something's got to be done about this."

"All I know is tonight's roast is on TSN," Brewitt said. Then he laid on a little soft soap: "You're absolutely the best MC we could have for this roast," he said.

I took this with a grain of salt, because I'd heard they tried to get Vancouver broadcaster John McGeachy as MC before I got the call.

The event was as badly organized as any I've ever attended. I tried repeatedly to get a list of the head-table guests and their biographies, but none was forthcoming. Two minutes before air-time I was still writing down names of dignitaries, speakers, and celebrities in the crowd. And for some reason, Howie Meeker sat all alone at one end of the head table, while the rest of the dignitaries sat elbow to elbow at the other end. Finally, I heard later that the event was poorly publicized, and they were asking people to come in off the street (no charge, folks) to help fill the empty seats at the tables.

If you're wondering whether I kept my promise to Eddie Shack to "cut him a new asshole" when it was his turn to speak, of course I didn't. I gave him the standard, "Here he is, folks, number 23 in your program, number 1 in your hearts, the Great Entertainer, Eddie Shack!"

I have encountered Shack several times since I blasted him in Vancouver and our conversations have generally been cordial if reserved. I guess I'm still not a big fan.

"Why, the Shacks and the McFarlanes are among our dearest friends," Andra Kelly once told my wife Joan. "We had no idea Eddie and Brian were at odds with each other."

Shackie is the guy who makes Andra laugh when he comes by the house and shouts through the kitchen window, "Andra, can Leonard come out to play?" Apparently, Andra and Red see things in Shackie that I have yet to discover.

To be fair, when he spoke in Hamilton a few months later, Shack lived up to his name—the Great Entertainer:

People often ask me how I got the name "Clear the Track." While playing for Toronto, I hit Rod

Gilbert and another New York Ranger one night. Both of them went to the ice and I didn't get a penalty for either. Paul Rimstead, a hockey writer with the *Telegram*, wrote a headline the next day that read "Clear the Track, Here Comes Shack." Then Brian McFarlane made up a song to go along with the name. He musta said, "Holy sheep shit, maybe I can do somethin' with this." He's a writer, he's got the books goin' and the rest of that stuff.

I always spent the beginning of the year in the minors. At that time of the year, if you misbehaved you were sent down to the minors for two weeks. So I always got sent down. When I played for Imlach it was absolutely hell. The lines were Keon, Armstrong, and Duff, then it was Kelly, Mahovlich, and Nevin, then it was Olmstead, Stewart, and somebody else, and it was always Shack and Harris and whoever the Christ wants to go with them.

While playing for Toronto, I didn't score many goals. I couldn't because I was always sitting on the bench. Punch Imlach used to say to me, "For Christ's sake, Shack, shuddup or it will cost you ten bucks to buy a ticket to watch the game."

Playing the game of hockey has been great for me. I've had a lot of fun. I got sent to so many clubs. My little wife—she's such a sweet little thing—told me we could make more damn money on the houses we bought than you can make playing hockey. When the price would go up, she'd say, "Shackie, act up again and let's get the hell out of here."

I'm from Sudbury, you know, that's where they grow potatoes, but the only way they can get 'em up is to blast 'em. I played Juniors for Guelph, which is pretty close to Hamilton and we used to play here. At that time it was great. It was always dynamite to come into Hamilton.

Hockey is absolutely fabulous. When I was with the Leafs and we were playing Montreal we always anticipated a scrap or two. We were always up for those games. I'd have to get Frank [Mahovlich] up for it because Frank would be in a little bit of a cloud. I mean, he's a good guy and everything, but holy shit! And Imlach loved me for that.

I happened to get on the ice against Montreal and remember I used to wheel around out there, skating all over and doing crazy things. I didn't mean to but I did—I mean my wife says "act up" and I act up. And who do I pick on but the smallest guy, Henri Richard. When you're a Ukrainian from Sudbury and you see a French guy you have a tendency . . . well, you just don't like him. You don't like the way he talks, you don't like how short he is, and you absolutely want to kick the shit out of him. I get a hold of Henri. The rule then was the third man in is out of the game. It was the best deal in hockey while I was there.

While I got a hold of Henri, who comes nosing around but John Ferguson. He wants to get at me. I'm trying to shake little Henri and I can't shake the little bugger so I said to myself, let's see if the little bugger can take this. And I bonked him with my head. Boom! I hit him just above the eye and now the blood is coming down and the bad language is pouring out of him, "Shit de shit de goddam my brudder from two an a 'aff rivers will kill you, Shack."

Now we have to go back and play in Montreal. Well, I was a nervous wreck. We're in the Forum skating around and there's a guy there blowing a big horn saying, "Shack the Nose, Shack the Nose." And Ferguson is shouting at me, saying he's going to get me. I'm hoping the game stays even. If one side or the other grabs a big lead, Imlach's going to send out my line.

We go through the gateway and who's sitting up there but Maurice Richard. You know, the guy who got two minutes for lookin' so good on television. Maurice cups a hand and yells down at me, "Shack! Thank God you didn't hit my brudder with your nose or you may have split him in two."

I don't usually lose my composure at a speaking engagement, but it happened in Burlington, Ontario, a couple of weeks before the Meeker roast. This event was also a roast, organized by my friend Don Koharski, the highly regarded NHL referee. Don and I, along with our wives, had been guest speakers at a golf tournament in the Maritimes earlier that summer and had enjoyed ourselves immensely. And the small but appreciative audience had laughed at all our jokes. So Don invited me to his fundraiser in Burlington, where Alan Eagleson, then the executive director of the NHL Players Association, served as a willing target for our jibes.

I shared the head table with Red Fisher, Dennis Hull, Harry Neale, and former NHL president John Ziegler, and MC Pat Marsden. I was well down the list of speakers. Red Fisher got up to speak, and the first thing he did was to steal two of Dennis Hull's best jokes.

There's a certain code of ethics that most speakers adhere to. When a story or joke is closely linked with a particular speaker, others tend to shy away from it as a matter of courtesy. Don't get me wrong. None of us is clever enough to do fifteen minutes of original material. We all resort to joke books, dressing-room quips, and now the Internet. I work hard to come up with material that's different from the other speakers, and I know Dennis does as well.

Harry Neale got up next and, to my amazement, started rattling off all my best one-liners. He'd copied them down at a speech I'd given in Oshawa a few weeks earlier—I saw him doing it. Now he was using them all right in front of me—and in the same order I tell them!

I was well aware of his reputation for writing down other people's jokes at banquets—and I don't understand it, because he's such a natural wit and shouldn't need to scoff other people's material.

There's a story I tell about my honeymoon, how I looked up and saw a mirror on the ceiling. I thought the mirror was great but my wife said, "Look, it's like the one on our car: it says, 'Objects are larger than they appear.'" When Harry used that line in Burlington, he not only annoyed me by stealing it, but he screwed up the punchline: "Look, it says, 'Objects are smaller than they should be.'" I was more hurt than angry because I thought Harry was a friend.

I was still teed off when Marsden introduced me. "Shit," I muttered. Then I said it again, louder. "Shit!" and threw my notes down.

I turned to Red Fisher and said, "Red, you're a bit of an asshole for stealing two of Dennis Hull's joke about his brother."

I looked at Harry Neale.

"Harry, *you're* an asshole for stealing all my best jokes from that banquet in Oshawa and using them here tonight."

The crowd began to laugh, but both Red and Harry looked uneasy. This was a first for me, calling two of my peers assholes in public. I can't recall what I said after that, what material I was able to salvage, but my gut feeling when I sat down was that I'd done all right, that I'd still been able to entertain and garner a few laughs.

I've never felt quite the same about Harry since that roast. But I try to see the best in people and in Harry's case, there's a lot of good to see. He has earned his vast popularity because he is a very decent man and a splendid hockey commentator.

Later, my wife said she was stunned by my outburst. But we both agree that, as we grow older, we tend to become more outspoken. I don't apologize for it. Hey, that's what made my CFRB colleague Gordon Sinclair so endearing. I plan to speak my mind a lot more often, and to a lot more people.

Popular coach Roger Neilson stole the show at a roast for Bob Gainey in Peterborough one night in 1983 when Gainey was at the peak of his career as a Montreal Canadien.

Roger began by apologizing for his hay fever. "It seems that anytime I get within a hundred miles of Harold Ballard my allergies start acting up," he said. He continued:

We all know Bob Gainey is a guy with a heart of gold—and hands of cement. Twelve goals he got last season, I mean, why are we honouring him? Tiger Williams got almost that many goals last year.

And Montreal can't give him away.

Gainey is one of those guys that you can hear stickhandling. [Habs coach] Bob Berry told me after he rushes up the ice a couple of times in practice, they have to change the pucks.

A Russian once—and he must have been at a party—called Gainey the greatest hockey player in the world. Now I know that when he's skating he looks like Bobby Orr. But when he gets the puck he looks like *Frank* Orr.

I see Doug Jarvis here tonight. He played with Bob for a long time. I think it's fitting that Jarvis should be here because he can't remember when he last scored, either.

Talk about slowing down. Last year in Washington they put a pylon out on the ice in practice, next to Jarvis, just to make sure he was moving. Jarvis spent the summer rafting on the Colorado River, and I think that's appropriate because he's been floating for about three years now.

But Jarvis is a nice guy, we all know that.

At this point a woman in the crowd shouted, "Right on!" It was Doug's mother. Neilson went on:

And it's nice to see Red Fisher at the head table. I didn't know he was still living.

I took one look and saw Red up here and I thought it was a telethon for senility. They had a birthday party for Red the other day and the candles on the cake turned on the air conditioning. I don't know what your favourite movie is, Red, but I know what it should be: *A Streetcar Named Retire*.

Then there's Dick Irvin. Good old Squeaky. He's kind of an eastern Howie Meeker. The ultimate test for those two guys would be to tie a Timex to their tongues.

And Alan Eagleson, Mr. Hockey. He's done for hockey what surfing has done for the economy of Saskatchewan. He's sort of a sex symbol for all those Canadian women who've reached an age where they no longer care. Al's about as sincere as Liz Taylor saying "ouch" on her honeymoon.

There's Kenny Dryden. Wake up, Ken.

Remember when he used to fall asleep leaning on his goal stick? Geez, Ken, don't lie down— somebody'll bury you.

I'm surprised Scotty Bowman showed up tonight. He was demanding a first-round draft choice to come here.

Then there's Brian McFarlane. He's one of those guys I've known for twenty years and I don't even know what he does. But he's always fighting with Harold Ballard, so he can't be all bad.

Brian is kind of a swinger on the road. I can see it now: He's in the hotel room with a woman. Out come the false teeth and they go into the drawer. Out come the contact lenses and into the drawer. Off comes the hair and into the drawer. The poor woman! She wouldn't know whether to get into the bed or get into the drawer.

Here in Peterborough we all know Bob Gainey as a big, gangly, awkward kind of a guy. You see him walking along, his knuckles almost touching the ground. He turned down George Street and four people gave him a banana.

I remember when he went to St. Peter's High School. His favourite grade was grade nine. He spent four years there. His instructor told us he had a room-temperature IQ. One day we were filling out an insurance questionnaire and the question was "Church preference." Bob wrote in, "Red brick."

It's so easy to say the wrong thing at the wrong time—to tell a joke or make a comment that seems innocuous at the time, but in retrospect might have been better left unsaid.

I have been guilty on occasion of making poor judgments as a speaker. After a Leo Boivin roast in Prescott, Ontario, I received a letter from a man in the audience, a man of the cloth, who suggested that a few of my "smutty jokes" were in poor taste. He said his criticism was meant to be constructive, and I took it that way, but how I agonized over the fact I might have upset or irritated some of Boivin's friends or family in the room that night.

I have worked many banquets with Dennis Hull over the years and no matter how often I hear his routines I always laugh. Dennis has the magic, that indefinable gift for humour. The fact that he laughs louder than anyone at his own jokes endears him to his audience. For years, performing gratis as we all do, Dennis has been a popular speaker at the Canadian Society dinner in New York.

Here's Dennis:

I get in a lot of trouble for what I say. Last week I got in trouble with Bob Pulford, the manager of the Chicago Blackhawks. I was being interviewed on TV in Chicago and they asked me to name the last amateur team that I played with. I said the Chicago Blackhawks. I have a bumper sticker that says "Go Hawks—And Take the White Sox With You." Pulford wasn't too crazy about that, either.

I had the rare opportunity to play in the Bing Crosby Golf Tournament last year. Not only to play, but to appear on the Crosby Clambake, an entertainment show. People appearing included Jimmy Dean, Kathryn Crosby, Roy Clark, Pat Boone, Perry Como, Hull, and a large lady who was an opera singer.

Well, I made a big mistake. You see, I followed this lady. She is six foot three inches tall, and six foot three inches wide. She had her dress cut down to her waist. It looked like she was hiding two Yul Brynners inside.

She didn't want to go up on stage because she didn't think the band knew her music, and she didn't think people would understand her singing, which was opera. I suggested perhaps they wouldn't know Dennis Hull who was following her—a hockey player from Canada, and this was in North Carolina. Anyway, she went out and knocked them dead—she was great. But I went out after her, and said something wrong, I suppose. I walked up on to the stage in front of ten thousand people and said, "You probably thought the show was over because the fat lady sang."

Despite the fact that people are willing to pay outrageous sums to hear him speak, Don Cherry has pretty well given up the banquet circuit, except for rare occasions. Grapes doesn't need the money or the aggravation that goes along with speaking—the travel, the fans who clamour for autographs, etc. Why, he can hardly go anywhere without being swamped. He's right up there with Shania Twain and Céline Dion as the most sought-after celebrities in Canada.

Grapes and I were head table guests a few years ago at a dinner in Colborne, Ontario, near my summer home. Here's how the conversation went when they called to invite me.

"We don't have a budget for speakers but we'd sure like you to come."

"That's okay," I said. "I should put something back into the community anyway. Who else will be there?"

"Well, we've lined up a couple of curlers and a jockey and we've got Don Cherry coming . . ."

"Wait a minute! You've got no budget and you've got Grapes coming? He gets big bucks for appearances. How'd you manage that?"

"Well, Molson's is picking up his fee."

"Well, maybe Molson's would pick up my fee as well. After all, we both work for *Hockey Night in Canada*. Why not ask them?"

"Brian, we already did."

"And?"

"And they said no."

Fair enough. I went anyway. Had a good time.

Former Leaf defenceman Jim McKenny has enjoyed a wonderful and productive post-NHL career. He became a popular sportscaster for CityTV in Toronto and a good after-dinner speaker. Here's part of a McKenny routine I caught at a sports celebrity dinner in Newmarket, Ontario.

You spend a lot of time hangin' around airports when you're a professional hockey player. You're in one town, then on to the next, and a lot of times when you're losing you're not allowed to go to the bar. I played for the Leafs for fifteen years so we didn't go to the bar too often. But our travel bags were always full, we didn't go thirsty and we weren't kiddin' anybody.

One of our favourite tricks on the road was putting a $100 bill into a boarding pass, tying a string to it, and dropping it on the floor at an airport. We'd see a guy look down, spot the hundred and reach for it. Then we'd yank the thread. You'd see guys almost pull their shoulders out trying to grab that bill. We had beige thread for O'Hare in Chicago 'cause that matched the linoleum there. We went out to Denver, they had the orange stuff on the floor there, it was tough gettin' that orange thread.

A lot of people ask me about my nickname—Howie. When I came from Ottawa to Toronto to play Junior with the Marlies I was fourteen years old. I was good when I was a kid, horseshit in pro, but as a Junior I had a lot of potential. We had another defenceman on the team and his name was Jim McEndry. They kept getting us mixed up, so they had to find a nickname for me. They started calling me Howie, because I had a facial resemblance to Howie Young, one of the finest alcoholics to ever strap on the blades.

Howie was in a movie once, *Home of the Brave*, with Frank Sinatra. They were shooting it in Hawaii. One day Howie got into his cups out on a yacht. He thought that Frank didn't look so great so he picked him up and threw him overboard. Four of Frank's goons promptly beat the hell out of Howie and they just dropped him off on a beach somewhere. When he woke up the next morning he thought he was in heaven.

One of the greatest things a coach can say about a player is he brings his all. I used to bring what was left. At least I had a good time, and I've still got a liver.

We went into the Forum one night, and Montreal hadn't lost at home for something like thirty eight games. We were playing well, too—we'd only lost four in a row. It was just a matter of time before we snapped out of it.

Johnny McLellan was our coach then, a good guy. Johnny gave us a great pep talk before the game. He said, "Geez, guys, my ass is on the line. I'm going to be fired pretty soon. Please just try and keep it close out there."

Hey, that was fair. We came in after the first period and the score was only 2–0 Canadiens, but they'd outshot us 21–1. John comes in and he says, "One shot? One goddamn shot? We're paying you guys millions of dollars to play hockey and you could only manage one bloody shot? I can't believe it." He almost tore the room apart, kickin' cans and everything. Then he went out the door and slammed it. Tim Ecclestone gets up and says, "Okay, who's the wise guy?"

Darryl Sittler has appeared at hundreds of sports dinners and usually comes well prepared. I was with him in Barrie for such an event back in 1985.

I can tell you a few stories about Eddie Shack. With the Leafs one year, he was at the stage in his career that I am going through now, where you're not playing a whole lot. You're on the bench, trying to keep alert and be involved, and it's not that easy at times.

Eddie got up behind the bench at Maple Leaf Gardens and started walking back and forth, making like he was loosening up his legs. He talked to the people behind the bench and got a little chant going. Red Kelly was the coach at that time. The next thing you know the fans start to pick up on it and there he is leading his own cheers. There are sixteen thousand people shouting, "We want Shack!"

When you're travelling with the guy he is always full of jokes and fun. I remember an incident where we were on an airplane. I was sitting beside Eddie, the rest of the players were in behind us. It was a fairly long flight. There was a bald fellow right in front of us. Didn't have a hair on his head, nice shiny scalp there. Shackie nudges me and whispers, "Watch this." He puts his hand in a glass of water—you know the size of those Eddie Shack hands. And then he goes ah-ah-ah-CHEW as he flicks his hand, spraying water all over the guy in front. To this day, I don't know if the guy knows that it was just water all over his head.

Often after practice guys go out and have a few refreshments and get talking about different things. We had a little group session one day at a bar and the guys were talking about investments and the stock market. We had a couple of fellows on our team who go back out west and farm every year and they were talking about how they've bought sections of land and when they're finished playing they're going to go back and farm. Eddie stood up and said to the guys, "Well, I'm starting to accumulate some land myself. In last night's game, I blocked a shot and now I have two achers."

Now a word about my record 10-point night 1976. Gerry Cheevers was not playing for Boston that night. The goalie was Dave Reece, a rookie. Unfortunately for Dave, that was his last game in the National league.

People ask me why things like that happen. Really, you can't explain it, because I know that there have been other games where I personally felt that I played better than I did that night, but the puck didn't go in, or I passed it and the other guy didn't put it in. But for some reason on this night everything went in.

The story goes that when Dave Reece got back to Boston he was pretty dejected and he couldn't sleep all the next night. So he got out of bed and decided he was going to commit suicide. So what he did was he jumped in front of a subway train—but fortunately for him it went right through his legs.

Back in the mid seventies, the Leafs had some real battles with the Philadelphia Flyers. I can remember the series in '76. We were going into the sixth game of the series. Philadelphia was up 3–2 and we were back at Maple Leaf Gardens. Red Kelly was our coach and we came in for the morning skate.

Coaches are always thinking of ways to motivate their players and how to get the best out of them. We went into the dressing room and Kelly had a number of pyramids placed in our dressing room. He made a big speech about what the pyramids do. The power apparently comes from the base and goes to the top and generates energy, so if you sit underneath one it will energize you and you will play better.

Well, you know hockey players—it doesn't take much to encourage us to try something like this. So that night we sat under the pyramids and then we went out and won the game and tied the series up 3–3.

The press picked it up, of course; there were headlines in all the papers. At that time the Philadelphia Flyers had their own good luck charm in Kate Smith. She sang "God Bless America" and every time she sang it they seemed to win. So for the seventh game they were going to trot out Kate Smith. I remember seeing the headline in the *Toronto Star*: "The Leafs' Pyramid Power Against Kate Smith and the Flyers."

We got into Philadelphia for the seventh game, walked into the dressing room and there was a 5-foot pyramid sitting there. So the guys started taking five minutes each, sitting under this pyramid, energizing themselves for the seventh game. Well, Tiger Williams was with us at the time and he pipes up, "Am I ever glad I'm not a Philadelphia Flyer. Can you imagine sitting under Kate Smith for five minutes?"

Really, I shouldn't get on Tiger like that. He's quite a team guy. Anytime there was a battle going on the ice, he was always out there helping out, and I was glad to have him on my side for many years.

There was one night—Kurt Walker was with us then—and he and "Houndog" Kelly were squaring off. They were staring into each other's eyes, trying to be tough guys, you know. The referee was Bryan Lewis and he says to them, "Come on, break it up, you guys. If you don't break it up, you are going to the box."

Tiger's on the ice and he says to Lewis, "Come on Bryan, between the two of them they only have an IQ of 11."

I always try very hard in my presentations to mix humour with hockey lore. For example, here's the text of a speech I made to a group in Dryden, Ontario, on March 24, 1999:

Folks, I hope there are no hecklers in the audience tonight. Because I don't know how to deal with hecklers. The last time I spoke, an elderly couple right down in front began to heckle me. "Get off the stage, you bozo. What do you know about hockey?" That sort of thing. And I was hurt because I knew these people. I even got them tickets for the event. Wouldn't you think a couple out celebrating their sixtieth wedding anniversary would be happy to have their son get up and say a few words?

I want you all to know I'm proud and pleased and flattered to be with you today. Proud to be part of this great hockey event [a hockey tournament], pleased to be here in Dryden, one of Canada's most enthusiastic hockey centres, and flattered that you considered me for the role of dinner speaker. Oh, I know I wasn't the committee's first choice to be your speaker, but that's all right.

They tried to get Don Cherry, but he couldn't make it. He said he had nothing to wear to such a prestigious event—and I think it must be true. Don looked in his closet this week and found that moths had chewed up three of his best outfits. And there they were—throwing up all over the floor.

Don got a call from Indianapolis this week. They want to use his jacket as the starter's flag at the Indy 500.

Don is living proof a guy can be a big success in Canada without speaking either of the official languages.

I had a terrible dream about Cherry last night. I dreamed I was stranded on a desert island with him and I only had one earplug.

So you're left with me, a broken-down old sports announcer who jumped at the chance to be here because I know all about your famous Northern Ontario hospitality.

I was born in Northern Ontario and I always enjoy coming back to be with people who love the game of hockey like I do.

In Toronto they make jokes about people from the north, and they're never funny.

Somebody said, "You know a guy's from Northern Ontario if he's been married three times and he still has the same in-laws."

Then he said, "They have big families up north. One guy had eleven brothers. He thought his name was 'Get some wood' until he was a teenager. His brother was 'Get some more wood.'"

But northerners love their hockey. Your chairman was just telling me that hockey is so popular here in Dryden that no other activity comes close to it in terms of popularity.

I said, "Really? Isn't there any night life in the city?"

He said, "There used to be, but she moved to Thunder Bay about six months ago."

I flew from Toronto to be with you today.

Somebody must have told the Air Canada pilot I was on board because he came on the intercom and said, "Ladies and gentlemen, we're in our final descent. Please fasten your seat belts—and Mr. McFarlane, would you please return the flight attendant to the upright position?"

I was really embarrassed.

So was Bruce, the flight attendant.

Then, when I got to Dryden, the committee arranged a police escort for me all the way in from the airport. That was really thoughtful—although I did get a little tired running in between those two motorcycles.

I went for a walk around town today and met some interesting people. I met your mayor, who, I'm told, is one of the finest politicians money can buy.

And I met a lady coming down the street—and I was surprised to see that she had one breast hanging out. So I stopped her and told her about it. She looked down and said. "My God, I've left my baby on the bus!"

But the people here are very friendly. I was waiting on a corner when a guy tapped me on the shoulder. He said, "Hey there, stranger, you want to buy some crack?" I said, "No thank you, officer."

I must say I was glad to get out of Toronto this week because it's been a rough week for me back home. This week my wife and I installed a skylight in our new apartment—and the people who live upstairs are really pissed off about that.

This week I discovered my dog is going deaf. I shouted "Sit" the other day and what a mess she made all over the kitchen floor.

This dog of mine used to be a big hockey fan. Years ago she'd watch every Leaf game on TV, and if the Leafs lost she'd lie down on the rug and cry her eyes out.

Somebody asked me once, "What does she do when they win?"

I said, "I dunno, I've only had her for about six months."

This week my wife's mother came to visit and I tried to make her feel right at home. I said, "Mom, my house is your house."

She said, 'Great, get the hell off my property.'

Actually, my mother-in-law's not so bad. She made me a nice cup of tea the other day and she said, "When's the last time a ninety-year-old made you a nice cup of tea like this?" I said, "Last week, Mom. On Air Canada."

My wife is mad at me this week. You see, I made a big faux pas the other night. She was getting dressed to go out for dinner when she said, "How do I look?"

I said, "Well, your stockings are a little wrinkled."

She said, "I'm not wearing any stockings tonight."

She got back at me in the restaurant. She ordered the roast beef, the baked potato, the salad.

The waiter said, "What about the vegetable, madame?"

She said, "Oh, he'll have the same thing I'm having."

My wife always gets the last word.

She said to me the other night, "What's the most useless thing on a woman?" I said, "I dunno." She said, "A man about your age."

A few years ago I told her I wanted to get a vasectomy and she said, "Dear, why not let sleeping dogs lie?"

Even on our honeymoon—and that was over forty years ago—she got the last word. I said, "You're awfully quiet when we make love." She said, "I wanted to moan, but I didn't have time."

A couple of years ago we went to New York on a second honeymoon but it wasn't the same. This time *I* ran into the bathroom and cried my eyes out.

My wife went to see her new doctor the other day. She came home and said, "Dr. Astaphan says a woman in my age bracket should be making love fifteen times a month." I said, "Great! Put me down for three."

I told that little story at a golf tournament last summer and Bobby Hull was in the room. He shouted out, "Put me down for the other twelve!" That's a true story. Maybe I'd have laughed harder if I felt he'd been joking.

Bobby's such a ladies' man. Although Dennis Hull told me Bobby once went twelve years without even thinking about sex.

But when he turned thirteen, he really made up for it.

Bobby was in divorce court a few years ago and the judge told him, "Mr. Hull, I'm going to give your wife $3,000 a month." Bobby said, "Why that's great, Your Honour, I'll try to chip in a few bucks myself."

One of my grandsons said to me the other day, "Grandad, can you make a noise like a frog?"

I said, "Sure, why?"

He said, "Grandma says when you croak we're all going to Disney World."

My latest grandson is the cutest little baby. If you hold him in a certain way he looks just like me. But my wife says we can't hold him that way very long or all the blood's going to rush to his head.

Kids are so smart these days.

One of my grandsons—at age six—can already recite the Gettysburg Address, and I think that's pretty amazing because Abraham Lincoln couldn't do it until he was fifty-four.

You have to have a sense of humour in my family.

My dad had a great sense of humour. He was always kidding around when I was growing up. I remember the day he told me he went out and joined Big Brothers. I said, "Hey, that's great, Dad." And he said, "Yeah, every week a ninety-year-old guy is going to come around and take me to the zoo."

My dad was a good father—a generous father. I remember the time he bought me some toys to play with in the bathtub: a toaster and a radio.

And the time he taught me how to swim by taking me out to the end of the dock and pitching me into 40 feet of water. Getting back to the dock was the easy part. Getting out of that damn bag was the tough part.

When it was hunting season, he'd take me with him out in the woods. Dress me in a bunny outfit. Give me a three-minute head start.

He taught me how to play golf. He even taught me how to cut a hole in my pocket in case I had to count to six.

The last time I played golf I hit two balls really hard. That's when I stepped on the rake in the sand trap.

When I played Junior hockey I remember a Leaf scout coming to the house one day, and he talked about signing me for $3,000.

My dad said, "Gee, we don't have that kind of money."

Unfortunately my dad never taught me anything about the facts of life growing up. So I never knew anything about sex. Well, I knew one thing. I knew I was going to go blind at any minute.

One day I saw two dogs stuck together and I asked my dad about it. He said they were merely dancing. No wonder I got thrown out of the junior prom that year.

One year he sold hearing aids door to door. But he quit because most of his best prospects never answered the bell.

My dad taught me many valuable lessons growing up. He would say things like: "Don't confuse your net worth with your self-worth." "Think classy, you'll be classy." "If you fail to prepare, you're prepared to fail." "Unless you're the lead dog, your view never changes." "If you want to lead the orchestra, you've got to turn your back on the crowd." "An ounce of mother is worth a ton of priest." "Remember, even a kick in the butt is a step forward." "One good friend is worth ten lousy relatives."

"If you always do what you've always done, you'll always get what you've always gotten." "Character consists of what you do on the third and fourth try." "Glory may be fleeting but obscurity is forever."

Maybe he got these sayings from the *Reader's Digest*, I don't know. But his words always made an impact on me.

Sometimes, just for laughs, my dad couldn't resist throwing in some really silly advice—stuff that made no sense at all.

He'd say, "Never accept a ride with a stranger unless he gives you candy first."

He'd say, "Never get in fights with ugly people because they have nothing to lose."

He'd say, "Never jump on an opponent unless he's down."

And he'd say, "Love your enemies in case your friends turn out to be a bunch of dickheads."

Now for some true stories.

I remember how some of the fans reacted to my early broadcasting work. I was coming through the crowd at Maple Leaf Gardens one night when a loudmouth fan shouted at me, "McFarlane, you're the reason I come to the games—I can't stand listening to you at home!"

There are certain individuals in hockey I place very high on my list of first-class people. Jean Beliveau comes to mind. What a gentleman. This man oozes class and I've never heard anyone utter a negative word about him.

Wayne Gretzky and Bobby Orr. I place these two men in a virtual tie at the top of my list of most talented players. Orr's moves were simply incredible. So were Gretzky's, even late in his career. And Gretzky gets my nod as hockey's greatest ambassador. He's known and revered throughout the world.

You can't mention the best players in the game without Gordie Howe's name surfacing. Imagine playing in the NHL alongside your two sons and scoring goals as a grandfather in the NHL—at the age of fifty-one. No, there'll never be another Howe. Or another Rocket Richard or Mario Lemieux, either.

I've mentioned a pair of centres and a right winger, so I'll throw in Bobby Hull's name as the greatest left winger I've ever seen. Dick Beddoes once said that Hull "transcended the game and took care of the crowd." Hull signed every autograph book and slip of paper and took time to ask a kid his name. Nobody walked way from the Golden Jet disappointed—not like today's players who scrawl something indecipherable and rush off.

And it's hard to argue with fans who say, "The Big M was just as good as Hull." Or, "Mike Bossy was a more prolific scorer."

The toughest player and best fighter? John Ferguson. Fergie still gets my vote, even though today's tough guys would tower over him and are much bigger and stronger. I still think Fergie—to use an old hockey expression—would beat the crap out of most of them.

On the golf course this summer, I asked Jerry Toppazzini, a former Boston Bruin, to tell me a story from his career. He said, "Brian, I'm the only guy in NHL history to score 4 goals in a game— in a 2–2 tie. I scored 2 goals on my own goaltender and 2 more on the Montreal goalie. How's that for a record?" Then he burst out laughing.

At the turn of the century, a player named Chummy Hill of Toronto once scored a Stanley Cup goal with half a puck. It happened in Winnipeg in 1902, when the puck split in two during a game. Hill fired half the puck into the net and the referee said, "That's good enough for me."

In that same game, the puck was hoisted high in the air and got caught in the rafters over the ice. Apparently there was only one puck, because the players gathered below and tossed their sticks skyward. The one who dislodged the stuck puck received quite an ovation from the fans.

Later in the game, the puck flew over the low boards—they were a couple of feet high—and in among the spectators. Instead of throwing it back, which was the usual custom, a fan put it in his pocket and refused to give it up. That man started a tradition that carries on to this day.

When a player got a penalty in those days, he was told to "sit on the fence." That meant he was obliged to sit on the boards surrounding the rink—there was no penalty box—until such time as the referee felt he'd sinned enough and was allowed back into the game. In all my research I have still not discovered when penalty boxes made their debut in hockey.

A few years later, in Montreal, some four thousand fans stood outside the arena waiting to buy tickets to a Stanley Cup playoff game. When the ticket sellers were tardy in opening the box office, the fans broke down all the doors and windows and sat in all the best seats.

Did you know that Harold Ballard saw some fans breaking down the doors at Maple Leaf Gardens a few years ago? But he caught them all and made them go back and see the rest of the Leaf game.

Early in the century, one team playing for the Stanley Cup put two goalies in the net at the same time. But the pair of netminders stumbled around and bumped into each other and that unique strategy was quickly abandoned.

The other day I discovered in my research the man who was paid less than any other NHLer. Dinny Dinsmore was the NHL's only dollar-a-year man. Yes, Dinny signed with the Montreal Maroons in 1929–30 for $1. He played in 9 games that season, so that works out to slightly more than 10¢ a game.

We've all heard of players who say they'd play for nothing. Dinny's the guy who came closest to doing so.

In modern-day hockey, we have goalies scoring goals, women goalies winning games in pro hockey—it happened three times in the minor leagues in the '90s—we have expansion after expansion, mammoth new arenas, multimillion-dollar salaries, ticket prices that are so far out of sight my grandchildren—and yours—may never see a game in the NHL except on television.

I don't know why anyone would want to own an NHL franchise—especially in Canada. We've lost Winnipeg and Quebec. Owners have to worry about the bottom line. They worry about season-ticket sales and broadcast rights and having to pay outrageous amounts—in U.S. dollars—to mediocre players who may leave on a whim, like Alexei Yashin, contract or not. Ron Bremner, the CEO of the Calgary Flames, told me once, "Every time the Canadian dollar drops half a cent the Calgary Flames have to find another $500,000 in their budget."

I really worry about the future of some of the small-market Canadian franchises. What a shame it would be to lose them. And who can blame an owner like Marcel Aubut in Quebec for selling out to U.S. interests if it eradicates all the day-to-day headaches while adding a few million dollars to his bank account?

Still, the game is what it is and what it has always been: a marvellous blend of skill on skates; a fast, exciting team game with the element of harsh body contact. Sometimes the latter alarms me because of the vicious nature of the contact, accompanied far too often by carelessly hurled sticks that can do permanent damage to an eye, a head, or a brain.

The lack of respect for life and limb saddens me, shocks me. If teams ever discard the ritual of shaking hands after the deciding game in a playoff series, I'll know that all respect is gone, all sportsmanship erased from the game.

What the NHL needs now is for the league moguls—executives and owners—and the NHLPA to get together and work hard on a reasonable solution to the game's problems, financial and otherwise.

It's a beautiful game to watch, an exhilarating game to play.

No wonder millions of young people gravitate toward hockey, a game that provides more fun, in my opinion, than any other.

If young men choose to make it a career, the opportunities are now so unlimited that many of Canada's top Junior players, and others who turn pro after U.S. college careers, will become rich and famous and play in cities spread all over North America. NHL salaries have risen so dramatically that there are now almost three hundred players who earn a million dollars a year or more.

On draft day their lives are changed forever and I wish them well. They are merely following a dream that has been the dream of most of us. They are young and talented and they have benefited from solid coaching and, in most cases, the love and support of their families.

I applaud the parents who have devoted so many hours and sacrificed so much in order for their children—boys and girls—to play the game. I hope they realize early on that only a select few will rise above the others and become professionals. Those who don't can still enjoy the game as much as those who do.

I applaud the coaches who hone the skills of our young players, and the league executives and officials who provide the proper environment for playing the game—these are the unsung heroes of hockey.

I'm sixty-eight and I thoroughly enjoy watching my six grandchildren play the game—four boys and two girls. I still play old-timers hockey myself three times a week and I'll quit only when the enjoyment that comes from suiting up in smelly equipment leaves me forever.

And I don't think we should worry about other nations turning out more skilled players than our Canadian boys and girls. Our young players will always be at or near the top—and if they're not, so what? Canadians should be proud that the game we discovered and honed and enjoyed for over a century is now being played all over the globe. We should be happy to share the joy we found in hockey with newcomers to the game. And if they master it and come to North America to display their abundant skills, we should admire and applaud them, not resent them.

I'll leave you with a story about a player who set goals for himself aside from hockey. I often conclude my verbal presentations with this anecdote.

Moe Mantha Sr. played in the American Hockey League for about fourteen seasons before deciding to retire and try his hand in the political world.

He went home to Nipissing, Ontario, where he sought the Conservative nomination in that riding. Mantha made a nice little speech in the town hall and all his friends showed up to applaud his presentation. He had no difficulty winning the nomination.

The following week he was back to speak again, this time at an all-candidates meeting.

Once again, Mantha made a lively speech. But just as he sat down a lady in the back of the room called out, "Mr. Mantha, before you sit down I'd like to know your thoughts on pro-life."

Mantha picked up the microphone and said, "Lady, I always liked the pro life. You see different cities, play in big arenas, have a few beers after the games. Yeah, it's a great life, the pro life."

Then he sat down.

Making a presentation to officials of the Timmy Tyke Hockey Tournament in 1982.

Game Over

And now it's done, the most difficult book I've ever written by far. It's not easy to write about yourself and your personal experiences. What to include? What to leave out? My hope is there'll be a sequel—I've got hundreds more taped interviews I've done with hockey personalities over the years.

Looking back on my nights in the gondola at Maple Leaf Gardens, through those deplorable Ballard years, I think my biggest thrill came early—the Leafs' Stanley Cup win of 1967. As for individual accomplishments, I give you Darryl Sittler's 10-point night in 1976. Or any time Wayne Gretzky played in Toronto in the eighties, when there was a buzz throughout the arena and interest in hockey peaked, sort of like it did when Bobby Orr was working wonders in the seventies.

The new millennium began without a hockey superhero. Sidney Crosby, Alex Ovechkiin, and Evgeni Malkin are filling the void. Time will tell if they are revered like number 99, Bobby Orr, Mario Lemieux, Gordie Howe, the Golden Jet, the Flower, or the Rocket.

The Maple Leafs have never been able to produce another team equal to the ones that won four Stanley Cups in the sixties, especially the gallant oldtimers of '67. Except for perhaps Curtis Joseph, there's never been a goaltender to match Johnny Bower and Terry Sawchuk, only one defenceman—Borje Salming—to compare with Tim Horton, Allan Stanley, Marcel Pronovost, Carl Brewer, or Bobby Baun. How many forwards in the past three decades have equalled Red Kelly, Dave Keon, Frank Mahovlich, Ron Ellis, Bob Pulford, or George Armstrong? Sittler, yes, and Lanny McDonald. And Doug Gilmour, despite the short time he spent in a Leaf uniform. Mats Sundin could skate in that company. And Wendel Clark. Possibly Rick Vaive. It's a very short list. Ten Hall of Famers emerged from that '67 squad (eleven counting the coach, Punch Imlach). How many Hall of Famers can you name from recent Leaf clubs?

It will take all of the collective skills of Brian Burke and Ron Wilson to bring another Stanley Cup to Toronto. May all Leaf fans live long enough to see it happen.

The McFarlane clan: daughter Brenda, the Hollywood playwright (back row, left); daughter Lauren and husband Brad Jackson (center); son Michael and wife Debbra (far right); and Joan and I up front. Joan still has trouble convincing people she's a senior.